ZION

The Pure in Heart

LARRY BARKDULL

Pillars of Zion Series Titles

Introduction: *Portrait of a Zion Person*

Book 1: *Zion—Our Origin and Our Destiny*

Book 2: *The First Pillar of Zion—The New and Everlasting Covenant*

Book 3: *The Second Pillar of Zion—The Oath and Covenant of the Priesthood*

Book 4: *The Third Pillar of Zion—The Law of Consecration*

Book 5: *The Pure in Heart*

Book 6: *No Poor among Them*

Pillars of Zion Publishing
Orem, Utah

Copyright and Permission

Publishing Imprint: Pillars of Zion Publishing, a division of Barkdull Marketing, Inc. Licensed for publication and distributed by BestBooks Publishing and Distribution, Spanish Fork, Utah. Phone: 801.815.5349.

Contact

Contact us at info@pillarsofzion.com
Visit our Website at www.PillarsOfZion.com

Disclaimer

This series is heavily documented with some 5,000 references and 400 works cited. Every effort has been made to achieve accuracy. This work is not an official publication of the Church of Jesus Christ of Latter-day Saints, and the views expressed within this work are the sole responsibility of the author and do not necessarily reflect the position of The Church of Jesus Christ of Latter-day Saints or any other entity.

LICENSE USE

Library of Congress Cataloging Publication Data is on file at the Library of Congress.
ISBN: 978-1-937399-13-9

Dedication

To Elizabeth Barkdull
Ron and Bonnie McMillan
David and Lorelea Anderson
Paul and Sharon Meyers

Acknowledgments

My wife, Elizabeth, and I would like to acknowledge a number of people, who, in one way or another, lent their support for the creation of this project.

Lawrence and Georgia Shaw
Lance and Jozet Richardson
Blaine and Kathy Yorgason
Scot and Maurine Proctor
Clay Gorton
Ted Gibbons
Grover Cardon
Gary and Bonnie Leavitt
Bud and Barbara Poduska
Dee Jay Bawden
Steve Glenn
Gavon and Tanya Barkdull

Production Staff

Thanks to Eschler Editing for editorial and design work.

Editors—Jay A. Parry and Michele Preisendorf
Graphic Artist—Douglass Cole
Typesetter—Sean Graham

Note about The Three Pillars of Zion

The complete Zion series contains seven books. The full bibliography, and index are included in each of the books for ease of referencing and navigation. Each volume includes its own table of contents except for the Introduction book, *Portrait of a Zion Person*, includes the table of contents for each volume in order to introduce the entire series.

Table of Contents

Book 5
The Pure in Heart

Book 5
The Pure in Heart

Introduction

"[Zion] commences in the heart of each person."[1]*—Brigham Young*

In this fifth book of The Three Pillars of Zion series, we will examine the journey that leads to Zion and discover along the way what it means to be pure in heart.

By way of review, we learned in book 1 that Zion was our origin and our destiny. She is our ideal and the antithesis of Babylon. Moreover, Zion is the standard among celestial and celestial-seeking people.[2] Joseph Smith said, "We ought to have the building up of Zion as our greatest object."[3] The obligation to become Zion people rests upon each of us individually.

We recall that the "law of the Church" (D&C 42) states that three covenants are sufficient to establish us as Zion people: "And ye shall hereafter receive church covenants, such as shall be sufficient to establish you, both here and in the New Jerusalem."[4] These covenants are:

1. The New and Everlasting Covenant. (D&C 132:4–7)
2. The Oath and Covenant of the Priesthood. (D&C 84:33–44)
3. The Law of Consecration. (D&C 82:11–15)

These covenants flow from the Atonement of Jesus Christ. In book 2, we learned that we accept the Atonement by formally receiving the new and everlasting covenant by baptism. The new and everlasting covenant is the first pillar of Zion and the umbrella covenant of the gospel. It consists of two primary covenants: (1) the covenant of baptism, and (2) the oath and covenant of the priesthood. The priesthood covenant is magnified by (1) ordination for worthy men; (2) temple covenants and ordinances for worthy men and women; and (3) the temple sealing covenant, which is called the covenant of exaltation,[5] for worthy

1 Young, *Discourses of Brigham Young,* 118.
2 D&C 105:5.
3 Smith, *Teachings of the Prophet Joseph Smith,* 60.
4 D&C 42:67.
5 Nelson, *The Power within Us,* 136; Smith, *Doctrines of Salvation,* 2:58. Note: Elder McConkie stated that men make a covenant of exaltation twice: once upon ordination to the Melchizedek Priesthood and again at the time of the marriage sealing: "Ordination to office in the Melchizedek priesthood and entering into that 'order of the priesthood' named 'the new and everlasting covenant of marriage' are both occasions when men make the covenant of exaltation, being promised through their faithfulness all that the Father hath (D&C 131:1–4; 84:39–41; 132; Num. 25:13)." (*Mormon Doctrine,* 167.)

men and women. The new and everlasting covenant provides a way to be cleansed from sin and separated from the world.

As mentioned, the new and everlasting covenant leads to the second pillar of Zion, the oath and covenant of the priesthood. The priesthood covenant provides us a way to receive God's authority, power, and knowledge—everything we need to become like him and inherit all he has.

The principles of the priesthood apply to both worthy men and women. The priesthood covenant is received by men at the time of ordination, but its principles are expansive and eventually lead to the temple. There, faithful men and women are endowed with priesthood covenants and ordinances that culminate at a marriage altar. Elder Bruce R. McConkie said, "This covenant, made when the priesthood is received, is renewed when the recipient enters the order of eternal marriage."[6] Plainly, both men and women are involved in the doctrines of the priesthood.

We discussed the history of the priesthood and men who were great examples of priesthood worthiness and power. We discussed priesthood keys and their importance in the restored Church of Jesus Christ. Then we surveyed our covenantal agreements and the Father's oath, instructions, and promises. Later we examined "The Constitution of the Priesthood," found in Doctrine and Covenants 121, and we discussed why many are called to eternal life but few are chosen. We also studied the Lord's instructions and rewards for the chosen few. We came to understand that priesthood is more than an ordination; it is a way of life and the power to pursue that life. Without the priesthood and its guiding principles, neither man nor woman can achieve Zion in his or her life and thus attain exaltation, the ultimate form of salvation.

In the fourth book of the Three Pillars of Zion series, we examined the law of the celestial kingdom,[7] which is the foundational law of Zion—the law of consecration, the third pillar of Zion. We demonstrated that this law is a template that can and has been used in a number of situations. Our living the guiding principles of the law of consecration results in equality and unity, two foundational characteristics that describe the celestial kingdom. To live this law, we must make a choice between God and mammon, which is the ultimate test of mortality. In the end, we learned that the law of consecration is all about love. It is a manifestation of "The Royal Law,"[8] which is this: "Thou shalt love the Lord thy God with all thy heart, and with all thy soul, and with all thy mind. This is the first and great commandment. And the second is like unto it, Thou shalt love thy neighbour as thyself." The royal law is "the first and great commandment," according to Jesus, and upon it "hang all the law and the prophets."[9] When all is said and done, we consecrate ourselves and all that we have and are because we love God and his children.

Now armed with the three pillars of Zion, we embark on the journey to Zion, and in the process we will become pure in heart. The journey necessitates our "falling" into this lone and dreary world. Here we encounter the wilderness of sin, which we enter when we

---

6 McConkie, *A New Witness for the Articles of Faith*, 313.
7 D&C 105:5.
8 James 2:8.
9 Matthew 22:36–40.

sin and fall away from the Lord, followed by the Lord's wilderness, into which the Lord takes us to purify and sanctify us. To escape the wilderness of sin, we must awaken to our awful situation and cry unto the Lord for deliverance. Rescue comes by making and keeping covenants, and thus we begin the transforming journey that ends in our own personal land of promise: Zion.

The journey is one of purification, elimination of contaminants, and sanctification (to change our purpose in life). To come forth as gold, we must submit to "crucible" periods, which are essentially times when we are thrown into the furnace of affliction. The purpose of these times is to change our nature and our disposition to sin. Only by submitting to this process can we one day be in a position for the Lord to perform our ultimate deliverance and usher us into his presence. Other purposes of crucibles are to weld us to the Lord under the Covenant, to teach us to have faith and to trust him, and to prove us trustworthy of the blessings of eternity.

To navigate the Lord's wilderness involves hard work, traveling by revelation, and journeying exactly as the Lord directs. We discover that angels attend us, and, despite the odds, we always enjoy the Lord's safety and security. To solidify this idea in our minds and to prepare us for the ultimate day of deliverance, the Lord delivers us multiple times from seemingly impossible situations. Occasionally, the Lord brings us, as he did Lehi, to our own Bountifuls, or places of reprieve. We use these reprieves as Sabbaths: to commune with the Lord, to enter into his rest, and to prepare us for the final and most difficult part of our journey, which becomes our ultimate test of faith.

Somewhere along the way we are confronted by Satan. Once and for all, we must choose between Satan and God. In some cases, this confrontation is also coupled with the equally necessary Abrahamic test. Overcoming Satan and sacrificing all things bring us to the point where we can fully take upon us the name of Jesus Christ, the ultimate manifestation of being born again. Now we are pure in heart and qualify to be ushered into the presence of the Lord. This wilderness journey is how we come to Zion and to Christ. The wilderness journey is the "adventure of discipleship, [the] trek of treks,"[10] the path called "strait and narrow."

We become pure in heart by increments. And, ultimately, the ideal of being pure in heart is to qualify to see God.

Indeed, we are commanded to seek the face of the Lord.

This is a process that involves knowing and living the higher law, receiving power from on high, and seeking more doctrine from the Lord. These things make us progressively more holy. To arrive at this point, we strive to become Zion people:

- Above all, pure in heart.
- Separate from Babylon.
- Of one heart and mind—unified with God and our fellowmen.
- Equal in opportunity for and access to God's blessings.
- Stewards, not owners, who are accountable to God.
- Those who have chosen God over mammon.

10 Maxwell, *The Promise of Discipleship*, i.

- Striving to labor for Zion and not to amass personal wealth.
- Those who have completely consecrated ourselves: our time, talents, and all that we have and are for the upbuilding of the kingdom of God and the establishment of Zion.

Now is the day of decision. President Lorenzo Snow said, "It is high time to establish Zion."[11] If we were to apply ourselves, said Brigham Young, we could qualify for the establishment of Zion in our lives, marriages, and families in as little as one year.[12] To do so, we must eliminate contention and anger and bring into our lives the other principles discussed in this series. The book of 3 Nephi is our latter-day guide to establishing Zion.

The account in 3 Nephi describes the ultimate reward for becoming pure in heart. Diligent striving to sanctify ourselves carries the promise that one day we—all of us—will return to the presence of the Lord and behold his face: "And blessed are all the pure in heart, for they *shall* see God."[13] Seeing him is only the beginning of blessings for the pure in heart. We read that the Lord bade the Nephites to come to him *one by one* and experience for themselves the reality of the Atonement and the sacrifice he had made in *each* person's behalf. From this account we learn that many blessings accompany this experience for each of us. For example, as we worship the Lord, rejoice, and bear testimony in his presence, we receive a greater endowment of knowledge and are healed of all our sicknesses and afflictions. Moreover, we hear him pray for us, and we are encircled about by angels. In his presence, we partake of the Lord's Supper and receive a greater endowment of the Holy Ghost. He wipes away all tears, recompensing and multiplying our blessings in proportion to our sacrifices and service, and compensating us for our sufferings, sorrows, and pain. The Lord also gives us greater revelations, prophecies, explanations, and commandments. When we are in his presence, he offers us the privilege of asking for and receiving a special, personalized gift, which we will consecrate back to him in the form of service to his children.

In the end, what we learn from our journey to Zion and our experience with the Lord is that Zion is beautiful! Whether Zion is found within an individual, a marriage, a family, or a priesthood community, Zion is "the perfection of beauty," where "God hath shined."[14] The interpretation of the following scripture has been hotly debated for centuries:[15] "How beautiful upon the mountains are the feet of him that bringeth good tidings."[16] Now we can answer the question of the ages: Who were the beautiful ones? The pure in heart—Zion people.

The blessings the beautiful ones receive are without equal: "And surely there could not be a happier people among all the people who had been created by the hand of God."[17] Happiness describes Zion and its people. Joseph Smith said, "Happiness is the

11 Snow, *The Teachings of Lorenzo Snow*, 181.
12 Young, *Journal of Discourses*, 11:300.
13 3 Nephi 12:8; emphasis added.
14 Psalm 50:2.
15 Ludlow, *A Companion to Your Study of the Book of Mormon*, 186.
16 Isaiah 52:7–10.
17 4 Nephi 1:16.

object and design of our existence; and will be the end thereof, if we pursue the path that leads to it." Then the Prophet defined the path: "This path is virtue, uprightness, faithfulness, holiness."[18] The path to happiness is also the path to Zion and the ultimate goal of our journey: "Happiness is the end of our existence."[19]

18 Smith, *Teachings of the Prophet Joseph Smith*, 255–56.
19 McKay, *Pathways to Happiness*, 208.

Section 1
Come to Zion: The Universal Journey to the Land of Promise

Eternal life is not easily won. It requires our entering into the covenant of salvation—the new and everlasting covenant—living by faith and obedience, sacrificing all things, and consecrating the entirety of ourselves and our possessions to God. Premortally, when we anticipated the journey to eternal life, we shouted for joy.[20] But as we might imagine, when the reality of mortality sets in, even the strongest of spirits sometimes shudder with feelings of inadequacy. Without a doubt, the journey to eternal life is not for the fainthearted. Only by grace can we succeed, "after all we can do."[21] If we did not keep *arrival* as our goal, we would certainly come up short and lose the prize.

Now that we are here in mortality, we realize that the grandest prize is Zion, with its promise of eternal life. Zion is the glorious land, or condition, of promise that lies at the end of a well-defined path called the "strait and narrow."[22] The word *strait* means confined, restricted, strict, or exacting.[23] There is no wiggle room on this path. Thus, the route to Zion is ordered, or *ordained*, with specific markers called *ordinances*, which are gifts of God received by covenant. Only by following this strict path and reaching the markers along the way can we hope to arrive in Zion and partake of eternal life.

From the outset of our journey, we realize that the path is going to be difficult and rugged. Everything along the way seems to be programmed to distract and oppose us. At times, we feel that we are running the most challenging race of our existence. As we travel, our true character and desires emerge. Elder Bruce R. McConkie promised that if we would step onto the path and gather the courage to hold faithfully to it until death, we would achieve our goal. Then, when we finally enter the next life, our calling and election will be assured.[24]

20 Job 38:7.
21 2 Nephi 25:23.
22 McConkie, Conference Report, Oct. 1955, 12.
23 *Webster's New World Dictionary*, s.v. "strait."
24 McConkie, "The Probationary Test of Mortality," 11.

The scriptures are replete with stories of journeys to lands of promise, all of which are representative of the journey to Zion. Moses' and Lehi's journeys figure prominently in the Bible and in the Book of Mormon. There are other "journey" stories: Abraham, Joseph of Egypt, Elijah, the brother of Jared, Alma the Elder, Alma the Younger, Limhi. All of these journey stories, of course, lead to Jesus and the ultimate promised land.. Here are some more examples: The parable of the prodigal son is a story that describes flight from sin and a journey home. In the latter days, we remember the story of the Mormon pioneers. The goal of these physical or spiritual treks remains the same: "Come unto Mount Zion, and unto the city of the living God, the heavenly Jerusalem, and to an innumerable company of angels; to the general assembly and Church of the Firstborn, which are written in heaven, and to God the judge of all, and to the spirits of just men made perfect, and to Jesus the Mediator of the new covenant."[25]

Significantly, each of these journeys was tailor-made to the people involved and to their circumstances. Just so, our own individual journey stories will be unique; nevertheless, we will arrive at the same destination. Examining scriptural journeys, we see a pattern emerge, a pattern we might expect to encounter as we travel toward Zion. In this chapter, we will explore some of the identifying milestones and conditions of the journey to Zion.

Zion Is Our Heritage

The condition of Zion is consistent with our heavenly home, that which we might call the "land of our first inheritance."[26] We were in the beginning with the Father.[27] At some point, our spirits were literally begotten of God and experienced a literal birth of the spirit. Our new spirit bodies carried the genotype of our exalted parents. Our spirit birth provided us a new and expanded identity: as sons and daughters of God, our spirit bodies contained seeds of divinity, with the potential to become exactly like our Heavenly Parents.[28] What remained to become like them was our choosing to walk the same path they had walked and to gain the same experience.

As much as the condition of Zion existed in our first heavenly home, the condition of Zion also existed in the first earthly home. Most certainly, the Garden of Eden was a Zion-like environment. After the Fall, Adam patterned his government after the government of heaven. Adam called upon the Lord, and "the Holy One of Zion . . . established the foundations of Adam-ondi-Ahman."[29] The fact that human life and the first government began this way accentuates and perpetuates our understanding of the reality of our noble heritage. Clearly, we descend from royalty: Our Heavenly Parents, the progenitors of our spirits, are the king and queen of heaven, and our earthly progenitors, Adam and Eve, are also royalty. Adam is the archangel Michael, our "prince forever."[30]

---

25 Smith, *Teachings of the Prophet Joseph Smith,* 12; see also Hebrews 12:22–24.
26 Alma 54:12.
27 D&C 93:21–23.
28 McConkie, *Mormon Doctrine,* 750–51.
29 D&C 78:15.
30 D&C 107:54–55.

Many of the scriptural journey stories contain references to a royal beginning. For example, Moses was the adopted son of Pharaoh; the sons of Mosiah were sons of the king, and Alma was the son of a prophet. The "certain man" who was the father of the prodigal son was obviously a prominent, wealthy man.[31] We likewise had a regal beginning. Our heritage is royal; our genesis was in the environment of Zion. As the poet William Wordsworth wrote:

> Our birth is but a sleep and a forgetting:
> The Soul that rises with us, our life's Star,
> Hath had elsewhere its setting,
> And cometh from afar:
> Not in entire forgetfulness,
> And not in utter nakedness,
> But trailing clouds of glory do we come
> From God, who is our home:
> Heaven lies about us in our infancy![32]

In the same way the genes of an infant's physical body hold in them the child's potential and destiny, spiritual genes carried in our spiritual bodies contain our divine prospects and future. Therefore, if our heavenly parents were kings and queens, we, their progeny, contain the programming to become like them. If they are Zion-like and exist in a Zion-like environment, then we, their children, have the potential to become Zion-like and live in Zion. We are products of Zion parents; our origin and our destiny is Zion.

God created us for a specific purpose: happiness. Lehi said, "Men are that they might have joy."[33] Again, Joseph Smith explained it this way: "Happiness is the object and design of our existence; and will be the end thereof, if we pursue the path that leads to it." Then the Prophet defined the path: "This path is virtue, uprightness, faithfulness, holiness."[34] In the same way that physical genes are programmed to determine the color of eyes, texture of hair, and height, spiritual genes are programmed to determine our happiness. Because we are children of God, we are creations of joy; "happiness is the end of our existence."[35] Happiness describes Zion, the end goal of our journey: "And surely there could not be a happier people among all the people who had been created by the hand of God."[36]

Perfect happiness involves inheriting God's crown. By entitlement of birthright, that crown is rightfully ours. But we cannot obtain it without making the journey, and we cannot make the journey without help. When Adam and Eve realized the distance between them, happiness, and the crown, they rejoiced that Heavenly Father had provided them a Savior to help them achieve their purpose.

---

31 Luke 15:11–32.
32 Wordsworth, "Ode on Intimations of Immortality," in *Narcissism and the Text*, 116–29.
33 2 Nephi 2:25.
34 Smith, *Teachings of the Prophet Joseph Smith*, 255–56.
35 McKay, *Pathways to Happiness*, 208.
36 4 Nephi 1:16.

> And in that day the Holy Ghost fell upon Adam, which beareth record of the Father and the Son, saying: I am the Only Begotten of the Father from the beginning, henceforth and forever, that as thou hast fallen thou mayest be redeemed, and all mankind, even as many as will.
>
> And in that day Adam blessed God and was filled, and began to prophesy concerning all the families of the earth, saying: Blessed be the name of God, for because of my transgression my eyes are opened, *and in this life I shall have joy,* and again in the flesh I shall see God.
>
> And Eve, his wife, heard all these things and was glad, saying: Were it not for our transgression we never should have had seed, and never should have known good and evil, *and the joy of our redemption,* and the eternal life which God giveth unto all the obedient.[37]

Adam and Eve could not hold back from telling their children the good news. "And Adam and Eve blessed the name of God, and they made all things known unto their sons and their daughters."[38] Suddenly, life had a defined purpose—happiness; a defined inheritance—a crown; and a defined destination—Zion. Adam and Eve told their children that if they would enter the path that led to happiness, their children could experience redemption and achieve happiness. Moreover, their children could progress to the point that they could see God, their heavenly progenitor, and eventually return home to the place of their origin, Zion, and there receive their crowns.

Ironically, the pathway to happiness leads through sorrow and adversity. Lehi explained that it is impossible to learn without experiencing opposites.[39] This law of opposition, or opposites, is central to our existence; without opposites, all things would be a "compound in one." That sameness would bring everything to an abrupt halt. In the way that an engine is propelled by electricity alternating between positive and negative poles, the purpose of existence is driven by harnessing the power of opposites. Hence, to ascend on high we must descend below all things so that we might comprehend all things, and thereby gain the ability to become as the Gods, who are above and in all and through all things.[40] For reasons we do not completely understand, employing the power of the law of opposites is the only way to become exalted.

Happiness, therefore, seems to be a byproduct of adversity. That is, by learning to channel the power of adversity, we achieve happiness. Heavenly Father constantly deals with heartfelt sorrow for his sinful children, and yet he describes his life as a "fulness of joy."[41] We can gain an appreciation for this principle through consecration. When we give

37 Moses 5:9–11; emphasis added.
38 Moses 5:12.
39 2 Nephi 2:11–12.
40 D&C 88:6.
41 3 Nephi 28:10.

him our complete selves, including our sorrows, weaknesses, sins, and challenges, he "shall consecrate [our] afflictions for [our] gain."[42] He knows how to do it. He has the ability to use negatives for positive purposes, and that is the way he launches us toward the end purpose of our creation: happiness. And happiness is a primary descriptor of Zion.[43]

The Fall

Earth life is a journey, not a destination. To arrive at our desired destination, we must *fall* into the lone and dreary world[44] and make our way through it by faith. We suddenly find ourselves in a foreign environment. The author of the book of Hebrews names a number of righteous individuals who fell into this environment and successfully traveled the path that we are on now. These individuals might speak for us: "These [righteous individuals saw their promises] afar off, and . . . confessed that they were strangers and pilgrims on the earth." As we traverse the lone and dreary, strait and narrow path, a troubling thought seems to nag at us, saying that things in this telestial environment are not "as they really are."[45] This telestial sphere is a contrived condition that we never have or will experience again. We are strangers here; we are seeking a better country, "that is, an heavenly [country]: wherefore God is not ashamed to be called [our] God: for he hath prepared for [us] a city."[46] That "city" is Zion, and we need to be constantly moving toward it.

The word *fall* is appropriate. We cannot comprehend the distance or the depth of the Fall precipitated by Adam. We fell physically, spiritually, and emotionally into a condition described by President Joseph F. Smith as "below all things."[47] We had, in effect, stood upon the safe ledge of the brilliant celestial kingdom and looked downward upon an ominous darkness, knowing that once we stepped off, we would forfeit our memory and power and become helpless—completely incapable of making it on our own. Worse, we would have no immediate comprehension that we had descended into a fallen world. Unless we were taught differently and gained a testimony of our true identity and heritage, we would be consigned to the belief that this mortal existence is all there is, and worse, that the conditions here are normal. Tragically, for a time, we might even embrace the luring dangers that permeate telestial life.

In her "Alma the Younger" series, Brigham Young University religion professor Catherine Thomas stated that in this mortal existence we "would begin to make choices before we had much knowledge or judgment or ability to choose right over wrong consistently and would inevitably make mistakes and sin. . . . As we grew in a fallen environment, we would form wrong opinions and make false assumptions, by which we would then govern our lives, and would unwittingly be programmed by many precepts of men. We would make many choices before we had grasped the significance of even the Light

42 2 Nephi 2:2.
43 4 Nephi 4:16.
44 McConkie and Millet, *Doctrinal Commentary on the Book of Mormon*, 3:276.
45 Jacob 4:13.
46 Hebrews 11:13–16.
47 Smith, *Gospel Doctrine*, 13.

that we had. Many would reach an advanced age before they really saw the Light. Some would never see it in this life."[48]

We cannot fathom the range of emotions that must have barraged us as we contemplated our descent into this lone and dreary world. Nevertheless, we had vigorously defended the Father's plan in the War in Heaven; we had dedicated our lives to Christ, who was to become our Savior and the central figure in the plan of salvation; we had hoped and prepared in every way for this moment; and yet, we must have been horrified to imagine that we, who stood with the noble and great ones, would come here and succumb to sin. In Catherine Thomas's words, "The period of descent was surely seen by the righteous premortal spirits as a great sacrifice. The most righteous did not want to sin. They knew the truth about sin. A veil was necessary so that they would make the descent . . . into spiritual darkness."[49] Only profound faith in Christ could have given us the strength to voluntarily fall from our Zion home.

Nevertheless, knowing that falling was the only way to obtain a physical body, make covenants, and gain an eternal kingdom, we stepped off the celestial ledge, armed with the light of Christ, and plummeted into this dark, telestial world. Imagine our courage, for because of agency no one would have been compelled to come; imagine our hope, for the transcendent possibilities of eternity lay before us. We knew the risks. We also knew that eternal life would be won only by our entering and keeping our second estate.[50] Therefore, we willingly fell into the unnatural condition of mortality and away from Zion in order to rediscover the principles of Zion and make our way back to Zion.

The Wilderness of Sin

In this fallen state, we encounter at least two experiences the scriptures refer to as "the wilderness." In both wildernesses, we gain experience in discerning between good and evil. One of the wildernesses is the wilderness of the Lord, which we will discuss shortly; we enter that wilderness by the Lord's design. The other wilderness is the wilderness of sin,[51] which, like a prison, people are consigned to as a consequence of their errant actions or which they choose, as did the prodigal son, by their sinful wanderings from the Lord.

In the parable of the prodigal son, the wilderness of sin is described as a "far country" in which there is famine, disloyalty, and widespread want. This is descriptive of Babylon, where neither it nor its citizens will ultimately support us. When we choose to go to the far country, we are left to suffer the harsh realities of our choices. The prodigal entered this wilderness because he had chosen "riotous living," wantonness, gross sin, and wastefulness.[52] In this wilderness, the idea of being of royal heritage is a thing of naught, and inheritances are sold for a mess of pottage.[53]

48 Thomas, "Alma the Younger, Part 1," n.p.
49 Thomas, "Alma the Younger, Part 1," n.p.
50 Abraham 3:26.
51 Exodus 16:1.
52 Luke 15:13–16.
53 Genesis 25:29–34.

On the other hand, the Lord cast Paul into the wilderness of sin when the resurrected Savior abruptly appeared and intervened in Paul's life. Paul's wilderness experience was compacted into three days of spiritual suffering and physical blindness: "And [Paul] arose from the earth; and when his eyes were opened, he saw no man: but they led him by the hand, and brought him into Damascus. And he was three days without sight, and neither did eat nor drink."[54] Then he was healed, and he devoted the rest of his life to the Lord.

Likewise, by the act of an angel, Alma was thrust into the wilderness of sin for three hellish days. His description of this wilderness is perhaps the most vivid in scripture:

> And it came to pass that I fell to the earth; and it was for the space of three days and three nights that I could not open my mouth, neither had I the use of my limbs. . . . But I was racked with eternal torment, for my soul was harrowed up to the greatest degree and racked with all my sins.
>
> Yea, I did remember all my sins and iniquities, for which I was tormented with the pains of hell; yea, I saw that I had rebelled against my God, and that I had not kept his holy commandments.
>
> Yea, and I had murdered many of his children, or rather led them away unto destruction; yea, and in fine so great had been my iniquities, that the very thought of coming into the presence of my God did rack my soul with inexpressible horror.
>
> Oh, thought I, that I could be banished and become extinct both soul and body, that I might not be brought to stand in the presence of my God, to be judged of my deeds.
>
> And now, for three days and for three nights was I racked, even with the pains of a damned soul.[55]

The wilderness of sin is designed to reclaim us. There we suffer the buffetings of Satan, which are so severe that we will eventually cry out for relief. Only the Lord's redemption can rescue us from this fate: "Inasmuch as ye are cut off for transgression, ye cannot escape the buffetings of Satan until the day of redemption."[56]

Satan knows the secret of sin, and if he can convince us to sin, he can torture us until we become as miserable as he is.[57] Because Satan is the exact opposite of God,

54 Acts 9:8–9.
55 Alma 36:10–16.
56 D&C 104:9; see also D&C 78:12; 82:21; 132:26.
57 2 Nephi 2:27.

whose life is marked by a "fulness of joy,"[58] Satan is most miserable being in the universe. In an effort to make us equally miserable, he seeks to enter and take over our bodies so that he can transform us into beings like himself. Because "light and truth forsake the evil one,"[59] he seeks to empty us of light and truth. He does this by persistent temptation. If he can persuade us to sin, he can cause a rupture in our spiritual system so that we hemorrhage light and truth: "That wicked one cometh and taketh away light and truth, through disobedience."[60]

The devil's tactic is terrifying: "And thus he flattereth them, and leadeth them along until he draggeth their souls down to hell; and thus he causeth them to catch themselves in their own snare."[61] Once he gains entrance to our souls by tempting us to sin, he can drain us of light and truth to the point that he can convince us, almost without restraint, to do anything and to follow him down to hell. Then he has what he wanted so much in the beginning—our agency—and many of us hardly put up a fight to protect and retain it. The scriptures reveal his strategy:

- "The temptations of the devil . . . blindeth the eyes, and hardeneth the hearts of the children of men, and leadeth them away into broad roads, that they perish and are lost."[62]
- "[The devil] is the founder of all these things; yea, the founder of murder, and works of darkness; yea, and he leadeth them by the neck with a flaxen cord, until he bindeth them with his strong cords forever."[63]
- "And others will he pacify, and lull them away into carnal security, that they will say: All is well in Zion; yea, Zion prospereth, all is well—and thus the devil cheateth their souls, and leadeth them away carefully down to hell."[64]

The Awakening

The prodigal son wandered in the wilderness of sin until, fully miserable, "he came to himself."[65] When we have had enough, we also come to ourselves, and turn back. We find ourselves miserable as we wallow in the wilderness of sin, and, as we have learned, misery is contrary to our nature: "Happiness is the object and design of our existence."[66] We can stand sin and misery for only so long. When we awaken and find ourselves in Babylon, we cry out for help to get back to Zion.

Often, we must be stirred up to repentance: "For the kingdom of the devil must shake, and they which belong to it must needs be stirred up unto repentance, or the devil will grasp them with his everlasting chains, and they . . . perish."[67] Being stirred up to

---

58 3 Nephi 28:10.
59 D&C 93:37.
60 D&C 93:39.
61 D&C 10:26.
62 1 Nephi 12:17.
63 2 Nephi 26:22.
64 2 Nephi 28:21.
65 Luke 15:17.
66 Smith, *Teachings of the Prophet Joseph Smith*, 255–56.
67 2 Nephi 28:19.

repentance is the Lord's way of calling us home: "And after their temptations, and much tribulation, behold, I, the Lord, will feel after them, and if they harden not their hearts, and stiffen not their necks against me, they shall be converted, and I will heal them."[68] But, as we have noted, before the healing we often must experience the Lord's chastisement, which is more than scolding; it is punishment with the Lord's rod: "Therefore I command you to repent—repent, lest I smite you by the rod of my mouth, and by my wrath, and by my anger, and your sufferings be sore—how sore you know not, how exquisite you know not, yea, how hard to bear you know not."[69] As we shall see, in the process of conversion the Lord also uses chastisement and the rod in a refining rather than a punishing sense.

Alma was chastised and stirred up to repentance in the wilderness of sin. He described his awakening this way: "And it came to pass that as I was thus racked with torment, while I was harrowed up by the memory of my many sins."[70] To be "racked with torment" summons images of medieval torture whereby the body is violently stretched, pulling apart vertebrae and tearing limbs from sockets. To be "harrowed up" recalls the image of a plow cutting deeply into the soil, unearthing roots and weeds and exposing the dark things that are underground to the sudden brightness of light. Only by embracing the light can one be delivered from being racked and from harrowing and escape the wilderness of sin.

Like Paul and Alma, we also are stirred up and awakened from our dire situation. As we have noted, "stirring up" can happen "by [the Lord] allowing financial reversals to occur, bringing loss of homes, cars, boats, and incomes; personal or corporate bankruptcy; and so forth. We might also experience a severe loss of health or death of a loved one, which can do the same thing by making worldly things [and sin] unattractive and meaningless."[71] We are awakened because of the seriousness of our situation. In desperation, we seek a way out, and, when we finally realize that nothing and no one can save us, we reach out to the Savior.

Alma recorded: "I remembered also to have heard my father prophesy unto the people concerning the coming of one Jesus Christ, a Son of God, to atone for the sins of the world. Now, as my mind caught hold upon this thought, I cried within my heart: O Jesus, thou Son of God, have mercy on me, who am in the gall of bitterness, and am encircled about by the everlasting chains of death. And now, behold, when I thought this, I could remember my pains no more; yea, I was harrowed up by the memory of my sins no more. And oh, what joy, and what marvelous light I did behold; yea, my soul was filled with joy as exceeding as was my pain!"[72] He had turned from Babylon and begun the journey back to Zion.

The Cry for Help

The Lord often allows us to linger in the wilderness of sin so that we can internalize lessons that can be learned only there. One of the best examples of the awakening and cry for help is the account of Limhi's people, who had been languishing in the wilder-

68 D&C 112:13.
69 D&C 19:15.
70 Alma 36:17.
71 Yorgason, *I Need Thee Every Hour,* 206.
72 Alma 36:17–20.

ness of sin because of their transgressions. Finally, after being crushed by the weight of their afflictions, they awakened from their wretched condition and cried out for deliverance: "And they did humble themselves even in the depths of humility; and they did cry mightily to God; yea, even all the day long did they cry unto their God that he would deliver them out of their afflictions."

Their situation was miserable and hopeless. Despite their repeated efforts to deliver themselves and their having risked everything, they, of themselves, could not break free of the chains that held them bound. This is a universal lesson that everyone in the wilderness of sin must learn: Only the Savior can deliver us. We are helpless without him. Evidently, Limhi's people needed to learn this lesson completely so that they would never again depart from it or yield to sin. Therefore, "the Lord was slow to hear their cry because of their iniquity."

Of course, the Lord had every right to chastise them. As every parent knows, punishing a child for misconduct is secondary to helping the child internalize a lesson. Therefore, to briefly chastise and then immediately reinstate priviledge is not always the wise course. Sometimes wrongdoing requires a season of torment to help the child rethink the attitude that resulted in his bad behavior. Such was the case of Limhi's people. Mormon informed us that the Lord indeed "did hear their cries," but the Lord temporarily withheld deliverance in an act of mercy beyond the ability or maturity level of most parents. The Lord used the natural consequences of sin to create an atmosphere in which he could help Limhi's people learn to trust and obey him. Then, as they learned their lessons, the Lord delivered them by degrees. That is, he eased their burdens in proportion to their repentance; but for the present, "the Lord did not see fit to deliver them out of bondage."[73]

The approach worked. The next thing we read is that the people drew together in love and adopted a form of consecration to take care of the widows and orphans.[74] They were discovering the principles of Zion and becoming Zion-like. That change of heart qualified them for deliverance, which miraculously occurred a short time later—and was a testimony of the Lord's intervention. Mormon told us plainly: "There was no way they could deliver themselves . . . , [they were surrounded] on every side."[75] They finally realized that they could only be delivered in turning to the Lord for salvation.

Alma the Younger's cry for help is one of the most poignant: "O Jesus, thou Son of God, have mercy on me, who am in the gall of bitterness, and am encircled about by the everlasting chains of death."[76] Likewise, when we awaken to our awful situation[77] and cry out, "O Jesus, thou Son of God, have mercy on me," he will respond and, in time, deliver us.

To escape the wilderness of sin requires our making or renewing the new and everlasting covenant, which is the covenant of deliverance. After Christ's Resurrection, Peter was teaching people who were in the wilderness of sin. Through the Spirit, his message

73 Mosiah 21:1–15.
74 Mosiah 21:16–17.
75 Mosiah 21:5.
76 Alma 36:18.
77 Ether 8:24.

pierced them, and suddenly they awakened to their awful state and cried out for help: "Now when they heard this, they were pricked in their heart, and said unto Peter and to the rest of the apostles, Men and brethren, what shall we do? Then Peter said unto them, Repent, and be baptized every one of you in the name of Jesus Christ for the remission of sins, and ye shall receive the gift of the Holy Ghost."[78]

Only the new and everlasting covenant, the covenant of deliverance, offers relief and safety: "Whosoever believeth in [Christ] should not perish."[79] A man cannot escape the wilderness of sin without being born of the water and of the Spirit. Jesus said, "Verily, verily, I say unto thee, Except a man be born of water and of the Spirit, he cannot enter into the kingdom of God."[80] As we have discussed, the new and everlasting covenant calls for us to live a new life; if we will do this, we receive in return the guarantee of deliverance. Hence, the Lord said, "Ye must be born again."[81] We are symbolically born again by baptism, then by the sacrament, and, finally, by the temple ordinances. Agreeing to live a new life is the price we pay for deliverance from the wilderness of sin. When we pay this price and indicate our willingness to remain firm in this decision, the Lord takes us out of the condition of Babylon and points us toward Zion.

The Lord's Wilderness

Interpreted broadly, mortality is a wilderness experience. But in mortality we experience, specifically, both the wilderness of sin and the Lord's wilderness. We leave the first wilderness only when we enter the second. Perhaps Lehi was describing the transition we all must make from one wilderness to the other: "Methought I saw in my dream, a dark and dreary wilderness [the wilderness of sin]. And it came to pass that I saw a man, and he was dressed in a white robe; and he came and stood before me. And it came to pass that he spake unto me, and bade me follow him. And it came to pass that as I followed him I beheld myself that I was in a dark and dreary waste [the Lord's wilderness]."[82] We might call this second "waste" Lehi had just entered the "Lord's wilderness" because within that wilderness was the tree of life.[83]

The purpose of the Lord's wilderness, which is traveled by means of the strait and narrow path, is not to reclaim but to:

1. Purify (eliminate impurities and cause the spirit to become contrite)
2. Sanctify (change the purpose of the soul's journey by causing the heart to be broken and pliable)
3. Deliver us into the presence of the Lord, where we will receive a crown.

We enter the Lord's wilderness to make our way to Zion. Faith and repentance prepare us to enter this wilderness. Marking the entrance of the Lord's wilderness is a gate, which is distin-

78 Acts 2:37–38.
79 John 3:16.
80 John 3:5.
81 John 3:6–7.
82 1 Nephi 8:5–7.
83 1 Nephi 8:10.

guished by two ordinances: baptism and confirmation. "For the gate by which ye should enter is repentance and baptism by water; and then cometh a remission of your sins by fire and by the Holy Ghost. And then are ye in this strait and narrow path which leads to eternal life."[84]

It is vitally important to understand that we are clean when we enter the Lord's wilderness. We are not in his wilderness to become clean; we are here to become Zion-like and to prepare to return to the presence of the Lord and receive eternal life. Therefore, when we encounter the refining environment of the Lord's wilderness, we must not allow ourselves to be deceived by Satan and imagine that we are being punished. The process of becoming perfected requires that a clean person submit to the Holy Ghost, who will make that person pure and sanctified. "Clean hands and a pure heart" is a description of the process, not just a list of virtues.[85] Job understood the process and declared, "He that hath clean hands shall be stronger and stronger."[86] We remain clean by doing all we can do (obeying the commandments, constantly repenting, worthily partaking of the sacrament, having humility, performing charitable service, and so forth), but we become pure in heart by the refining motions of the Holy Ghost in the Lord's wilderness.

Experiencing Opposites

In some ways, the Lord's wilderness can be a harsher environment than the wilderness of sin. Of course, both have similarities. For example, in each wilderness the Lord allows us to experience opposition in its extreme. However, in the Lord's wilderness, we must prove our worth by descending below all things in order to gain the power to rise above all things.[87] President Joseph F. Smith taught, "Had we not known before we came the necessity of our coming, the importance of obtaining tabernacles, the glory to be achieved in posterity, the grand object to be attained by being tried and tested—weighed in the balance, in the exercise of the divine attributes, god-like powers and free agency with which we are endowed; whereby, after descending below all things, Christ-like, we might ascend above all things, and become like our Father, Mother and Elder Brother, Almighty and Eternal!—we never would have come; that is, if we could have stayed away."[88]

At the outset of his wilderness experience, Moses discovered the highs and lows of universal powers. What began as a remarkable face-to-face experience with the Lord suddenly turned to Moses being left to himself and face-to-face with Satan. When Moses detected and overcame the devil through the name of Jesus Christ, he returned to the presence of the Lord. This cycle of *blessing-descent-blessing* or *revelation-testing- greater revelation* is a cycle wilderness wanderers experience time and again. With each cycle, we grow to know the Savior more intimately and eternal life comes into finer focus. With each cycle, we learn to discern between Babylon and Zion, and that enhanced ability to discern gives us greater power to make exalted choices.

84 2 Nephi 31:17–18.
85 Psalm 24:4.
86 Job 17:9.
87 D&C 88:6.
88 Smith, *Gospel Doctrine*, 13.

Strangers and Pilgrims

In the Lord's wilderness, we find ourselves in a lone and dreary world—a major discovery!—and we long to go home to Zion. We feel like strangers and pilgrims in a hostile land. Soon a dawning of realization settles upon us: This place is not home. It is a contrived, fallen condition that in no way resembles home or "things as they really are."[89]

Adults look back upon their school days as foreign to the realities of adult life, and yet in their youth they needed that schooling to help prepare them for life. Just so, the school of mortality is a foreign atmosphere to us as compared to our heavenly home; but mortality is necessary for what lies ahead. Any school environment is temporary, controlled, set apart from real-world conditions, and strict. In school, we are relegated to a place that is not home and that does not even resemble home. But when we complete our schooling, life will never be the same. The Lord's wilderness is no different. Here in the wilderness, we experience the extremes of joy and difficulty, but through them we acquire the indispensible education required to bring us back home equipped with knowledge and understanding. The Lord's wilderness is much like a preparatory school where we get to practice being Zion-like in a telestial experience.

Lehi described how foreign and weighed down he felt in his wilderness travels: "And after I had traveled for the space of many hours in darkness, I began to pray unto the Lord that he would have mercy on me, according to the multitude of his tender mercies."[90] This place was not Lehi's home, and he knew it. He was a stranger and a foreigner here. This stark realization caused him to set his sights on getting through the wilderness and going home to where he belonged. And he knew that he could not do it alone. He had neither a compass to guide him nor adequate power to persevere. Therefore he cried out to the Lord for help.

Separation from Babylon

A purpose of the Lord's wilderness is to separate us from Babylon. The call to leave Babylon is accompanied by deliverance from the wilderness of sin. During our sojourn in the Lord's wilderness, we will experience deliverance from time to time, and those experiences will prepare us for the ultimate deliverance: entering into our promised land. Our personalized promised land is always symbolic of Zion. From the moment we enter the Lord's wilderness until we are delivered, we hear the Lord's voice beckoning us to come to him and behold his face, an event which attends ultimate deliverance.

> Behold, that which you hear is as the voice of one crying in the wilderness—in the wilderness, because you cannot see him—my voice, because my voice is Spirit; my Spirit is truth; truth abideth and hath no end; and if it be in

89 Jacob 4:13.
90 1 Nephi 8:8.

> you it shall abound. And if your eye be single to my glory, your whole bodies shall be filled with light, and there shall be no darkness in you; and that body which is filled with light comprehendeth all things. Therefore, sanctify yourselves that your minds become single to God, and the days will come that you shall see him; for he will unveil his face unto you, and it shall be in his own time, and in his own way, and according to his own will.[91]

No tragedy could be worse than being delivered from the wilderness of sin and entering the Lord's wilderness only to turn back. The possibility is as real as it is potent. The ever present lure of Babylon permeates our environment. Nephi reported, "And it came to pass that as we journeyed in the wilderness, behold Laman and Lemuel, and two of the daughters of Ishmael, and the two sons of Ishmael and their families, did rebel against us; yea, against me, Nephi, and Sam, and their father, Ishmael, and his wife, and his three other daughters. And it came to pass in the which rebellion, they were desirous to return unto the land of Jerusalem."[92] This dangerous condition caused Nephi to grieve; the entire expedition was suddenly at risk because of Laman and Lemuel's persistently trying to mix Babylon and Zion.

Likewise, if we who have been delivered from Babylon and the wilderness of sin look back and return to it, our condition will be worse than it was before we were delivered. Peter taught, "For if after they have escaped the pollutions of the world through the knowledge of the Lord and Saviour Jesus Christ, they are again entangled therein, and overcome, *the latter end is worse with them than the beginning.* For it had been better for them not to have known the way of righteousness, than, after they have known it, to turn from the holy commandment delivered unto them."[93]

The conditions of the Lord's wilderness require rejecting Babylon completely, trusting in the Lord absolutely, being willing to exist day to day by the grace of Jesus Christ, surrendering our hearts to him, and traveling as the Lord directs. Upon entering the Lord's wilderness, our source of security shifts from the world to the Lord, and, in the process, our faith is sometimes sorely tried. No wonder, then, that we often look back and long for the life Babylon offers. No wonder, then, that the Lord continually calls us away from Babylon: "Go ye out from among the nations, even from Babylon, from the midst of wickedness, which is spiritual Babylon."[94] He pleads with us to stay focused on the journey: "After a person has faith in Christ, repents of his sins, and is baptized for the remission of his sins and receives the Holy Ghost, (by the laying on of hands), which is the first Comforter, then let him continue to humble himself before God, hungering and thirsting after righteousness, and living by every word of God, and the Lord will soon say unto him, Son, thou shalt be exalted."[95]

---

91 D&C 88:66–68.
92 1 Nephi 7:6–7.
93 2 Peter 2:20–21; emphasis added.
94 D&C 133:14.
95 Smith, *Teachings of the Prophet Joseph Smith,* 150.

When we separate ourselves from Babylon and enter the Lord's wilderness, we figuratively, and sometimes literally, leave behind everything associated with Babylon. We simply cannot take anything of Babylon with us as we travel toward Zion. Lehi and his family literally left everything superfluous behind: "And it came to pass that he departed into the wilderness. And he left his house, and the land of his inheritance, and his gold, and his silver, and his precious things, and took nothing with him, save it were his family, and provisions, and tents, and departed into the wilderness."[96] We learn that Limhi and his people "did depart by night into the wilderness with [nothing but] their flocks and herds."[97] Likewise, Alma's people took only their flocks and grain "and departed into the wilderness,"[98] and later, when they had built the beautiful city of Helam, they left everything again and fled into the Lord's wilderness with only their flocks.[99] These people's flights are reminiscent of the Latter-day Saints leaving Ohio, Missouri, then Nauvoo, to cross the wilderness with nothing except what they could carry in a wagon or on a cart.

Separation is a sacrifice, and it can be painful. Jesus said, "He that loveth father or mother more than me is not worthy of me: and he that loveth son or daughter more than me is not worthy of me. And he that taketh not his cross, and followeth after me, is not worthy of me."[100] We separate from Babylon and enter the Lord's wilderness as a test of our loyalty to the Lord and to the new and everlasting covenant: "For if ye will not abide in my covenant ye are not worthy of me."[101] The Lord allows no excuses; despite the difficulty of the sacrifice, he requires that we come out of Babylon completely and never turn back: "Behold, I, the Lord, who was crucified for the sins of the world, give unto you a commandment that you shall forsake the world."[102]

Fleeing for Safety

We flee Babylon into the Lord's wilderness for our own safety. Lehi fled to save his life; the Israelites fled to escape Pharaoh; the brother of Jared fled to preserve the individuality of his people and their language. Abraham, who was faced with losing his life and the prospect of a devastating famine, received the following commandment from the Lord: "Get thee out of thy country, and from thy kindred, and from thy father's house, unto a land that I will show thee."[103] To arrive at that "land," or, our Zion we must traverse the Lord's wilderness.

Hugh Nibley wrote: "Babylon's time is all but used up, and the only thing for the Saints to do is to get out of her."[104] Her destiny and the destiny of her people is complete and utter collapse, the extent of which the world has not experienced since the Flood and the annihilation of the nations of the Jaredites, Nephites, and the Jews: "And there

96 1 Nephi 2:4.
97 Mosiah 22:11.
98 Mosiah 23:1.
99 Mosiah 24:18–20.
100 Matthew 10:37–38.
101 D&C 98:15.
102 D&C 53:2.
103 Abraham 2:3.
104 Nibley, *Approaching Zion*, 31.

followed another angel, saying, Babylon is fallen, is fallen, that great city, because she made all nations drink of the wine of the wrath of her fornication."[105]

Both Alma the Elder and Alma the Younger were told to get their people out of their respective Babylons. To the elder Alma the Lord said, "Haste thee and get thou and this people out of this land."[106] To the younger Alma he said, "Get this people out of this land, that they perish not; for Satan has great hold on the hearts of the Amalekites, who do stir up the Lamanites to anger against their brethren to slay them; therefore get thee out of this land; and blessed are this people in this generation, for I will preserve them."[107] No matter how persuasive Babylon's propaganda, our remaining within her spiritual and physical precincts is deadly. In our individual and collective lives, we must escape Babylon and flee to the Lord's wilderness for safety. Blaine Yorgason wrote:

> For those who would enter the wilderness of the Lord, a separation of sorts must occur as they leave behind those who do not wish, for whatever reasons, to travel where they are going. In our day this separation will usually be more spiritual and emotional than physical, but it will be just as real and difficult as a physical separation might be. It will usually mean that world-oriented loved ones will have less and less in common with the wilderness travelers, conversations about things of the Spirit will decrease as the wilderness travelers' knowledge concerning the things of God increases, and the wilderness sojourners' increasing sense of responsibility for the spiritual welfare of their loved ones will often be unappreciated.
>
> Wilderness travelers must look forward to a certain amount of loneliness. If they talk of their experiences with others who are not fellow travelers (and truthfully there never seem to be many), they will either be misunderstood or, worse, maligned and mocked. One or two such encounters, and they soon learn to keep their mouths closed and to lean wholly upon the strength of the Lord for companionship. Thus does their journey become private and even occasionally secret.[108]

While our departure from Babylon into the Lord's wilderness might be without fanfare, the wilderness journey will nevertheless save our spiritual and physical lives. Hugh Nibley wrote:

105 Revelation 14:8.
106 Mosiah 24:23.
107 Alma 27:12.
108 Yorgason, *I Need Thee Every Hour,* 248.

> "He leadeth away the righteous into precious lands, and the wicked he destroyeth, and curseth the land unto them" (1 Nephi 17:38). Such was always the Lord's way. When he brought Lehi out of Jerusalem, "no one knew about it save it were himself and those whom he brought out of the land." Exactly so did the Lord bring Moses and the people in secret out of the wicked land of Egypt, and Abraham fled by night and secretly from Ur of the Chaldees as Lot did from Sodom and Gomorrah, and so was the city of Enoch removed suddenly to an inaccessible place. And in every case, the wicked world thus left behind is soon to be destroyed, so that those who leave the flesh-pots and the "precious things" behind and lose all for a life of hardship are actually losing their lives to save them.[109]

The Crucible

The Lord's wilderness is temporary, but its duration is tailor-made to each person. The commonality of the Lord's wilderness for each of us is that it always results in deliverance for its travelers. In some cases, the Lord's wilderness leads to deliverance in the form of death. Perhaps that is why an extreme, sanctifying trial often precedes death, as if that trial were a final preparation for the promise of eternal life.

Both the duration of the wilderness experience and the distance traveled are punctuated by *crucible* periods. A crucible is a container that receives raw ore and is placed by a metallurgist in a furnace. When the ore becomes molten, the properties of the ore separate, and the metallurgist can divide the pure from the impure. The result is steel, silver, gold, or some other unalloyed metal. Job entered the Lord's wilderness and submitted to his crucible. At a point of intense heat, he cried out his allegiance and testified: "When [God] hath tried me, I shall come forth as gold."[110] The transformation of the raw natural man to the purified Saint requires that he, like Job, submit to the refining process so that he can emerge as a new creature[111] in the image of God.[112] The scripture reads: "And [the Lord] shall sit as a refiner and purifier of silver; and he shall purify the sons of Levi, and purge them as gold and silver, that they may offer unto the Lord an offering in righteousness."[113]

Any number of conditions can qualify as a crucible: relationship challenges, spiritual tests, financial setbacks, illnesses, caring for a sick or afflicted person, or any combination of these things. A crucible can also come in the form of persecution, when the world

---

109 Nibley, *An Approach to the Book of Mormon*, 139.
110 Job 23:10.
111 JST, 2 Corinthians 5:17.
112 Alma 5:19.
113 3 Nephi 24:3; D&C 128:24.

rejects, hates, and fights against us.[114] Job's crucible involved the loss of family, fortune, health, and honor. He lost the loyalty of his friends, and the relationship with his wife was strained. At one point, even his spirituality seems to have taken a beating.

Sometimes crucibles are called "trying" or "chastisement," and we are required to endure the process or forfeit our eternal inheritance: "My people must be tried in all things, that they may be prepared to receive the glory that I have for them, even the glory of Zion; and he that will not bear chastisement is not worthy of my kingdom."[115]

During the crucible periods of our lives, we are not only thrown into the furnace to burn out impurities, but we are also straitened by the Lord's rod.[116] As we have learned, to straiten is to confine by strict and exacting measures.[117] A rod is a straight stick used to punish, which is how it is used in the wilderness of sin. A rod is also a staff, or scepter, carried as a symbol of office, rank, or power. Additionally, a rod is used to measure.[118]

It is easy to see why the Lord would use the terms *straiten* and *rod* in connection with the crucible experience. Because he is the Purifier, he places us in a temporary, confined environment where he can extract from us all impurities. He accomplishes this by strictness and chastisement, and he measures our worth by how we submit to the process. He does all of this in love, of course; punishment occurs only in the wilderness of sin. Straitening by the rod has a different purpose in the Lord's wilderness; that purpose is to chasten, which in the Lord's wilderness means, among other things, "to make chaste,"[119] or in other words, to make us "pure in thought and act."[120] The author of Hebrews says, "For whom the Lord loveth he chasteneth, and scourgeth every son whom he receiveth. If ye endure chastening, God dealeth with you as with sons; for what son is he whom the father chasteneth not?" Knowing that we are being *loved* into the image of God might make the purifying experience bearable but it does not necessarily make it easier: "Now no chastening for the present seemeth to be joyous, but grievous: nevertheless afterward it yieldeth the peaceable fruit of righteousness unto them which are exercised thereby."[121]

Thus, in the Lord's wilderness, straitening by the rod equals loving chastisement, which makes us chaste (pure in thought and act). The process increases our level of righteousness until we approach perfection. This is the purpose of the Lord's wilderness: to purify, sanctify, and perfect us until we "come forth as gold."[122] Joseph Smith's translation of Hebrews 11:40 reads: "God having provided some better things for them through their sufferings, for without sufferings they could not be made perfect."

In the Gethsemanes—a word meaning "olive press"—of our lives, we are crushed and pressed until impurities are bled from us. Often, at critical moments, we call for the

114 Kimball, "A Gift of Gratitude," 1.
115 D&C 136:31.
116 1 Nephi 17:41.
117 *Webster's New World Dictionary*, s.v. "strait."
118 *Webster's New World Dictionary*, s.v. "rod."
119 *Encyclopedia of Mormonism*, 264.
120 *Merriam-Webster Collegiate Dictionary*, s.v., "chaste."
121 Hebrews 12:6–7, 11.
122 Job 23:10.

Lord's servants, the elders, to bless us by means of the sacred ordinance of administration.[123] Perhaps the tears and perspiration that flow during crucible experiences act like a sacred washing, which prepares us to be anointed with oil while we are administered to. Then the elders, who act in the name of Jesus Christ, bless us with healing, instruction, and comfort. It is no wonder, then, that when we are delivered from a physical malady by means of the administration ordinance, we are also delivered spiritually, and, remarkably, our sins are forgiven.[124]

Something of eternal value is being forged if we will endure the pain of the crucible: "Ye cannot behold with your natural eyes, for the present time, the design of your God concerning those things which shall come hereafter, and the glory which shall follow after much tribulation."[125] The greatest miracle in time or eternity is about to take place: A god is about to emerge from the ashes of a natural man! But, if we had not been willing to enter the Lord's wilderness and endure its crucible—the straitening, the rod, and the chastisement—we simply would not have been able to accomplish our mission in life or achieve the apex of our potential. Abraham, Job, Nephi, Alma, and Joseph Smith are all examples of individuals who entered the Lord's wilderness, submitted to the fire of the crucible, and came forth as gold.

As we have said, the Lord's wilderness and its crucible periods are temporary; nevertheless, they are individualized and of indeterminate length. Nephi traveled eight years in the wilderness before he reached Bountiful. The Israelites wandered forty years before they crossed the Jordan River into the promised land. We often see fourteen years as a common wilderness measurement. For example, the sons of Mosiah served fourteen years among the Lamanites. From the time Ishmael was born, Sarah waited fourteen years for her promised Isaac. Jacob served fourteen years for the privilege to wed Rachel. Joseph of Egypt was imprisoned fourteen years before he was released. Joseph Smith's ministry was fourteen years long (1830–1844) and ended with his death. Once we enter the Lord's wilderness or begin a crucible experience within the wilderness, the Lord will keep us there until the purifying and sanctifying work is complete. Then, when we are pure and sanctified, he will deliver us from his wilderness into Zion, and we will come forth as gold.

When we take into account the purpose of the Lord's wilderness and the crucible periods, we gain insight into a possible reason why some health blessings are delayed. It might be that the Lord's timetable calls for more time for the purification process to reach its goal. If we fail to understand the Lord's crucibles, we might become discouraged and confused when healing is not forthcoming. How do we square that delay with scriptures that state unequivocally that the sick and afflicted "shall be healed" unless they are "appointed unto death"?[126] Unmistakably, we need to broaden our view. Beyond the issue of faith is the issue of the crucible and the Lord's timing, which perhaps takes precedence. In the meantime, the administration ordinance is absolutely valid,

123 James 5:14; D&C 42:43–52.
124 James 5:15.
125 D&C 58:3.
126 D&C 42:48.

and the healing will take place according to individual needs and the timing and methods of the Lord.[127] Elder James E. Talmage wrote: "Not always are the administrations of the elders followed by immediate healings; the afflicted may be permitted to suffer in body, perhaps for the accomplishment of good purposes."[128] The point is this: We cannot and should not attempt to remove people from the Lord's wilderness or its crucibles. We can, however, bless them and place their delivery under the direction of the priesthood; then we can labor to ease their burdens while they endure the heat of the purification process. We are told that during the Savior's crucible experience in Gethsemane an angel came to strengthen him.[129] The angel did not remove the Savior's burden, but he did strengthen him. We can be angels to people who are working through their crucible experiences.

The Lord's wilderness with its attendant crucibles has defined boundaries. Beyond these boundaries lies a promised land; the Lord's deliverance ushers us there. We will not have to endure chastening one moment longer than is necessary to claim the blessings. When we emerge, we will come forth from the fiery furnace as did the three Hebrew youths, without even the "smell of fire."[130] We will be infinitely valuable, like pure gold,[131] having "become holy, without spot."[132] This is the condition of Zion people.

The Tragedy of Murmuring

The wilderness and its crucibles are demanding. Occasionally, we encounter periods of extreme difficulty, "emotional trauma and turmoil," wrote Blaine Yorgason, "the despair of believing that all [is] hopeless and that there could be no positive end to the experience." Paradoxically, our fighting through these trials by means of a cheerful attitude is a key to our deliverance. Our resisting and complaining about the lessons of the wilderness only prolongs the process. "Both Lehi and Sariah found some of the trials of the wilderness to be almost more than they could bear. They each murmured, repented, and then bore powerful testimonies as to the goodness of God in allowing them to enter their wilderness (see 1 Nephi 5:1–3, 16:20)."[133]

Murmuring is more than complaining; it is complaining against God. By murmuring, we are criticizing his way of handling things. Essentially, we are accusing him of being unaware of our situation, or lacking power to change things, or being indifferent to our plight. By murmuring, we charge him with not loving us enough to do something about our situation. The irony of murmuring is that while we are accusing God, we are simultaneously acknowledging that he exists, that he is aware of us, and that he has the power to reverse things. The moment we murmur, we halt the process of purification and

127 Oaks, "He Heals the Heavy Laden," 6–9.
128 Talmage, *Articles of Faith,* 205.
129 Luke 22:43.
130 Daniel 3:19–27.
131 Job 23:10.
132 Moroni 10:33.
133 Yorgason, *I Need Thee Every Hour,* 257.

sanctification and we become God's enemies rather than his students. And, judging from what happened when Laman and Lemuel murmured, the result is tragic.

Conversely, the dual miracles of sanctification and deliverance materialize from a positive attitude: "Therefore, dearly beloved brethren, let us cheerfully do all things that lie in our power; and then may we stand still, with the utmost assurance, to see the salvation of God, and for his arm to be revealed."[134] Unless cheerfulness in the midst of adversity is grounded in absolute trust in the Lord, that cheerfulness will be false, and it will not have power to sustain or deliver us. Such feigned cheerfulness cannot be maintained. True cheerfulness is a product of faith in Jesus Christ and the safety guaranteed by the new and everlasting covenant.

The result of true cheerfulness is peace, which is a gift of the Spirit that cannot be duplicated. The peace that Jesus offers us is unlike the peace offered by the world. The Lord's peace emerges from our relationship with him; it calms the troubled heart, jettisons fear,[135] and allows us to relax and move forward with cheerful confidence. The Lord's wilderness experience teaches us that even in our darkest moments, God never leaves us and always comes to our rescue. Nephi sought to remain cheerful and chose to trust in the peace that comes from the Lord. He rejoiced, saying, "O Lord, I have trusted in thee, and I will trust in thee forever. I will not put my trust in the arm of flesh; for I know that cursed is he that putteth his trust in the arm of flesh. Yea, cursed is he that putteth his trust in man or maketh flesh his arm."[136]

Finding Joy in the Journey

It is indeed a challenge to find joy amidst our trials in the Lord's wilderness. Nevertheless, finding joy is possible. We recall that God created us with his genotype, which contains the potential for true happiness. Happiness is one of the predominant characteristics of our nature. We recall that Joseph Smith said that happiness is the purpose of our life here on earth.[137] Zion is a condition or environment of matchless happiness: "Surely there could not be a happier people among all the people who had been created by the hand of God."[138]

In Nephi's wilderness journey, he continually used the word *delight.* He wrote of delighting "in the things of the Lord," "in the scriptures," and "in the great and eternal plan" of our Father in Heaven.[139] Former general Young Women's president Susan W. Tanner noted that in times of great trial, Nephi was quick to remember the sources of his delight, which empowered him to focus on things of eternal consequence. Delighting in the Lord and his blessings allows us to "lift" our hearts in the midst of affliction and cause to "rejoice."[140]

134 D&C 123:17.
135 John 14:27.
136 2 Nephi 4:34.
137 Smith, *Teachings of the Prophet Joseph Smith,* 255.
138 4 Nephi 1:16.
139 2 Nephi 4:15–16; 11:2–8.
140 "Tanner, My Soul Delighteth in the Things of the Lord," 81–83.

Often we wonder how happiness can be achieved when conditions are so difficult. We find our answer in yet another gospel irony called "affliction brings joy." Former general Relief Society president Barbara W. Winder gave this explanation of joy:

> Joy, it seems, is not only happiness, *but the resultant feeling of the Holy Ghost manifested within us.* How can we provide a climate in our lives to foster the presence of the Holy Ghost, that our lives may be more joyful? Just as a reservoir stores water to bring relief and replenish the thirsty land, so we can store experiences, knowledge, and desires to replenish and fortify our spiritual needs. Four ways may be helpful in developing reservoirs of righteousness and spiritual self-reliance. We prepare by—
>
> 1. Developing a cheerful disposition wherein the Spirit can dwell.
> 2. Learning the Savior's will for us, that we may know our divine potential.
> 3. Understanding and accepting his atoning sacrifice and repenting of our sins.
> 4. Keeping his commandments and having a firm determination to serve him.[141]

Joy, like peace, is a gift of the Spirit. We cannot conjure it up, and Satan cannot duplicate it.[142] Only the Holy Ghost can produce joy, and, amazingly, he produces it from the seedbed of affliction. Prefacing his report on the mission of the sons of Mosiah, Mormon hinted at the connection between affliction and joy: "And this is the account of Ammon and his brethren, their journeyings in the land of Nephi, their sufferings in the land, their sorrows, *and their afflictions, and their incomprehensible joy.*"[143] Elder Bruce C. Hafen explained that Adam and Eve could never have experienced joy without experiencing affliction:

> Lehi taught his children that if Adam and Eve had not transgressed, they would have remained in the Garden of Eden. Had that happened, Adam and Eve "*would have had no children;* wherefore they would have remained in a state of innocence, having no joy, for they knew no misery; doing no good, for they knew no sin. . . . Adam fell that men might be; and men are, that they might have joy" (2 Nephi 2:23–25; italics added). . . . Without

141 Winder, "Finding Joy in Life," 95; emphasis added.

142 Cannon, *Journal of Discourses,* 15:375–76; see also Dew, "Living on the Lord's Side of the Line," Brigham Young University devotional, Mar. 21, 2000.

143 Alma 28:8; emphasis added.

> being expelled from the innocent comfort of Eden into the turbulence of mortality, Adam and Eve would not only have had no children, and no misery, but they would never have found joy; *hence, the very meaning of life would have been lost on them.* There really is a deep connection between the hard things of life and the best things of life.[144]

Remarkably, through the power of the Atonement, the Lord has the power to "consecrate [our] afflictions for [our] gain"[145] and turn misery into joy. Elder Hafen wrote: "Because they received the Atonement of Jesus Christ, Adam and Eve were able to learn from their experience without being condemned by it."[146]

Coupled with this idea is the probability that finding joy in the journey contributes to our deliverance. For example, when Paul and Silas were imprisoned and beaten, they reacted joyfully by praying and singing praises: "And at midnight Paul and Silas prayed, and sang praises unto God: and the prisoners heard them. And suddenly there was a great earthquake, so that the foundations of the prison were shaken: and immediately all the doors were opened, and every one's bands were loosed."[147] The Jaredites followed a similar course of action: "And they did sing praises unto the Lord; yea, the brother of Jared did sing praises unto the Lord, and he did thank and praise the Lord all the day long; and when the night came, they did not cease to praise the Lord. And thus they were driven forth; and no monster of the sea could break them, neither whale that could mar them; and they did have light continually, whether it was above the water or under the water."[148] And, as we have mentioned, to the suffering Latter-day Saints, the Prophet wrote, "Therefore, dearly beloved brethren, let us cheerfully do all things that lie in our power; and then may we stand still, with the utmost assurance, to see the salvation of God, and for his arm to be revealed."[149]

Elder Hafen reminded us that the condition of the Lord's wilderness is not one of punishment but one of discovery and experience: "Through sometimes bitter experience, they [Adam and Eve, who are the models for all married couples] could come to really understand life and meaning and joy. 'They taste the bitter,' the Lord explained to Adam, 'that they might know to prize the good' (Moses 6:55). In fact, He said, 'If they [Adam and Eve] never should have bitter [experiences] they *could not know the sweet*' (D&C 29:39; italics added). In other words, sometimes the twists and turns of life *are* the straight and narrow path."[150]

Here, then, is the ironic connection between affliction and joy: God created man to have joy, which we all want, but joy can be realized only by experiencing its opposite,

144 Hafen, *Covenant Hearts*, 65–66; emphasis added.
145 2 Nephi 2:2.
146 Hafen, *Covenant Hearts*, 66.
147 Acts 16:25–26.
148 Ether 6:9–10.
149 D&C 123:17.
150 Hafen, *Covenant Hearts*, 66; emphasis added.

affliction, which we do not want. Moreover—and this is another irony—if joy is a gift of God, so is affliction. Spiritually mature people develop both the capacity and the perspective to express gratitude for their joys *and* their afflictions. They are not necessarily trying to be noble, nor are they in denial; rather, they have learned something the Gods know: there can be no joy without affliction.

With this understanding, we begin to appreciate the Lord's wilderness as a condition of love and not one of condemnation. The wilderness is a condition of the Fall, which "introduced the process by which we can *learn from our experience, which is the central meaning of existence*. . . . Learning from hard things is what life is all about."[151] Despite present difficulties, the Lord's promise of joy is always before us, and we are expected to discover it. And we will. Because God is a God of truth who cannot lie,[152] we are assured that his promise will be fulfilled: "After much tribulation come the blessings [joy]."[153] Ultimately, afflictions will result in joy, and will help rather than injure us.

Consider the example of Nephi. After all he suffered, he was still able to say that he lived after the manner of happiness.[154] Somewhere along the journey to the promised land, we too must discover the great plan of happiness,[155] and when we do, we must cling to it in the midst of afflictions. Then we will discover the invaluable connection between affliction and joy, as we see how the Savior sanctifies our afflictions for our eternal gain.[156] As we experience the Lord's sustaining and transforming miracles, our relationship with him will solidify, and eventually that relationship will lead us to a "fulness of joy."[157] Therefore, as we survey the Lord's wilderness and summon courage to take the first step into it, we need to understand that joy through adversity will be the discovery and that a fulness of joy will be the end result.

Conditions of the Lord's Wilderness

The wilderness experience has specific purposes and conditions. As we have mentioned, if we were viewing the Lord's wilderness from an eternal perspective, it would surely appear contrived. The condition of Zion is much more natural to us (meaning our innocent spirits) than the condition of mortality. Telestial life is often described as a school; we are to be "in the world but not of the world."[158] Here, we temporarily set aside "things as they really are,"[159] and enter into an educational environment.

Joseph Smith explained that the things of men are so dissimilar from "the conditions of God's kingdom . . . that all who are made partakers of that glory, are under the necessity of learning something respecting it previous to their entering into it." That process takes time, he said. "No man ever arrived in a moment: he must have been

151 Hafen, *Covenant Hearts*, 71–72; emphasis added.
152 Ether 3:12.
153 D&C 58:4.
154 2 Nephi 5:27.
155 Alma 42:8.
156 2 Nephi 2:2.
157 3 Nephi 28:10.
158 McKay, *Gospel Ideals*, 399.
159 Jacob 4:13.

instructed in the government and laws of that kingdom by proper degrees, until his mind is capable in some measure of comprehending the propriety, justice, equality, and consistency of the same." To that end, the Lord enrolls us in his wilderness school. For example, Joseph Smith said the Lord found Jacob "in a desert land, and in the waste, howling wilderness; He led him about, He instructed him, He kept him as the apple of His eye, etc.; which will show the force of the last item advanced, that it is necessary for men to receive an understanding concerning the laws of the heavenly kingdom, before they are permitted to enter it: we mean the celestial glory."[160]

No one who wishes to attain Zion and enter the celestial kingdom can avoid the Lord's wilderness school. Blaine Yorgason wrote: "Jesus went fasting into the wilderness for forty days so He could learn directly from the Father; Moses did the same. Adam called his wilderness experience being driven into the lone and dreary world, and Lehi called his experience the wilderness of his affliction. Both Ether and Moroni were well acquainted with wilderness schooling, and John the Baptist received his preparation there. The Lord has always required of those who desire to be His people a withdrawal from the world and its telestial ways. If we so desire, we can have the same sanctifying experience."[161]

Living by Manna

Achieving a Zion-like life is possible only if we learn to trust God implicitly and consecrate our hearts to him. To facilitate those goals and point us toward Zion, the Lord mercifully gave us what we might call the "manna principle." Wilderness travelers share the common experience of living by the Lord's grace from day to day. The manna principle states that we can gather only enough manna to last for one day; nevertheless, manna will always be there when we need it.

The manna principle persuades us to surrender our will to God as it brings us to the point where we will ask him to manage the affairs of our lives. To accomplish that goal, God often creates a situation that renders us temporarily powerless. Then, when we give our will to him, he provides us manna in return. Elder Maxwell said, "The submission of one's will is placing on God's altar the only uniquely personal thing one has to place there. The many other things we 'give' are actually the things He has already given or loaned to us. However, when we finally submit ourselves by letting our individual wills be swallowed up in God's will, we will really be giving something to Him! It is the only possession which is truly ours to give. Consecration thus constitutes the only unconditional surrender which is also a total victory."[162]

The manna principle also allows that we will have sufficient for our needs, but not excess. In other words, the Lord gives us enough of what we need, but no more. Moreover, the manna principle causes our vision to become restricted: when we attempt to look into the future, we see little except for uncertainty. The conditions of having *suf-*

160 Smith, *Teachings of the Prophet Joseph Smith*, 51.
161 Yorgason, *I Need Thee Every Hour*, 215.
162 Maxwell, *If Thou Endure It Well*, 54.

ficient but not excess and *limited vision* are apparently designed to drive us to our knees, where, by necessity, we must continually plead to the Lord for help to get through the day. Of course, the Lord does help, but, according to plan, he often sends his help at the very last minute, and then as a miracle. As uncomfortable as this process feels at times, it nevertheless multiplies our hope and faith. What happens after we have experienced a number of these miracles? We begin to expect them. Over time, we learn about the personality and characteristics of the Giver of Miracles. We learn that he is aware of us, he has great power, he loves us, he is consistent, and that he treats us uniquely but just as well as he does any another person. That discovery is essential to our forging a trusting relationship with him, which is paramount to establishing Zion in our lives.

Despite the length of our wilderness journey and the harshness of its occasional crucible experiences, we will emerge from it recognizing that we were always cared for. To the Israelites, Moses said, "For the Lord thy God hath blessed thee in all the works of thy hand: he knoweth thy walking through this great wilderness: these forty years the Lord thy God hath been with thee; *thou hast lacked nothing*."[163] The absence of lack and the presence of abundance are characteristics of Zion. Although the journey to Zion is rigorous, we will be fed by manna, and we will lack for nothing.

Hard Work

The Lord's wilderness is an experience of hard work, and it is hard work that propels us toward a Zion-like life. Kirtland, Jackson County, Far West, Nauvoo, Salt Lake City—the Mormon pioneers were forever building homes, neighborhoods, cities, and temples by the sweat of their faces, which is the law of mortal existence.[164] The Lord told the brother of Jared, "Go to work and build, after the manner of barges which ye have hitherto built. And it came to pass that the brother of Jared did go to work, and also his brethren, and built barges after the manner which they had built, according to the instructions of the Lord."[165] Similarly, Joseph of Egypt instructed his people to labor for seven years to store provisions against the coming famine.[166] Noah was told to labor and build an ark,[167] and Nephi was commanded to create tools and build a ship by his labor.[168]

Significantly, these people were called upon to labor in situations that were foreign to them: temples, cities, massive storage projects, and seaworthy submarines and ships. Such projects would have been impossible without the Lord aiding them. We learn a lesson from their accounts: Labor we must, but we are divinely helped in proportion to our effort. Only by partnering with the Lord is success made possible. It is by faith in Jesus Christ and receiving his grace (Jesus making up the difference after we do all we can do) that we survive the wilderness and go forward to our own personal promised land of Zion.

163 Deuteronomy 2:7; emphasis added.
164 Genesis 3:19.
165 Ether 2:16.
166 Genesis 41:46–49.
167 Genesis 5:13–16.
168 1 Nephi 17:8, 10–11, 16.

Partnering with the Lord is the Zion way to labor. Our motivation, goals, and results become different from the way we labor in Babylon. Working hard in the Zion way presents us with the ongoing opportunity to see the Lord's hand in our lives, and by continually partnering with him, we grow to count on him, love him, and trust him.

Zion work is cooperative and exalting whereas Babylon work focuses on selfishness, independence from God, and self-congratulation. Babylon work advances the philosophy of the anti-Christ: succeeding in life according to personal management, prospering according to one's genius, conquering according to one's strength, and setting personal interpretations on ethics.[169] On the other hand, Elder McConkie wrote, "Work is the great basic principle which makes all things possible both in time and in eternity. Men, spirits, angels, and Gods use their physical and mental powers in work. 'My Father worketh hitherto, and I work,' Jesus announced. (John 5:17.) Also: 'I must work the works of him that sent me, while it is day.' (John 9:4.)"[170]

In either environment, Zion or Babylon, we are required to work hard. But there are questions that determine in which camp we are laboring: With what attitude are we approaching our work? And, For what motivation are we working?

Traveling by Revelation

By scanning the scriptural record, we discover that people entered the Lord's wilderness and journeyed toward their Zion by revelation; that is, they traversed the wilderness as the Lord directed. As we study the accounts of righteous wilderness travelers, the purpose of dependency begins to come clear: The Lord's wilderness is designed to teach us to recognize and respond to the voice of the Lord. Only by revelation and absolute obedience to it can we survive the experience and arrive safely home in the embrace of God. Elder Maxwell wrote: "He cannot fully receive us until we fully follow Him."[171] Upon this principle pivot our eternal salvation and ultimate safety. Joseph Smith said, "A man is saved no faster than he gets knowledge [from God], for if he does not get knowledge [from God], he will be brought into captivity by some evil power in the other world, as evil spirits will have more knowledge, and consequently more power than many men who are on the earth. Hence [we need] revelation to assist us, and give us knowledge of the things of God."[172]

Blaine Yorgason stated: "What the Lord is asking from wilderness wanderers is nothing less than absolute trust, absolute faith, absolute obedience. And why is that? Because in this way only can we gain godly, godlike knowledge."[173] To survive the wilderness and gain its blessings, we must "feast upon the words of Christ; for, behold, the words of Christ will tell [us] *all* things what [we] should do."[174] Elder Maxwell explained, "What the Lord is asking us to do is to see with His eyes, to think with His mind, and

169 Alma 30:17.
170 McConkie, *Mormon Doctrine*, 847.
171 Maxwell, *Even as I Am*, 33.
172 Smith, *Teachings of the Prophet Joseph Smith*, 217.
173 Yorgason, *I Need Thee Every Hour*, 234.
174 2 Nephi 32:3.

to feel with His heart. Those in the city of Enoch made their mark in this regard (see Moses 7:18). Though we cannot really do that to anything approaching a full degree, we can further trust Him by letting our will be further 'swallowed up' in His."[175] We cannot achieve Zion in our lives or do the Lord's will unless we learn the Lord's will; otherwise, our efforts are guesswork.

Often, the Lord gives us a physical object to help us with the spiritual process of receiving revelation. For example, Abraham, the brother of Jared, Aaron, King Mosiah, and Joseph Smith each received a Urim and Thummim to assist them in obtaining revelation.[176] Lehi received the Liahona, an object that was both a compass and a revelation device.[177] Today, we have the Book of Mormon, our Liahona,[178] which Joseph Smith called "the most correct of any book on earth, and the keystone of our religion." Pertaining to its revelatory power, the Prophet said "a man would get nearer to God by abiding by its precepts than by any other book."[179]

Upon entering the Lord's wilderness, we are given the gift of the Holy Ghost, who is our guide, our purifier, and our revelator. Joseph Smith said, "You have received the Holy Ghost. Follow its teachings. Sometimes it will seem to you as though it was hardly the right way. No matter, follow its teachings, and it will always lead you right, and if you do so it will, by and by, become to you a principle of revelation, so that you will know all things."[180] Beyond the Spirit's ability to guide, comfort, purify, and protect, the Holy Ghost reveals the Father and the Son. Specifically, what are we to learn about them? Joseph Smith had the answer: "First, the idea that [God] actually exists. Secondly, a correct idea of his character, perfections, and attributes. Thirdly, an actual knowledge that the course of life which he is pursuing is according to his will. For without an acquaintance with these three important facts, the faith of every rational being must be imperfect and unproductive; but with this understanding it can become perfect and fruitful, abounding in righteousness, unto the praise and glory of God the Father, and the Lord Jesus Christ."[181]

With some degree of certainty, we could state that every experience related to the Lord's wilderness is calculated to draw us to him; reveal his character, perfections, and attributes; bring our lives in line with his; and forge an eternal relationship. Blaine Yorgason wrote: "The course of study we have entered into, then, is designed by God to assist us in growing into the principle of revelation, this in order that Christ can communicate to us a correct and ultimately perfect understanding of who He is, His 'character, perfections, and attributes,' as well as an understandable witness that our own life is moving in appropriate ways toward our being like Him. In short, his school teaches us how to become gods and goddesses."[182]

175 Maxwell, *That Ye May Believe,* 119.
176 Abraham 3:1; Exodus 28:30; Mosiah 8:13–19; Ether 3:21–28; JS–H 1:35.
177 1 Nephi 16:10, 26–29; Alma 37:38.
178 Dellenbach, "Hour of Conversion," 41.
179 Smith, *Teachings of the Prophet Joseph Smith,* 294.
180 Smith, *Journal of Discourses,* 26:131–32.
181 Smith, *Lectures on Faith,* 3:3.
182 Yorgason, *I Need Thee Every Hour,* 218.

Journeying According to the Lord's Will

Of necessity, the Lord's wilderness is fraught with risks, twists, turns, and dangers. To negotiate the wilderness safely, we must learn to travel exactly as the Lord directs. To Abraham, the Lord said, "Behold, I will lead thee by my hand."[183] We read that the Jaredites "did travel in the wilderness, and did build barges, in which they did cross many waters, being directed continually by the hand of the Lord."[184]

Blaine Yorgason expounded on the journey of the Israelites: "Moses, who led the recalcitrant children of Israel into their wilderness experience, said: 'We turned, and took our journey into the wilderness by the way of the Red Sea, as the Lord spake unto me' (Deuteronomy 2:1; see also Exodus 13:17–18). Later, the Lord directed that they circle a certain mountain again and again until a particular lesson had been learned. Only then would He allow them to proceed along their very specific course (see Deuteronomy 2:1–7)."[185]

Likewise, as we traverse the Lord's wilderness, we must do so by revelation, and, at each junction of decision, we will encounter the issues of obedience, faith, truth, and dependency.

Angels Attend Us

Our present consciousness does not permit us to calculate the immensity of the impact of the Fall of Adam and Eve. Its effects were so devastating and long lasting that only a God could remedy the situation by the sacrifice of his life. Evidently, according to one apocryphal source, the prospect of sending his Well-beloved Son to rescue Adam and his posterity caused even God the Father to pause. In a conference address in April 2000, Elder Russell M. Nelson cited a passage from a fourth-century document known as the "Discourse on Abbaton." This text contains a passage in which the narrator rehearses a conversation between the Father and the Son:

> He . . . made Adam according to Our image and likeness, and he left him lying for forty days and forty nights without putting breath into him. And He heaved sighs over him, saying, "If I put breath into this [man], he must suffer many pains." And I said unto My Father, "Put breath into him; I will be an advocate for him." And My Father said unto Me, "If I put breath into him, My beloved Son, Thou wilt be obliged to go down into the world, and to suffer many pains for him before Thou shalt have redeemed him, and made him to come back to his primal state." And I said unto My Father, "Put breath into him; I will be his advocate, and I will go down into the world, and will fulfil Thy command."[186]

183 Abraham 1:18.
184 Ether 2:6.
185 Yorgason, *I Need Thee Every Hour*, 233.
186 Nelson, Russell M., Conference Report, April 2000.

In this text, Jesus described his willingness to come to this benighted telestial world in an effort to save us. Here in the Lord's wilderness we are to learn the same lessons our first parents learned in order to survive and achieve deliverance from the wilderness, and in order to go on to Zion and gain our exaltation. For these reasons and for every other consideration that emerges from the wilderness, we need heavenly help. Blaine Yorgason explained:

> Adam's quest to obtain messengers, once he had entered the lone and dreary world of his wilderness experience, is no idle tale. Beginning with him, all who entered the Lord's wilderness anciently, if they wished to understand the gospel thoroughly, sought for such visitations. And if they remained faithful in gospel study, strict obedience, mighty prayer, and the proper attitude during both the hard times and the Bountifuls, they grew stronger in the Spirit and closer to the Lord until they were blessed with the ministering of angels. Thus, after Adam's profound personal anguish and diligent prayer, an angel finally appeared to him (can his relief even be imagined?) and instructed him in the law of sacrifice and obedience (see Moses 5:6–7).[187]

The ministering of angels, seen or unseen, mortal or immortal, is common to the wilderness experience. Upon leaving the safety of the Garden of Eden, Adam and Eve "fell" into the Lord's wilderness and immediately sought angelic help. This is a pattern we must follow if we too would merit protection, instructions, comfort, and deliverance. Blaine Yorgason reminded us that Abraham was rescued from the sacrificial altar by an angel.[188] "Jacob obtained his endowment and new name (Israel) from an angel."[189] Nephi and his brothers were instructed and encouraged by an angel.[190] Later, Nephi received a panoramic vision of the earth's history from an angel and from Christ.[191] King Benjamin was visited by an angel who gave him the text of his final sermon.[192] An angel visited Amulek to prepare the way for Alma.[193] Helaman's son, Nephi, was ministered to by angels daily.[194] "Many of King Lamoni's people saw angels."[195]

We need only survey the Doctrine and Covenants and the journals of our faithful forebears to read about angels consistently ministering to the Saints. With little doubt,

187 Yorgason, *I Need Thee Every Hour,* 283.
188 Abraham 1:15.
189 Genesis 32:24–30.
190 1 Nephi 3:29–30.
191 1 Nephi 11:14.
192 Mosiah 3:2–27.
193 Alma 10:7.
194 3 Nephi 7:18.
195 Yorgason, *I Need Thee Every Hour,* 284; Alma 19:34.

we believe in the ministering of angels,[196] and we have evidence that from the days of Adam to the present that angels help righteous people traverse and survive the Lord's wilderness and safely arrive in the condition of Zion.

Safety and Security

We are faced with at least two facts when we exit Babylon and enter the Lord's wilderness: (1) Choosing Zion, we become enemies of Babylon. Babylon will no longer support us. We can expect an all-out war, and attacks may be waged on our finances, our health, and our relationships. (2) Babylon is destined to fall. If we have anchored our safety and security there, we will become part of the fallout. Hence, a curse is placed upon wilderness travelers who attempt to place their trust in the "arm of flesh" rather than trusting in the arm of the Lord.[197]

The transition from Babylon to Zion is daunting and can be frightening. We might ask ourselves, "What will become of us if we attempt to step away from Babylon and fully embrace the laws and principles of Zion?" The answer is always the same: "Seek ye first the kingdom of God and his righteousness, *and all these things shall be added unto you*."[198] The guarantees of safety and security are embedded in the new and everlasting covenant: the Lord will support us, sustain us, stand beside us, and keep us safe. Enoch said, "Surely Zion [the people] shall dwell in safety forever."[199] Safe in the Covenant, we no longer need worry as we did in Babylon. What Jesus said to his Apostles could apply to anyone in the Covenant: "Therefore take no thought, saying, What shall we eat? or, What shall we drink? or, Wherewithal shall we be clothed? For your heavenly Father knoweth that ye have need of all these things."[200] Again we quote President Kimball, who said, "What are we to fear when the Lord is with us? Can we not take the Lord at his word and exercise a particle of faith in him? Our assignment is affirmative: to forsake the things of the world as ends in themselves; to leave off idolatry and press forward in faith; to carry the gospel to our enemies, that they might no longer be our enemies. We must leave off the worship of modern-day idols and a reliance on the 'arm of flesh,' for the Lord has said to all the world in our day, 'I will not spare any that remain in Babylon.'"[201]

Consider the example of Nephi. After having traversed the wilderness and arrived in his promised land (his land of Zion), he was able to say that he had lived after the manner of happiness,[202] a remarkable statement considering all he had suffered. This quality of life, *happiness*, President Faust explained, is a product of absolute faith in Jesus Christ.[203] Because the Lord is who he is and because he and we are bound together in

196 D&C 107:20.
197 2 Nephi 4:34; 28:31.
198 Matthew 6:33; emphasis added; see also 3 Nephi 13:33.
199 Moses 7:20.
200 3 Nephi 13:31–32.
201 Kimball, *The Teachings of Spencer W. Kimball*, 417, quoting D&C 64:24.
202 2 Nephi 5:27.
203 Faust, "Standing in Holy Places," 62.

the Covenant, we are absolutely safe. Gospel writer Ted L. Gibbons describes our safety as being "on belay."[204] As rock climbers scale dangerous mountains, the one leading the way anchors the rope so that it is secure; then he calls to the climber below: "You are on belay." That is, "You are safe to proceed and follow me; I've got the rope and you are secure." The Savior has us safely on belay. Therefore, should we not exercise a particle of faith in him? Although we might slip and crash into the sides of the mountain from time to time, we cannot fall. We are tethered to Jesus by the seal of the new and everlasting covenant. When we understand the power, safety, and security resident in that Covenant, we, like Nephi, can feel at peace in the eye of the storm and live after the manner of happiness.

The assurance that the Lord is in control is the agent by which all Saints, from Adam to the present day, have been able to experience peace and happiness while enduring the wilderness and its crucibles. The Lord is our shadow by day and our pillar by night,[205] just as he was for the Israelites; that is, he protects us from the scorching sun and the dark of night; he is our "place of refuge, and . . . a covert from storm and from rain."[206] Moreover, the Lord's Zion, which is foremost a condition of the heart, is "a land of peace, a city of refuge, a place of safety for the saints of the Most High God."[207]

The Lord's wilderness is designed to build faith rather than destroy it. Thus, the Lord has no intention of letting us down. That would confuse us and shatter our faith. The reality of his perfect attributes of character and the power of the Covenant hold us on belay, and, despite our occasional feelings to the contrary, we are absolutely safe.

Deliverance Experiences

By definition, deliverance is necessary only when conditions exceed our ability to cope—when we stand in desperate need of help from a greater power. What the Lord said to Nephi he could say to every wilderness traveler: "I will also be your light in the wilderness; and I will prepare the way before you, if it so be that ye shall keep my commandments; wherefore, inasmuch as ye shall keep my commandments ye shall be led towards the promised land; *and ye shall know that it is by me that ye are led. . . . After ye have arrived in the promised land, ye shall know that I, the Lord, am God; and that I, the Lord, did deliver you from destruction; yea, that I did bring you out.*"[208]

The Lord's wilderness is designed to prepare us for ultimate deliverance by allowing us to experience periodic deliverances. For example, we recall that angels came to push the handcarts before ultimate deliverance came to the Martin and Willie companies.[209] Seagulls came to devour the plague of crickets before the Saints could establish a stronghold in the tops of the mountains.[210] Abraham's wife, Sarah, was spared twice from

204 Gibbons, *Be Not Afraid*, 142–43.
205 Exodus 13:21–22; Isaiah 4:6.
206 Isaiah 4:6.
207 D&C 45:66.
208 1 Nephi 17:13–14; emphasis added.
209 Hinckley, "Our Mission of Saving," 54.
210 Pratt, *Journal of Discourses*, 21:277–78.

the clutches of Pharaoh and the king of Gerar[211] before she experienced her true "deliverance" from her personal bondage with the birth of Isaac. Before Nephi was delivered into his promised land, he was delivered by an angel from a severe beating.[212] He was delivered from starvation following the breaking of his bow,[213] and he was delivered from being bound with strong cords onboard ship.[214] Plainly, the Lord's periodic deliverances prepare us for our ultimate deliverance, or deliverance into Zion, meaning the condition of a purified heart.

The ancient Israelites are examples of successive deliverance experiences that prepared them for their ultimate deliverance. The angel of death passed over them in Egypt.[215] They were delivered from Pharaoh's army, first by a column of fire and later as they passed through the Red Sea.[216] In the wilderness, when they had no water, the Lord delivered them by healing the bitter waters[217] and later by drawing water from a rock.[218] When they were hungry, the Lord delivered them by providing manna from heaven.[219] When they were faced with an overwhelming foe, the Lord delivered them by helping to defeat their enemy.[220] When they were bitten by poisonous serpents, the Lord delivered them with the miracle of the brazen serpent, an agent of healing.[221] Then when the day of ultimate deliverance finally came, the Lord delivered them by parting the waters of the Jordan River, allowing them to cross over on dry ground to their effectual Zion—their promised land.[222]

Like these and other wilderness travelers, we will also be delivered from time to time until the Lord effects our ultimate deliverance. Then we, like Alma, will able to testify: "I have been supported under trials and troubles of every kind, yea, and in all manner of afflictions; yea, God has delivered me from prison, and from bonds, and from death; yea, and I do put my trust in him, *and he will still deliver me*."[223]

The Fourth Watch

The timing of our deliverance is an important condition of the wilderness. Late one night when the Lord was absent, his Apostles found themselves in a crucible experience.

> And when even was come, the ship was in the midst of the sea, and he alone on the land. And he saw them toiling in rowing; for the wind was contrary

211 Genesis 12:14–20; 20:1–13.
212 1 Nephi 3:28–30.
213 1 Nephi 16:18–25.
214 1 Nephi 18:11–22.
215 Exodus 13:14.
216 Exodus 14:13–31.
217 Exodus 15:23–27.
218 Exodus 17:1–6.
219 Exodus 16:2–4.
220 Exodus 17:8–13.
221 Numbers 21:6–9.
222 Joshua 3:14–17.
223 Alma 36:27; emphasis added.

> unto them: and about the fourth watch of the night he cometh unto them, walking upon the sea, and would have passed by them. But when they saw him walking upon the sea, they supposed it had been a spirit, and cried out: For they all saw him, and were troubled. And immediately he talked with them, and saith unto them, Be of good cheer: it is I; be not afraid. And he went up unto them into the ship; and the wind ceased: and they were sore amazed in themselves beyond measure, and wondered.[224]

The Lord will always come—even if he has to cross the sea on foot, he will come. But very often he will come in the "fourth watch"—at the very last minute, in the darkest time of night just before the dawn. Because he is who he is, his motive for waiting is not a cruel one. As we have noted, everything about the wilderness experience is calculated to engender, not destroy, faith and trust. During the fourth watch, the question should never be, Will he come? Rather, the question is, Will we endure in faith until he comes?

The Lord came in the fourth watch when young Abraham was ready to be sacrificed by the wicked priest.[225] Similarly, the Lord came in the fourth watch when Isaac was bound on an altar and ready to be sacrificed.[226] The Lord came to Sarah, who conceived at age ninety, beyond the time any rational being would say a woman could bear a child.[227] In the fourth watch, both Limhi's and Alma's people were miraculously delivered. To drive home the point, Mormon reminded us three times that "none could deliver them but the Lord their God."[228] In the fourth watch, the Lord saved Daniel's companions from a fiery furnace and later Daniel himself from the lions.[229]

Each of us wilderness travelers could add our stories to these. Time and again, we have seen the Lord come to our rescue when all other options have failed, when the only view before us was imminent disaster. Such last-minute deliverance experiences seem to have a purpose. At the least they help us be resolved on the issues of the Lord's existence and character. Could another method of timing better convince us that he is real, aware, loving, and powerful? Moreover, could another experience better demonstrate that he takes seriously the new and everlasting covenant we made with him?

While we do not know the mind of the Lord, we nevertheless come to know by experience that he abides the terms of the Covenant he's made with us, which stipulate that he will stand beside us in times of trouble. Thus, in the crucibles of the Lord's wilderness, we are being proven. The question is always: Will we abide in the Covenant by waiting for his certain deliverance?

---

224 Mark 6:47–51.
225 Abraham 1:15.
226 Genesis 22:10–12.
227 Genesis 21:2.
228 Mosiah 23:23; 24:21; Alma 36:2.
229 Daniel 3:19–27; 6:16–22.

Lessons to Be Learned in the Lord's Wilderness

As ironic as it might seem, the Lord's wilderness is a place of spiritual refreshment, a place where spiritual giants have retreated to find and commune with God and to be nourished by him. Jesus sought the wilderness before embarking on his ministry. Likewise, the brother of Jared, Abraham, Moses, King David, Lehi, Helaman and his stripling warriors, John the Baptist, Brigham Young, and many others sought God in the wilderness.

In the Lord's wilderness, our spirits receive what the world cannot supply them: solitude, quiet, serenity, and reliance on God. The spirit craves these things while Babylon despises them. In the wilderness, we are forced to look toward heaven and continually realign our settings to the Polar Star for direction.[230] Finally, when we emerge from the wilderness, we are filled with spiritual power, as were these mighty individuals. We know better who we are, and we know our God better. Therefore, what the Lord said of the Church as a whole could be said of us individually: "Before the great day of the Lord shall come, [we] shall flourish in the wilderness."[231] We will come out "clear as the moon, and fair as the sun, and terrible as an army with banners."[232]

Preparation to Live the Higher Law

The Lord's wilderness urges us to grow beyond the level of the schoolmaster law, and it prepares us that we might live the higher law of Zion.

Elder McConkie wrote: "Though the newly called saints of the nineteenth century failed to build their promised Zion, yet they retained the glorious gospel, with all its hopes and promises. They were left in that state which now exists among us. What we now have is a schoolmaster to prepare us for that which is yet to be. We are now seeking to build Zion in our hearts by faith and personal righteousness as we prepare for the day when we will have power to build the city whence the law will go forth when He rules whose right it is." The Lord has been merciful to the latter-day children of Israel. When our ancient Israelite forefathers rejected the fulness of the gospel, and when Moses pled with them "to sanctify [your]selves and receive the fulness of his glory while in the wilderness," only a few "gained wondrous gifts and power, but the generality of the people, obeying only in part, rose no higher in spiritual stature than provided for in the lesser law. And yet in that law, always and everlastingly, there was a call to higher things. The very law itself was a schoolmaster to prepare the people for the fulness of the gospel."[233]

On the other hand, the Lord has given us the totality of the everlasting gospel, and all of its blessings are within reach. Elder McConkie referred to the Beatitudes, as they define the higher law of Zion, explaining, "If the . . . saints overcome anger; if they are reconciled with their brethren; if they rise above lewd and lascivious thoughts and commit no adultery in their hearts; if they cast away their sins, as though severing an offending hand; if their

230 Hinckley, "Till We Meet Again," 89.
231 D&C 49:24.
232 D&C 5:14.
233 McConkie, *A New Witness for the Articles of Faith*, 611.

every spoken word is true as though sworn with an oath; if they do not retaliate when others offend them; if they turn the other cheek and resist not evil impositions; if they love their enemies, bless those who curse them, and pray for those who despitefully use them and persecute them—if they do all these things, they will become perfect even as their Eternal Father is perfect."[234]

Zion is more than a destination; Zion is a condition of the heart and a way of life. In the Lord's wilderness school, taught Joseph Smith, we "receive an understanding concerning the laws of the heavenly kingdom, *before* [we] are permitted to enter it."[235] As evidence that this is true, we recall that the Lord first extended only his *promise* of lands of promise to Abraham, Moses, Lehi, the Jaredites, and the early Latter-day Saints; then, to achieve that goal, these people were required to travel through his wilderness to obtain the promise. In the process of traveling through the wilderness, they prepared for their future blessings by shedding their sins and developing spiritual skills, until at last they were finally ready to receive their promised Zion.

This is the pattern.

As we travel through the Lord's wilderness, our experiences will enlarge us by "proper degrees," taught Joseph Smith, and this will happen "in proportion to the heed and diligence given to the light communicated from heaven to the intellect." The journey will either make or break us; the family of Lehi is an example. But if we will allow the wilderness experience to do its work, it will refine us and prepare us to live the higher law and embrace its blessings. In the process, an amazing transformation will take place. The Prophet continued by saying, "The nearer man approaches perfection, the clearer are his views, and the greater his enjoyments, till he has overcome the evils of his life and lost every desire for sin; and like the ancients, arrives at that point of faith where he is wrapped in the power and glory of his Maker and is caught up to dwell with Him."[236] Thus, the Lord's wilderness prepares us to become gods whereby we may gain an eternal "land of promise"—our Zion—in our Father's kingdom.

Putting Off the Natural Man

As we have noted, marriage symbolizes many elements of the new and everlasting covenant. One element is that of death and rebirth. At the altar, the husband and wife "die" as to their former lives, then arise together, "alive," as one. Just so, we enter the Lord's wilderness to die as to the former natural man; then, when we give ourselves to Christ in the new and everlasting covenant, we begin the process of coming alive in Christ. When we emerge from the wilderness, we will belong completely to the Lord, having forged an eternal relationship with him.

King Benjamin spoke of the necessity of the death of the natural man and the renewal of life: "For the natural man is an enemy to God, and has been from the fall of Adam, and will be, forever and ever unless he yields to the enticings of the Holy Spirit,

234 McConkie, *The Mortal Messiah*, 2:143.
235 Smith, *Teachings of the Prophet Joseph Smith*, 51.
236 Smith, *Teachings of the Prophet Joseph Smith*, 51.

and putteth off the natural man and becometh a saint." How is the transformation to take place? "Through the atonement of Christ the Lord." What will be the characteristics of this reborn Saint? "[He] becometh as a child, submissive, meek, humble, patient, full of love, willing to submit to all things which the Lord seeth fit to inflict upon him, even as a child doth submit to his father."[237] No more willfulness, assertiveness, pride, impatience, contention, complaining, or resistance—the natural man is dead, and the Saint is alive in Christ.

We need only compare the lives of those who entered and later departed the wilderness to see this remarkable conversion. These people were never the same again. The Anti-Nephi-Lehies are an example of this. Once they had repented and taken upon themselves the gospel covenant, they entered the Lord's wilderness and experienced God's chastening hand, which transformed them. Then, when they finally were delivered from the wilderness and gained their land of promise—their Zion—they had no semblance of the natural man.[238] Their example of faithfulness became the standard of excellence for the Nephite nation for generations, and we have no record that they ever departed from that standard.

Another example is the Nephites who survived the destruction accompanying Christ's death. Initially, they were unable to enter his presence. Evidently they entered the Lord's wilderness by putting off the natural man because about a year later,[239] the Lord appeared to them at the temple in Bountiful. There he taught them the higher law and delivered them into Zion.[240] Whereas the Lord had chastised them twelve months earlier,[241] now he blessed them with abundance. Their remarkable transformation caused Mormon to exult: "And it came to pass that there was no contention in the land, because of the love of God which did dwell in the hearts of the people. And there were no envyings, nor strifes, nor tumults, nor whoredoms, nor lyings, nor murders, nor any manner of lasciviousness; and surely there could not be a happier people among all the people who had been created by the hand of God."[242]

Even the greatest of souls is tempered and prepared in the wilderness. The brother of Jared received divine correction when he failed to call upon God for four years.[243] Nephi came face-to-face with his own weakness, or the side of him called the "natural man," when he apparently became angry while dealing with his older brothers in the land of promise.[244] Blaine Yorgason wrote: "All of these wilderness travelers discovered—to their sorrow—that despite their desires to remain free from sin, they were continually beset by it. Thus, they seemed to need an inordinate amount of time on their knees repenting, and even more time on their feet as they went about their daily tasks castigating themselves and feeling godly sorrow that they were such weak servants of the Lord."[245]

237 Mosiah 3:19.
238 Alma 23–25, 27.
239 3 Nephi 10:8:5; 10:18.
240 3 Nephi 11:8–11.
241 3 Nephi 9:13, 22.
242 4 Nephi 1:15–16.
243 Ether 2:14–15.
244 2 Nephi 4:27.
245 Yorgason, *I Need Thee Every Hour,* 271–72.

Faced with his own carnal nature, Nephi cried, "O wretched man that I am! Yea, my heart sorroweth because of my flesh; my soul grieveth because of mine iniquities. I am encompassed about, because of the temptations and the sins which do so easily beset me."[246] Then Nephi asked himself some hard questions, "most certainly paralleling the questions other wilderness sojourners have been plagued with. Why do we continue in sin, even when we know better?"[247] "O then, if I have seen so great things," Nephi said, "if the Lord in his condescension unto the children of men hath visited men in so much mercy, why should my heart weep and my soul linger in the valley of sorrow, and my flesh waste away, and my strength slacken, because of mine afflictions? And why should I yield to sin, because of my flesh? Yea, why should I give way to temptations, that the evil one have place in my heart to destroy my peace and afflict my soul? Why am I angry because of mine enemy?"[248]

Referring to the writings of Alma, Elder McConkie wrote, "Mortal man is by nature carnal, sensual, and devilish (Alma 42:10), meaning that he has an inherent and earthly inclination to succumb to the lusts and passions of the flesh. This life is the appointed probationary estate in which it is being determined whether he will fall captive to temptations or rise above the allurement of worldly things so as to merit the riches of eternity."[249] Yorgason said,

> To Moroni the Lord declared: "If men come unto me I will show unto them their weakness. I give unto men weakness that they may be humble" (Ether 12:27). Note that the word "weakness" is not plural here and so cannot refer to the multitude of sins we all struggle with. Being singular, it must refer to the aspect of mortality that is also called "the natural man" (see 1 Corinthians 2:14; Mosiah 3:19; Alma 26:21; D&C 67:12) or our "carnal nature" (see D&C 67:12; Mosiah 16:5; Alma 42:10).
>
> Because of this mortal weakness, we all have an inherent tendency to commit sin. That tendency, according to what the Lord told Moroni, was intentionally "given" to us by God. How was it given? Through genetic traits, conditions under which we are raised, the tormentings of Satan and his evil horde, circumstances we are forced to live through, and so forth. And why was it given? To help keep us humble, penitent, and filled with faith.[250]

246 2 Nephi 4:17–18.
247 Yorgason, *I Need Thee Every Hour,* 273.
248 2 Nephi 4:26–27.
249 McConkie, *Doctrinal New Testament Commentary,* 3:249.
250 Yorgason, *I Need Thee Every Hour,* 273–74.

In the makeup of our nature, then, we find the seeds both of our education and of our deliverance. As we come face-to-face with our natural man and mourn, as did Nephi, for the inherent weakness in our souls, we seek the Lord in humility and plead with him to strengthen and help us overcome by his grace—his enabling power. Partnering with the Lord assists us in rising above our fallen state, and over time it forges a relationship with him that cannot be broken. We enter the Lord's wilderness as a natural man, but we are delivered from it as a new creature, that is, a Saint, a Zion person.

Learning the Formula of Obedience

Learning the formula of obedience is a fundamental lesson of the Lord's wilderness. A child takes a huge step forward in maturity when he ceases being obedient simply because rules are in place and begins to be obedient because he understands the benefits of those rules. Wisdom comes when he finally comprehends that rules are instruments of power by which great works can be accomplished and marvelous blessings gained. To become holy like God is the preeminent goal of obedience. President James E. Faust taught: "Holiness is the strength of the soul. It comes by faith and through obedience to God's laws and ordinances. God then purifies the heart by faith, and the heart becomes purged from that which is profane and unworthy."[251]

Once we enter into the new and everlasting covenant, we must be obedient to the Covenant, exhibiting as much diligence as did the Savior: "even unto death, that you may be found worthy."[252] The terms of the Covenant require that we apply the formula of obedience to God's commandments, which will lead us to become perfect as God is perfect.[253] That is, we must keep all of God's commandments as he does, and if we do so, we will receive, as he did, a "fulness," and we will become an heir of God and joint-heir with Jesus Christ.[254]

God places enormous weight on obedience. Elder McConkie called it "the first law of heaven."[255] We recall that in the beginning, God created a master law to which all other specific laws are dependent: "There is a [master] law, irrevocably decreed in heaven before the foundations of this world, upon which all [specific] blessings are predicated—And when we obtain any [specific] blessing from God, it is by obedience to that [specific] law upon which it [the specific blessing] is predicated."[256] That is, the master law of heaven stipulates that each law of God be comprised of set consequences and blessings. With that in mind, here is one of the most definitive statements on the formula of obedience: "For all who will have a blessing at my hands shall abide the [specific] law which was appointed for that [specific] blessing, and the conditions thereof, as were instituted from before the foundation of the world."[257] If we are obedient, these blessings are guar-

251 Faust, "Standing in Holy Places," 62.
252 D&C 98:14.
253 Matthew 5:48.
254 Smith, *Teachings of the Prophet Joseph Smith*, 308–9.
255 McConkie, *Mormon Doctrine*, 539.
256 D&C 130:20–21.
257 D&C 132:5.

anteed according to the terms of the master law of heaven. God is a God of truth and cannot lie.[258] He said, "What I the Lord have spoken, I have spoken, and I excuse not myself; and though the heavens and the earth pass away, my word shall not pass away, but shall all be fulfilled, whether by mine own voice or by the voice of my servants, it is the same."[259] That is, the Lord binds himself to deliver the promised blessings associated with every obeyed law: "I, the Lord, am bound when ye do what I say; but when ye do not what I say, ye have no promise."[260]

Therefore, the formula of obedience is this: (1) God creates eternal laws with set and eternal consequences and blessings; and (2) when we obey one of his laws, God obligates himself to deliver the promised blessing.

Nephi learned the formula of obedience early: "I will go and do the things which the Lord hath commanded, for I know that the Lord giveth no commandments unto the children of men, save he shall prepare a way for them that they may accomplish the thing which he commandeth them."[261] That is, as we obediently get up and get going, a way will open before us—it is guaranteed. Like Nephi, we wilderness travelers are wholly dependent upon the Lord; like Nephi, we cannot access the Lord's power unless we go and do as the Lord commands. This is according to the formula of obedience.

When the Lord commanded Nephi to build a ship, the first words out of the prophet's mouth were, "Lord, whither shall I go that I may find ore to molten?"[262] Nephi had learned the formula of obedience well. Once again, at the Lord's command, Nephi was ready to go and do, and he expected to be able to surmount the obstacles before him. Likewise, Adam was obedient and offered sacrifice, although he did not have a complete understanding of the ordinance's significance or power.[263] Eventually, Adam's obedience resulted in the guaranteed blessing. Abraham followed suit. From the outset of his record, he explained that his exercising obedience would be the key that would open the door to the supernal blessings he desired: happiness, peace and rest, the rights to the priesthood, great knowledge, becoming the father of many nations, the prince of peace, and receiving instruction from God.[264]

These great individuals are our models. We who sojourn in the Lord's wilderness must mature in the principle of obedience and apply its formula in order to make it a principle of power in our lives. Our very survival and success in accomplishing the purposes of the wilderness depend upon our learning this formula.

As much as blessings are guaranteed for obedience to God's laws, so are consequences guaranteed for disobedience. The penalty for disobedience is always weighty: "Therefore I command you to repent—repent, lest I smite you by the rod of my mouth, and by my wrath, and by my anger, and your sufferings be sore—how sore you know not, how exquisite you know not, yea, how hard to bear you know not. . . . Which suffering

258 Ether 3:12.
259 D&C 1:38.
260 D&C 82:10.
261 1 Nephi 3:7.
262 1 Nephi 17:9.
263 Moses 5:5–8.
264 Abraham 1:2.

caused myself, even God, the greatest of all, to tremble because of pain, and to bleed at every pore, and to suffer both body and spirit—and would that I might not drink the bitter cup, and shrink."[265] In a way, if we return to sin and suffer the consequences of disobedience while we are in the Lord's wilderness, this is a tragedy that sends us back to the dire conditions of the wilderness of sin, where we were buffeted by Satan. Joseph Smith said, "The devil has no power over us only as we permit him. The moment we revolt at anything which comes from God, the devil takes power."[266] Satan encircles us "about by the bands of death, and the chains of hell, [with] an everlasting destruction . . . await[ing] [us]."[267] Yorgason explained, "Satan's power over us *always* hinges upon our obedience or disobedience—our willingness or unwillingness to submit to the mind and will of the Father."[268]

Significantly, obedience is always accomplished by sacrifice: "Verily I say unto you, all among them who know their hearts are honest, and are broken, and their spirits contrite, and are willing *to observe their covenants by sacrifice—yea, every sacrifice which I, the Lord, shall command*—they are accepted of me."[269] The disposition to be obedient through sacrifice has the power to sanctify a person, and it is sanctification that is the key to our gaining great power. Obedience through sacrifice results in sanctification, which sanctification results in power.

Our effort to obey is always worth the price. Adam discovered that obedience results in greater knowledge and understanding of God and his purposes.[270] We are told that those who are willing to live the law of obedience and apply its formula will "have glory added upon their heads for ever and ever."[271] Obedience results in "liberty and eternal life,"[272] the very blessings we seek in the Lord's wilderness. Mother Eve taught us that eternal life is the gift "which God giveth unto all the obedient."[273] The discipline of obedience requires "the heart and a willing mind," but if we will apply to it, we shall receive the promised blessing: "the willing and obedient shall eat the good of the land of Zion in these last days."[274]

Learning to Trust God: The Universal Lesson

Perhaps no lesson is as common to wilderness travelers as learning to trust God. Why trust is *the* central issue in mortality can be an enigma. To learn to trust God almost always requires that we first be reduced to a powerless situation in which we *must* trust God to sustain and rescue us. A gospel irony is this: power is attained from our becoming powerless and our admitting to it. Only then can our dependency on God and our trust-

265 D&C 19:15, 18.
266 Smith, *Teachings of the Prophet Joseph Smith*, 181.
267 Alma 5:7.
268 Yorgason, *I Need Thee Every Hour*, 348.
269 D&C 97:8; emphasis added.
270 Moses 5:5–12.
271 Abraham 3:26.
272 2 Nephi 2:27.
273 Moses 5:11.
274 D&C 64:34.

ing him graft us into the True Vine[275] from which we can draw nourishment. This results in self-sufficiency (sufficiency in God) and independence (dependency on God).

Like so many other things, Babylon distorts the terms *self-sufficiency* and *independence*; Babylon twists the meanings and methods so much that they finally become exactly opposite from celestial law and its purpose. Are we supposed to become self-sufficient and independent? Of course. But not in Babylon's way. The very anti-Christ philosophy we are trying to shed in the Lord's wilderness is that: (1) Reliance on Christ is unnecessary; (2) every man fares in this life according to his individual management; (3) every man prospers according to his genius; and (4) every man conquers according to his strength.[276] To root any semblance of the anti-Christ philosophy from our souls, the Lord renders us helpless and powerless so that we might learn humility, dependency, and trust. Then we will be filled with faith, self-reliance, and independence from the world *in him*, and we learn to become trusting and trustworthy.

Trust is always developed and tested at the limits of our capability. To the spiritually immature, the Lord's allowing us to be pushed to the edge before rescuing us might seem cruel. Nevertheless, for a divine purpose, he consistently brings us to the point where no earthy solution could help. Then, and only then, he delivers us. As much as we might dislike this procedure, it nevertheless serves a purpose. In the process of being delivered time and again, we see a pattern emerge:

- Difficulty arises
- We attempt solutions
- Difficulty increases
- We try more options
- The difficult becomes the impossible
- No options remain
- Christ delivers us at the last moment

This is part of the reason, perhaps, why the Lord is called the Deliverer.[277] Obviously, we do not need deliverance from *possible* situations; we need deliverance only from *impossible* circumstances that require unearthly intervention.

As we have noted, it is because the Lord's purposes are best served by this method (and because the Lord's deliverance is always miraculous and cannot be duplicated) that we are "cursed" when we look elsewhere for deliverance.[278] Not only will all other methods fall short, but the Lord's objectives for us will be frustrated. Nephi understood the pattern of deliverance so well that he shuddered at the idea of placing his trust elsewhere: "O Lord, I have trusted in thee, and I will trust in thee forever. I will not put my trust in the arm of flesh; for I know that cursed is he that putteth his trust in the arm of flesh. Yea, cursed is he that putteth his trust in man or maketh flesh his arm."[279]

275 John 15:1.
276 Alma 30:17.
277 D&C 138:23.
278 2 Nephi 4:34; 28:31.
279 2 Nephi 4:34.

That is not to say we sit back and wait for the Lord to deliver us. Our best effort is always required to summon the Lord's blessings. Moreover, our deliverance will often come by means of other people. As we have noted, President Kimball said, "God does notice us, and he watches over us. But it is usually through another person that he meets our needs. Therefore, it is vital that we serve each other in the kingdom."[280]

The writer of Proverbs gave us the formula for trust, with its divinely mandated promise: "Trust in the Lord with all thine heart; and lean not unto thine own understanding. In all thy ways acknowledge him, and he shall direct thy paths."[281] The heart represents the most holy part of the soul. If the body is the temple of God,[282] the heart surely must be the altar, the center and most sacred place, the holy location where sacrifices and covenants are made, and where two people are bound together for eternity. To purify the heart so that the soul might regain the presence of God is the purpose of the wilderness. When we trust God with all our heart, we submit our will to his with the complete confidence that he will not forsake us. That assurance supersedes our need to place our trust elsewhere and precludes our frantically darting about and searching for solutions or pridefully clinging to our own genius or self-sufficiency. How easy it is to expect that another person's understanding is greater or more accessible than God's. But if we truly trust God—who he is and what he is—we do not go searching for a "second opinion," and we will not be disappointed. Our truly trusting him bids us acknowledge that he most certainly is involved in every facet of our lives, "in the details," as Elder Maxwell taught us.[283] When we truly trust him, when we stop inappropriately depending on outside understanding, when we acknowledge his hand in all areas of our lives, we qualify for his help to lead us carefully through the wilderness and to our promised land.

To cement the concept of trust, multiple deliverances will happen along our journey. Alma taught his son Shiblon that deliverance comes in proportion to our trust in God: "And now my son, Shiblon, I would that ye should remember, that as much as ye shall put your trust in God even so much ye shall be delivered out of your trials, and your troubles, and your afflictions, and ye shall be lifted up at the last day."[284] The more we trust, the more—and perhaps the *faster*—we are delivered.

The Lord never lets us down; that fact serves to forge a relationship of trust with him. Because the wilderness forces us to live by faith from day to day as we constantly encounter opposition and occasionally experience crucibles, we find ourselves continually being driven to our knees. In those moments, we learn at least three essential lessons of trust: (1) We discover the character, attributes, and perfections of God, those things that make him trustworthy; (2) we see that God takes our covenant relationship seriously—hence, we are absolutely safe with him in the Covenant; and (3) we come to understand the need to discover that we, too, are trustworthy. Before Abraham made his sacrifice, God already knew what Abraham would do. What remained was for Abraham

280 Kimball, *The Teachings of Spencer W. Kimball*, 252.
281 Proverbs 3:5.
282 John 2:21; 1 Corinthians 6:19.
283 Maxwell, *One More Strain of Praise*, 103–4.
284 Alma 38:5.

to know. Therefore, God gave Abraham a way to make this discovery about himself by asking him to sacrifice Isaac. Only through this experience could Abraham know for certain that he was truly trustworthy—that he had the faith necessary to do whatever the Lord would require of him.

As we have discussed, there are three primary reasons *not* to trust some*one*: (1) I don't know you well enough; (2) My past experience with you was disappointing or inconsistent; and (3) I don't think you can help me. Ultimately, our faith in the Lord is strengthened or weakened based on our trust in his divine attributes of character and our belief in the efficacy of our mutual covenant relationship. Moreover, if we personally are not trustworthy, it is difficult to imagine trustworthiness in someone else, especially God, whom we cannot see.

Trust requires that we are willing to be led as if we were blind. Our limited vision is the fertile ground into which the seeds of faith and trust are planted. In the wilderness, we are allowed to see only today, and we are obliged to hand tomorrow over to God. Except that we know that the outcome will eventually be positive, we are otherwise given little information about our present situation. We know neither the duration of time nor the twists and turns nor the extent of the difficulties we might face. We are absolutely blind, and we must extend our hand to the only One who knows the way and can help us. Until the day of our deliverance, we will enjoy scant understanding and perspective. In the wilderness we are forced to hope for things that are not seen; vision returns and perspective becomes clear only after the trial of our faith.[285] And that requires trust.

Trusting God is not limited to mortality. Often we give lip service to our desire to become part of his kingdom without thinking about what that decision will entail. As we have discussed, consecration is the governing law of the celestial kingdom. Under that law we will be given eternal stewardships—trusts—for which we will be held accountable. These trusts are severally denominated as "kingdoms, thrones, kingdoms, principalities, and powers, dominions, all heights and depths,"[286] and mansions of many sizes.[287] Evidently, these lesser kingdoms within the greater kingdom are overseen by the Church of the Firstborn, the heavenly Church.[288] Perhaps in a similar way that we are given family and ecclesiastical stewardships in The Church of Jesus Christ of Latter-day Saints (the earthly kingdom of God), we will be given family and ecclesiastical stewardships in the Church of the Firstborn (the kingdom of heaven).

Almost certainly the same principles that need to be manifest in stewardships here (unity, equality, agency, stewardship, accountability, labor, etc.) will apply there—and framing the foundational relationships that govern our stewardships will be the overriding issue of trust. Our sustaining the prophet is our model and our training in this life. In other words, will we, without reservation, accept God as the one and only sovereign and governor of the kingdom of heaven and trust the way he rules—just as we accept the prophet as our governor on earth? Will we accept Jesus Christ as the one and only

285 Ether 12:6.
286 D&C 132:19.
287 D&C 98:18.
288 D&C 88:5; 93:22; 107:19.

head of the Church of the Firstborn—just as we accept the prophet as our leader on earth? Will we rear our eternal families and serve obediently and trustworthily forever in the kingdom of heaven and the Church of the Firstborn—just as we faithfully rear our families and serve on earth? Clearly, our training in the Lord's wilderness prepares us for the responsibilities, opportunities, and trusts of eternal life.

We must learn the lessons of trusting in God and becoming trustworthy well enough that these lessons endure eternally. Therefore, we, like Abraham and Isaac, are often brought to "the point of the knife" to learn these lessons. "In the wilderness," Blaine Yorgason explained, "our temporal needs are strictly incidental to our spiritual needs. Like the widow who fed Elijah, our temporal needs will be met only after our faith has been tried sufficiently for spiritual growth to have occurred."[289] It is during the trying of our trust in God and the simultaneous trying of our trustworthiness that we proclaim our allegiance to God when we cry to him for relief, "Nevertheless not my will, but thine, be done."[290] The three Hebrew youths cried their allegiance at the mouth of the fiery furnace: "If it be so, our God whom we serve is able to deliver us from the burning fiery furnace, and he will deliver us out of thine hand, O king. But if not, be it known unto thee, O king, that we will not serve thy gods, nor worship the golden image which thou hast set up."[291] In the midst of his crucible, Job declared his allegiance: "Though he slay me, yet will I trust in him."[292] Each of these people trusted God and proved their trust at "the point of the knife." Here is the principle of power: To be able to cry allegiance and continue to trust in the Lord when all options have failed summons the Lord's deliverance.

The Lord urged Lehi's family to become trustworthy, and he guaranteed his own trustworthiness: "And I will also be your light in the wilderness; and I will prepare the way before you, if it so be that ye shall keep my commandments; wherefore, inasmuch as ye shall keep my commandments ye shall be led towards the promised land; and ye shall know that it is by me that ye are led. Yea, and the Lord said also that: After ye have arrived in the promised land, ye shall know that I, the Lord, am God; and that I, the Lord, did deliver you from destruction."[293]

In an episode from the New Testament, Jairus's daughter was dying; all of his options had failed. The account seems to suggest that when Jairus heard that Jesus was coming, he sat on the seashore all night anticipating the Lord's arrival. When Jesus stepped from the boat Jairus "besought him greatly, saying, My little daughter lieth at the point of death: I pray thee, come and lay thy hands on her, that she may be healed; and she shall live." Jesus obliged. As they were going to Jairus's house, "there came from the ruler of the synagogue's house certain which said, Thy daughter is dead: why troublest thou the Master any further? As soon as Jesus heard the word that was spoken, he saith unto the ruler of the synagogue, Be not afraid, only believe."[294] Notice that when the negative voices began to trumpet doom, Jesus immediately focused Jairus's attention on

289 Yorgason, *I Need Thee Every Hour*, 270.
290 Luke 22:42.
291 Daniel 3:17–18.
292 Job 13:15.
293 1 Nephi 17:13–14.
294 Mark 5:21–24, 35–43.

the issue of trust. Jesus bade Jairus not to listen to the voices and to trust him. When all seems lost, *trust*! We know the outcome. Jesus restored the child to life and once again proved himself trustworthy.

Jesus gave the same, never-too-late message of his trustworthiness to a grieving Martha, who was inconsolable at the death of her brother Lazarus: "Jesus said unto her, I am the resurrection, and the life: he that believeth in me, *though he were dead, yet shall he live*."[295] Imagine—even then, even though Lazarus had lain in the grave for four days, even when all evidence pointed to Lazarus's complete and unalterable demise, Jesus asked Martha to trust him. And Martha rose to the occasion! Although she was distraught, she trusted the Savior and his saving power: "But I know, that even now, whatsoever thou wilt ask of God, God will give it thee." Jesus confirmed her trust in him: "[He] saith unto her, Thy brother shall rise again."[296] And Lazarus did rise again. Jesus "cried with a loud voice, Lazarus, come forth. And he that was dead came forth, bound hand and foot with graveclothes: and his face was bound with a napkin. Jesus saith unto them, Loose him, and let him go."[297]

If trust is *the* most crucial and universal issue in the Lord's wilderness, the Lord will not disappoint us. We can expect him to give us multiple opportunities to learn this essential lesson. As we have said, he is not in the business of confusing us or destroying our faith in him. He does not start us down the path to eternal life only to lead us over a cliff. If his purpose is to build our faith and trust in him, we can rely on him to always come to our rescue, fight our battles, feed us manna, quench our thirst, clothe us, stand beside us, teach us, and love us. He will always keep his promises, and he will never let us down.

We need to learn these lessons thoroughly, because, as the scriptural accounts of wilderness travelers attest, deliverance is always preceded by an extraordinary test of faith; our survival and deliverance depend on our being good pupils. We must trust the Lord enough to pass that test. It is vitally important to our deliverance that we are trustworthy and obedient to his instructions. Our arrival in the promised land—our Zion—pivots on our ability to trust the Lord with all our heart. We must never listen to the alternative voices or imagine that it is too late. We must believe that at any moment, anywhere, and in any situation, the Savior can call to us, as he did to Lazarus, and we will emerge whole. We might be decaying in the bowels of the tomb, bound with the grave clothes, and we will hear the Savior say, "Loose him, and let him go." The Lord is absolutely trustworthy—this is the universal lesson—and we must internalize that lesson so well that it lasts eternally.

Bountiful—A Reprieve

The Lord grants us places and times of rest from the sometimes exhausting journey through his wilderness. During the eight years that Lehi and his family traveled in the wilderness, they "suffered many afflictions and much difficulty." The land Bountiful was

295 John 11:25; emphasis added.
296 John 11:22–23.
297 John 11:43–44.

a welcome relief. Whereas they had been living day to day by their skill as hunters, now they "did come to the land which we called Bountiful, because of its much fruit and also wild honey; and all these things were prepared of the Lord that we might not perish." It is no wonder, then, that they "were exceedingly rejoiced."[298]

After the persecutions and sufferings in Missouri, the Lord granted the Saints a temporary reprieve in Nauvoo. For a season, they recovered, experienced peace, grew in faith, and prospered. Likewise, Moroni recorded that the Jaredites also found reprieve in the land of Moriancumer, another place like Bountiful: "Behold, it came to pass that the Lord did bring Jared and his brethren forth even to that great sea which divideth the lands. And as they came to the sea they pitched their tents; and they called the name of the place Moriancumer; and they dwelt in tents, and dwelt in tents upon the seashore for the space of four years."[299]

Interestingly, the lands of Moriancumer and Bountiful were located on the shores of the great seas the people would need to cross. We learn a lesson here: The reprieves the Lord allows us are places to regroup, grow in spiritual stature, and prepare to cross over to the land of promise. But we must use these reprieves for the right reasons, as did Nephi, who took full advantage of Bountiful by communing often with the Lord and by building a ship to complete the journey.[300] On the other hand, the brother of Jared temporarily sat back, relaxed, and ceased to pray, as if he were setting up permanent camp in Moriancumer. We recall that the Lord chastised the brother of Jared, and, to his credit, he repented.[301] Bountiful is not Zion; it is a temporary reprieve, a place to prepare to become Zion-like. Bountiful is not where we become spiritually lax; Bountiful is a place to prepare to go to Zion and enter into the rest of the Lord.[302] Bountiful is like a Sabbath experience, a place to rest in the Lord to prepare for the coming week. Bountiful is where "the intensity of the wilderness schooling will be eased. During those times, we are expected to prepare for further wilderness experiences by taking advantage of all the Lord gives us. We are also expected, as were Nephi and the brother of Jared, to use that time of respite to draw ever nearer to the Lord through fasting and mighty prayer."[303]

Abraham experienced at least two significant reprieves. The first was in Haran, the place to which he escaped "from the terrible famine that pervaded his wilderness experience." When the famine abated, "he left Haran and made his way toward the land of Egypt, for though the famine was everywhere else, in Egypt there was plenty, and Abraham prospered there."[304] In each place, Haran and Egypt, he built altars, communed with God, grew spiritually stronger, and prepared for the next leg of his wilderness experience, which would end in a temple setting at an altar atop Mount Moriah.

We note from Abraham's story that reprieves are also places of refuge. For example, Alma and his people escaped captivity and "departed into the wilderness; and when

298 1 Nephi 17:5–6.
299 Ether 2:13.
300 1 Nephi 17:7–8.
301 Ether 2:13–15; 1 Nephi 17:17–55.
302 D&C 84:24.
303 Yorgason, *I Need Thee Every Hour*, 280.
304 Yorgason, *I Need Thee Every Hour*, 279–80; see also Abraham 2:4–5, 21.

they had traveled all day they pitched their tents in a valley, and they called the valley Alma, because he led their way in the wilderness." Notice that they used their reprieve correctly: "Yea, and in the valley of Alma they poured out their thanks to God because he had been merciful unto them, and eased their burdens, and had delivered them out of bondage; for they were in bondage, and none could deliver them except it were the Lord their God. And they gave thanks to God, yea, all their men and all their women and all their children that could speak lifted their voices in the praises of their God." But their reprieve was to be short-lived. "And now the Lord said unto Alma: Haste thee and get thou and this people out of this land, for the Lamanites have awakened and do pursue thee; therefore get thee out of this land, and I will stop the Lamanites in this valley that they come no further in pursuit of this people."[305]

The valley of Alma was much like the reprieves in our lives, a place with set boundaries beyond which our enemies or afflictions cannot pass. For example, we might experience such a reprieve by emerging from financial distress, away from the reach of creditors. Or we might experience healing after a season of sickness and feel the freedom of having distanced ourselves from the illness. From such reprieves, we regroup and move forward to our land of promise: "And it came to pass that they departed out of the valley, and took their journey into the wilderness. And after they had been in the wilderness twelve days they arrived in the land of Zarahemla; and king Mosiah did also receive them with joy."[306]

Confronting Satan

At some time during our wilderness journey, we must confront Satan. In the cases of Jesus and Moses, the wilderness experience itself served as a preparation to confront the adversary.[307] By means of these confrontations, we decide once and for all where our loyalties lie. Moreover, the confrontations with Satan prepare us to be delivered from the wilderness. They also prepare us to reenter it as an emissary of the Lord for the purpose of aiding other people along their way or helping to deliver them. Jesus, Moses, and Joseph Smith are examples of men who confronted Satan then reentered the wilderness to help other travelers.

The confrontation with Satan can occur in any combination of temptations, demands, threats, or afflictions—for example, temptations to self-indulge, pamper the appetite, seek honor, power, or money; demands for our loyalty; or attempts to destroy us. In these confrontational situations, we are forced to make a concrete decision about whom we will follow and worship. If we choose God, we so indicate by calling upon him to help us defeat and cast away our enemy, and he will not disappoint us. Often, exercising the priesthood is the means by which the confrontation ends.

The confrontation with Satan provides us with an essential key to being delivered from the Lord's wilderness. When Jesus, Moses, and Joseph Smith had confronted and

305 Mosiah 24:20–23.
306 Mosiah 24:24–25.
307 Matthew 4:3–11; Moses 1:12–22.

overcome Satan, they experienced an unbelievable outpouring of the Spirit—a type of deliverance. Consider the accounts of their deliverance:

- Jesus: "Then the devil leaveth him, and, behold, angels came and ministered unto him."[308]

- Moses: "And it came to pass that when Satan had departed from the presence of Moses, that Moses lifted up his eyes unto heaven, being filled with the Holy Ghost, which beareth record of the Father and the Son; and calling upon the name of God, he beheld his glory again, for it was upon him; and he heard a voice, saying: Blessed art thou, Moses, for I, the Almighty, have chosen thee, and thou shalt be made stronger than many waters; for they shall obey thy command as if thou wert God."[309]

- Joseph Smith: "Just at this moment of great alarm, I saw a pillar of light exactly over my head, above the brightness of the sun, which descended gradually until it fell upon me. It no sooner appeared than I found myself delivered from the enemy which held me bound. When the light rested upon me I saw two Personages, whose brightness and glory defy all description, standing above me in the air. One of them spake unto me, calling me by name and said, pointing to the other—*This is My Beloved Son. Hear Him!*"[310]

Blaine Yorgason explained that we cannot successfully confront Satan unless we comprehend him.

> Oliver Cowdery wrote that after Joseph had tried to take the plates and couldn't and then prayerfully repented, the angel Moroni "said, 'Look!' and as he thus spake [Joseph] beheld the prince of darkness, surrounded by his innumerable train of associates. All this passed before him, and the heavenly messenger said, 'All this is shown, the good and the evil, the holy and impure, the glory of God and the power of darkness, that you may know hereafter the two powers and never be influenced or overcome by that wicked one. Behold, whatever entices and leads to good and to do good, is of God, and whatever does not is of that wicked one: *It is he that fills the hearts of men with evil, to walk in darkness and blaspheme God*; and you may learn from henceforth, that his ways are to destruction, but the way of holiness is peace

308 Matthew 4:11.
309 Moses 1:24–25.
310 JS–H 1:16–17.

> and rest. . . . You have now beheld the power of God manifested and the power of Satan: You see that there is nothing that is desirable in the works of darkness; that they cannot bring happiness; that those who are overcome therewith are miserable, while on the other hand the righteous are blessed with a place in the Kingdom of God where joy unspeakable surrounds them'" (*The Papers of Joseph Smith*, edited by Dean C. Jessee [Salt Lake City: Deseret Book Company, 1989], 1:87–88).
>
> Part of our comprehending Satan is accomplished through the ordinances of the holy temple. As Brigham Young stated, "The Spirit of the Lord and the keys of the priesthood, hold power over all animated beings" (Nibley, *Nibley on the Timely and the Timeless*, p. 88). Joseph Smith discussed this power over all animated beings when he said, "I preached in the grove on the keys of the kingdom, charity, etc. The keys are certain signs and words by which false spirits and personages may be detected from true, which cannot be revealed to the elders till the temple is completed. . . . There are signs in heaven, earth and hell; the elders must know them all, to be endowed with power, to finish their work and prevent imposition' (*Discourses of the Prophet Joseph Smith*, p. 152)."[311]

The Abrahamic Test

The prize of eternal life is won by the sacrifice of all things—that is, we place all that we have and are on the altar as a consecration to God. This sacrifice forms the foundation of the law of consecration. Often we call this sacrifice the Abrahamic test because it is reminiscent of Abraham being willing to offer Isaac as a sacrifice, which in turn is in similitude of the Father's willingness to sacrifice his Beloved Son. Just as Abraham climbed Mount Moriah and built an altar of sacrifice, so must we climb our own figurative Mount Moriahs and build altars of faith and sacrifice. Then, holding back nothing and of our own free will, we must lay our all on the altar and offer it to God. Joseph Smith taught:

> Let us here observe, that a religion that does not require the sacrifice of all things never has power sufficient to produce the faith necessary unto life and salvation; for, from the first existence of man, the faith necessary unto the enjoyment of life and salvation

311 Yorgason, *I Need Thee Every Hour*, 342–43.

> never could be obtained without the sacrifice of all earthly things. It was through this sacrifice, and this only, that God has ordained that men should enjoy eternal life; and it is through the medium of the sacrifice of all earthly things that men do actually know that they are doing the things that are well pleasing in the sight of God. When a man has offered in sacrifice all that he has for the truth's sake, not even withholding his life, and believing before God that he has been called to make this sacrifice because he seeks to do his will, he does know, most assuredly, that God does and will accept his sacrifice and offering, and that he has not, nor will not seek his face in vain. Under these circumstances, then, he can obtain the faith necessary for him to lay hold on eternal life.[312]

Any number of situations could qualify as an Abrahamic test: health problems, financial reversals, loss of a loved one, giving extended service, or anything else or any combination of things that the Lord requires.

Abraham's particular test consisted of at least four elements:

1. He was required to give up someone (something) he loved very much.
2. He was required to do something he did not want to do.
3. He was required to do something he did not fully understand.
4. He was required to do something thick with irony.

The Lord explains that we must "be chastened and tried, even as Abraham, who was commanded to offer up his only son. For all those who will not endure chastening, but deny me, cannot be sanctified."[313] We recall that *chastening*, as the term is used in this instance, means "to make chaste" or "pure in thought and act." The sacrifice we make of all things seems to be connected to our being chastened and tried. Additionally, we will make our sacrifice in full view of God and all his holy angels. These holy beings are more than observers; they are participants who cheer, encourage, help us, and record our actions and our prayers: "Behold, this is pleasing unto your Lord, and the angels rejoice over you; the alms of your prayers have come up into the ears of the Lord of Sabaoth, and are recorded in the book of the names of the sanctified, even them of the celestial world."[314]

The results of the sacrifice of all things include the fulfillment of the Lord's promises of deliverance and inheritance, promises he now seals, or makes "more sure." Another result is that the Lord makes right, or restores, any losses we have suffered to make our sacrifice: "Verily I say unto you my friends, fear not, let your hearts be comforted; yea, rejoice evermore, and in everything give thanks; waiting patiently on the Lord, for your

312 Smith, *Lectures on Faith*, 6:7.
313 D&C 101:4–5.
314 D&C 88:2.

prayers have entered into the ears of the Lord of Sabaoth, and are recorded with this seal and testament—the Lord hath sworn and decreed that they shall be granted. Therefore, he giveth this promise unto you, with an immutable covenant that they shall be fulfilled; and all things wherewith you have been afflicted shall work together for your good, and to my name's glory, saith the Lord."[315] A discovery we make at the end of the sacrifice of all things is that it was not a sacrifice after all; rather, it was the instrument that provided us the greatest of all blessings.

We who submit to the Abrahamic test by traveling the Lord's wilderness, climbing our Mount Moriah, building an altar of faith, and making a freewill sacrifice will receive the blessings of Abraham: (1) Our posterity will have the right to receive all the blessings of the gospel and priesthood; (2) we will receive an inheritance in Zion both now and in eternity; and (3) we will be blessed with "eternal lives,"[316] meaning that our eternal marriage will be blessed to produce endless posterity. If our desire is to claim these blessings of Abraham, we must "do the works of Abraham."[317]

Lehi "did the works of Abraham," offering the sacrifice of all things and, like Abraham, was blessed with a promised land.[318] The brother of Jared did the same by climbing a mountain into a temple setting to present his offering to the Lord.[319] The Lord rewarded his sacrifice by giving him a land of promise. The Anti-Nephi-Lehies sacrificed everything, even to giving their lives rather than reject their covenant.[320] Their king set the example by saying, "I will give up all that I possess, yea, I will forsake my kingdom, that I may receive this great joy."[321] These people were blessed with a land of promise in Jershon, which became their Zion.[322] Joseph Smith sacrificed all things, including his life, and obtained a celestial inheritance.[323] The Latter-day Saints followed suit, gaining a land of promise in the tops of the mountains,[324] and will yet obtain the land of Zion.[325]

All blessings follow testing: "I would show unto the world that faith is things which are hoped for and not seen; wherefore, dispute not because ye see not, for ye receive no witness until after the trial of your faith."[326] During the trial of our faith we hope but cannot see the outcome. Nevertheless, by the immutable promise of the Lord, the day of testing will someday end, he will deliver us, and our sacrifice will be recorded in "the book of the names of the sanctified, even them of the celestial world."[327] Then we, like Joseph of Egypt, will be exalted from prisoner to prince and attain our eternal inheritance.

315 D&C 98:1–3.
316 D&C 132:24.
317 D&C 132:32.
318 1 Nephi 2:4, 20.
319 Ether 3:1–5.
320 Alma 24:17–19.
321 Alma 22:15.
322 Alma 27:22–27; 28:1.
323 D&C 135:1–7.
324 Isaiah 2:2.
325 D&C 101:43; 103:15–18; 105:9, 13.
326 Ether 12:6.
327 D&C 88:2.

Taking upon Us the Name of Jesus Christ

The greatest wilderness experience—that which takes place at the summit of our mountain—is to come face-to-face with Christ. The necessary preparation for this supernal event is the sum of the experiences described above. All of these experiences have served to create a new and pure heart, a heart that has "no more disposition to do evil, but to do good continually."[328] There remains but one essential step to attain this consummate experience—taking upon us *fully* the name of Jesus Christ. By fully taking upon us the Lord's name we approach the ideal of Zion.

The Book of Mormon contains several Zion accounts. The most obvious is found in 3 Nephi. There we are introduced to people who initially were unprepared for Zion but who diligently changed their lives so that the Lord could come and establish Zion among them. But there is another account that begs our attention, the account of the people of King Benjamin. These people *were* prepared for the establishment of Zion; they had been diligently keeping the commandments of the Lord,[329] and they were ready to ascend to a higher level of spirituality. As we have discussed in the oath and covenant of the priesthood section, King Benjamin used his priesthood to facilitate a spiritual experience that took them to that higher level. This level is where the ideal of Zion becomes possible in a person's life; it is this level where preparations are finally complete so that we can come into the presence of the Lord. This level is marked by fully taking upon us the name of Jesus Christ.

To fully take upon us the name of Christ requires at least three things: (1) intervention by the priesthood, (2) receiving all of the temple covenants and ordinances, and (3) living worthy of all that we have received. Elder David B. Haight taught us of the responsibility and the opportunity of a priesthood holder to bring those under his stewardship to a point where they can fully take upon them the name of Jesus Christ. Referring to "a sacred experience in which he viewed the Savior's ministry and came to a greater understanding of the power of the priesthood,"[330] he said, "During those days of unconsciousness [brought on by illness] I was given, by the gift of the Holy Ghost, a more perfect knowledge of His mission. *I was also given a more complete understanding of what it means to exercise, in His name, the authority to unlock the mysteries of the kingdom of heaven for the salvation of all who are faithful.*"[331]

King Benjamin understood his priesthood role to act as an advocate for the people and "to unlock the mysteries of the kingdom for [their] salvation." By the authority of the priesthood, he facilitated a spiritual experience whereby his people received a greater endowment of the Spirit in a temple setting. We must remember that the responsibility of the priesthood is to bring people to the Holy Ghost, whose responsibility is to bring people to Jesus Christ—whose responsibility is to bring people to the Father. King Benjamin sanctified himself, thus changing his purpose from being

328 Mosiah 5:2.
329 Mosiah 1:11.
330 Thomas, "Benjamin and the Mysteries of God," 281.
331 Haight, "The Sacrament—and the Sacrifice," 59; emphasis added.

king and protector to a savior for his people. The priesthood is the power to facilitate a conversion opportunity for those of one's stewardship, to bring people to Christ so that they might more fully take upon themselves his name, and to unlock the mysteries of the kingdom of heaven that can be learned only by revelation. This astounding idea links priesthood authority, the name of Christ, and the unlocking of blessings for those whom we serve.

Taking upon Us the Name of Christ through Baptism and the Sacrament

To review, the process of taking upon ourselves the name of Christ begins at baptism,[332] and it continues by our subsequently partaking of the sacrament, in which we indicate our *willingness* to take upon ourselves the name of Jesus Christ.[333] In both cases, however, our ability to fully take upon ourselves the name of Christ, which is sometimes termed being "born again" or being "born of God," is usually something that happens later. Elder Bruce R. McConkie explained:

> Mere compliance with the formality of the ordinance of baptism does not mean that a person has been born again. No one can be born again without baptism, but the immersion in water and the laying on of hands to confer the Holy Ghost do not of themselves guarantee that a person has been or will be born again. The new birth takes place only for those who actually enjoy the gift or companionship of the Holy Ghost, only for those who are fully converted, who have given themselves without restraint to the Lord. Thus Alma addressed himself to his "brethren of the church," and pointedly asked them if they had "spiritually been born of God," received the Lord's image in their countenances, and had the "mighty change" in their hearts which always attends the birth of the Spirit. (Alma 5:14, 31.)[334]

Beyond the ordinance of baptism and ordination to the priesthood for men, to fully take upon us the name of Christ requires at least three things:

1. The intervention or assistance of the priesthood.
2. Receiving all of the temple covenants and ordinances.
3. Living worthy of all that we have received.

332 2 Nephi 31:13.
333 Moroni 4:3; D&C 20:37.
334 McConkie, *Mormon Doctrine,* 101.

Common Ways of Taking upon Ourselves the Name of Christ

There are several ways we commonly take upon ourselves the name of Christ.

One way that we take upon ourselves his name is to accept him as the father, or head, of the earthly church to which we belong, the Church that bears his name: The Church of Jesus Christ of Latter-day Saints.[335] Our acceptance of him in this role transcends this world, for it is in the next world that we, having taken upon ourselves his name, will more fully see and accept him as the "Mighty God, the Everlasting Father,"[336] the eternal head of the *heavenly* church to which we will belong: The Church of the Firstborn.[337]

Another way that we take upon ourselves his name is by taking upon ourselves his priesthood. The Lord said to Abraham, "Behold, I will lead thee by my hand, and I will take thee, to put upon thee my name, even the Priesthood of thy father, and my power shall be over thee."[338]

Moreover, we take upon ourselves the name of Jesus Christ when we bear testimony of him. Testimony bearing and taking upon ourselves Christ's name are linked in the latter-day commandment: "Take upon you the name of Christ, and speak the truth in soberness."[339] Peter said, "Sanctify the Lord God in your hearts: and be ready always to give an answer to every man that asketh you a reason of the hope that is in you."[340] Bearing witness of the Lord is to commend him to others and to testify of his reality, his ability, and his works.[341] This recommendation and witness qualify as a form of taking upon us the name of Christ.

We take upon ourselves the name of Jesus Christ by assuming his work. Significantly, the Twelve Apostles are "special witnesses of the name of Christ in all the world."[342] By delegation, we take our part in the work of the Twelve, and thus we take upon us the work and name of Christ.

Born of God—The Mystery of Spiritual Rebirth

But there is another way of taking upon ourselves the name of Jesus Christ. This way speaks of a future event that is foreshadowed each time we partake of the sacrament and witness our *willingness* to take upon ourselves his name in this ultimate way. M. Catherine Thomas refers to this future event as "the mystery of spiritual rebirth."[343]

The idea of spiritual rebirth was introduced to Nicodemus by Jesus: "Ye must be born again."[344] The concept of birth invokes the image of parents or progenitors. When we are born again by baptism, we agree to accept Jesus as our spiritual father and give

335 D&C 115:4; 3 Nephi 27:7–8.
336 Isaiah 9:6; 2 Nephi 19:6.
337 D&C 76:54, 71, 76, 94; 93:22; 107:19.
338 Abraham 1:18.
339 Oaks, "Taking Upon Us the Name of Jesus Christ," 80, quoting D&C 18:21.
340 1 Peter 3:15.
341 Ether 12:41.
342 D&C 107:23.
343 Thomas, "Benjamin and the Mysteries of God," 277.
344 John 3:7.

ourselves to being adopted into his family, which is his Church. Hence, forevermore, we are called by the name of our adopted father—*Jesus Christ*—which is also the name of our new family. We accept Jesus as our adopted father in the sense that he becomes the father, or progenitor, of our salvation; that is, our salvation is born of him. King Benjamin said, "Because of the covenant ye have made ye shall be called the children of Christ, his sons and daughters; for behold, this day he hath spiritually begotten you."[345] Elder McConkie wrote:

> Those who are born again not only live a new life, but they also have a new father. Their new life is one of righteousness, and their new father is God. They become the sons of God; or, more particularly, they become the sons and daughters of Jesus Christ. They bear, ever thereafter, the name of their new parent; that is, they take upon themselves the name of Christ and become Christians, not only in word but in very deed. They become by adoption the seed or offspring of Christ, the children in his family, the members of his household which is the perfect household of perfect faith.[346]

That is not to say that we abandon our Heavenly Father, who is the progenitor of our spirit bodies, in favor of Jesus Christ, who is our elder brother. Conversely, Heavenly Father initiates the mandate that we take upon us the name of his Son, Jesus Christ, by our entering in the waters of baptism. Moreover, as we have said, each time we partake of the sacrament, we witness unto the Father our willingness to take upon ourselves the name of Jesus Christ, that is, to prepare ourselves and look forward to the day when we fully take upon ourselves the name of Jesus Christ.

It should be clear by now that taking upon ourselves the name of Jesus Christ is the central issue and objective of the gospel. Possibly nothing is more important to our salvation and eventual exaltation than taking upon ourselves this holy name.

Fully Taking upon Us the Name of Jesus Christ

This brings us to the account of King Benjamin and how he used his priesthood to facilitate a spiritual experience by which his people could fully take upon themselves the name of Jesus Christ—"the mystery of spiritual rebirth."

We recall that the prophet-king sanctified himself and thus fully took upon himself the name of Christ. Now he was in a position to help others. Jesus set the example for this process. In his great intercessory prayer, he said to the Father, "And for their sakes [the Apostles] I sanctify myself, that they also might be sanctified."[347] That is to say, he

345 Mosiah 5:7; see also Alma 5:14; 36:23–26.
346 McConkie, A New Witness for the Articles of Faith, 284.
347 John 17:19.

was about to magnify, or increase, his purpose through his atoning sacrifice so that he could fully become the Savior. He said that he was going to do this so that he could facilitate a sanctifying opportunity for his Apostles, "that they also might be sanctified." Likewise, King Benjamin sanctified himself, fully took upon himself the name of Christ, and then prayed earnestly for priesthood power to bring his people into the presence of the Lord. The process moved him from being a great king and protector to being a great prophet and priest, or more specifically, a savior to his people.

In response to King Benjamin's prayer, an angel appeared, granting him permission to gather the people for the purpose of giving them an endowment that would cause them to "rejoice with exceedingly great joy"[348] and be "filled with joy."[349] These terms are connected with being born again.[350] The central message of the angel involved King Benjamin's giving the people "a name, that thereby they may be distinguished above all the people which the Lord God hath brought out of the land of Jerusalem." Without a doubt, these people were righteous and highly favored. But what had they done to deserve the honor of being granted this "name"? King Benjamin explained that it was because "they have been a diligent people in keeping the commandments of the Lord." For that reason, they would be blessed with "a name that never shall be blotted out, except it be through transgression."[351]

From that point forward, the king's entire effort—gathering them to the temple, administering to them a sermon that was structured like the temple endowment,[352] making references to their being "sealed" to Christ in order to receive eternal life[353]—focused on helping his people fully take upon themselves the name of Jesus Christ.

It is worth emphasizing that these people were righteous people who had been diligent in keeping the commandments, which we may assume would mean that they had received baptism and so had already taken upon themselves the name of Christ. Now King Benjamin, through his priesthood, served as an advocate with God to provide these good people a new and fuller experience with the name of Christ. Obviously, they had never before taken upon themselves the name of Christ to this degree. What happened when they did so? Catherine Thomas said they attained to "a higher spiritual plain in their quest to return to God. . . . The people tasted of the glory of God and came to a personal knowledge of him; through the power of the Holy Spirit they experienced the mighty change of heart and the mystery of spiritual rebirth."[354] This poignant experience resulted in a "profound transformation from basic goodness to something that exceeded their ability to even describe. This much they did say, 'The Spirit of the Lord Omnipotent . . . has wrought a mighty change in us, or in our hearts, that we have no more disposition to do evil, but to do good continually' (Mosiah 5:2)."[355]

348 Mosiah 3:13.
349 Mosiah 4:3.
350 Thomas, "Benjamin and the Mysteries of God," 285–86.
351 Mosiah 1:11–12.
352 Thomas, "Benjamin and the Mysteries of God," 292.
353 Mosiah 5:15.
354 Thomas, "Benjamin and the Mysteries of God," 293.
355 Thomas, "Benjamin and the Mysteries of God," 290.

President Joseph F. Smith explained the result of taking upon ourselves the name of Jesus Christ and experiencing the mighty change of heart: "If our hearts are fixed with proper intent upon serving God and keeping His commandments, what will be the fruits of it? What will be the result? . . . Men will be full of the spirit of forgiveness, of charity, of mercy, of love unfeigned. They will not seek occasion against each other; nor will they take advantage of the weak, the unwary, or the ignorant; but they will regard the rights of the ignorant, of the weak, of those who are dependent and at their mercy, as they do their very own; they will hold the liberties of their fellow-men as sacred as their own liberties; they will prize the virtue, honor and integrity of their neighbors and brothers just as they would appreciate and prize and hold sacred their own."[356] Zion indeed!

The Temple and the Name of Christ

The key to understanding "the mystery of spiritual rebirth" is in the fact that King Benjamin's people fully took upon themselves the name of Christ in a temple setting. We cannot overstate the significance of this fact. The temple is a house dedicated to "the name" of the Lord.[357] The Lord's "name shall be put upon this house."[358] When we partake of the sacrament, we implicitly indicate our willingness to go to the temple to fully take upon ourselves the name of Christ and receive the blessings of exaltation.[359] Expounding on our receiving the fulness of the name of Christ, Elder Bruce R. McConkie wrote, "God's name is God. To have his name written on a person is to identify that person as a god. How can it be said more plainly? Those who gain eternal life become gods!"[360] Thus, it is in the temple that we fully receive the name of Jesus Christ through the covenants and ordinances of salvation that ultimately lead to our becoming gods.

In the temple we are purified, sanctified, and anointed to become kings and priests, queens and priestesses in the similitude of Jesus Christ.[361] It is in the temple that we receive the keys of his knowledge and power. It is in the temple that we make successive covenants that define a Christlike lifestyle.[362] It is in the temple that we are transformed into saviors on Mount Zion, with his "name written always in [our] hearts,"[363] and it is there that the price he paid for each of us becomes very real. We recall that the Nephites had something like a temple experience when the Savior invited them, one by one, to step forward and touch his wounds and thus come in contact with the reality of the Atonement on an individual basis.[364] As they effectively *received* the marks of the Atonement, they were transformed into saviors in the similitude of the Savior; that is, their ability to perform a saving service in behalf of others greatly increased, as evidenced in the beginning verses of 4 Nephi. In that encounter with the resurrected Savior, in a very

356 Smith, *Teachings of Presidents of the Church: Joseph F. Smith*, 425.
357 1 Kings 3:2; 5:5; 8:16–20, 29, 44, 48; 1 Chronicles 22:8–10, 19; 29:16; 2 Chronicles 2:4; 6:5–10, 20, 34, 38.
358 D&C 109:26.
359 Oaks, "Taking Upon Us the Name of Jesus Christ," 80.
360 McConkie, *Doctrinal New Testament Commentary*, 3:459.
361 Smith, *Teachings of Presidents of the Church: Joseph Smith*, 22.
362 *Encyclopedia of Mormonism*, 454–56.
363 Mosiah 5:12.
364 3 Nephi 11:14–17.

literal way, they took upon themselves the name of Christ, whereas previously they had received his name symbolically.

It is in the temple that we are bound to Jesus with a seal that cannot be broken—except by our own sin. There we symbolically ascend to where he is, to become what he is, and to achieve oneness with him as he is one with the Father. It is in the temple that we receive by marriage a kingdom within his kingdom. Everything about the temple experience points to fully taking upon ourselves the name of Jesus Christ.

The Name of Christ and Coronation

Moreover, everything about the temple experience points to our coronation in God's kingdom.[365] What we do in the temple symbolically we will one day do literally.[366] We recall that the kings of the Nephites typically received a new name when they ascended to the throne. At first, that name was Nephi.[367] Just so, when we ascend to our throne we are given a new name—a coronation name. That royal name is Jesus Christ; we become joint heirs with him. Thus, to fully take upon us the name of Jesus Christ opens the door to be nominated a candidate for a throne and exaltation.

The prophet Jeremiah rejoiced when he read, understood, and internalized the import of the word of the Lord as it applied to taking upon himself the name of Jesus Christ: "Thy words were found, and I did eat them; and thy word was unto me the joy and rejoicing of mine heart: for I am called by thy name, O Lord God of hosts."[368] Elder McConkie taught,

> We have the ability and the capacity and the power to attain unto that status [sons and daughters of God] after we accept the Lord with all our hearts (see D&C 39:1–6). Now the ordinances that are performed in the temples are the ordinances of exaltation; they open the door to us to an inheritance of sonship; they open the door to us so that we may become sons and daughters, members of the household of God in eternity . . . if we thereafter continue faithful, to receive eventually the fullness of the Father. The temple ordinances open the door to gaining all power and all wisdom and all knowledge. Temple ordinances open up the way to membership in the Church of the Firstborn. They open the door to becoming kings and priests and inheriting all things.[369]

365 *Encyclopedia of Mormonism*, 1464; McConkie, Conference Report, Oct. 1955, 13.
366 D&C 76:55–58.
367 *Encyclopedia of Mormonism*, 191.
368 Jeremiah 15:16.
369 McConkie, Conference Report, Oct. 1955, 13.

We conclude with Catherine Thomas's thoughts: "King Benjamin's people received an endowment of spiritual knowledge and power which took them from being good people to Christlike people—all in a temple setting. What they experienced through the power of the priesthood was a revelation of Christ's nature and the power to be assimilated to his image."[370] Plainly, those who fully take upon themselves the name of Jesus Christ qualify to come into his presence, receive their exaltation, and become gods. This is "the mystery of spiritual rebirth."[371]

Coming to Christ

Taking upon ourselves the name of Jesus Christ brings us to Christ and then into his presence. Of course, as we have discussed, we come to Christ and take upon us his name by degrees. Our progress is measured by how much we have become like him, how much we want what he wants, and how much we assume his work as our own.

Enos, in his wilderness experience, wrestled in the spirit to come to Christ, and in the process he experienced a mighty change of heart. From his account, we learn that the closer a person comes to Christ, the more his heart expands and the more he wants to bring an increasing number of people into its embrace. A pure heart continually reaches out, trying to save and bring people to Christ. Joseph Smith taught: "A man filled with the love of God is not content with blessing his family alone, but ranges through the whole world, anxious to bless the whole human race."[372] When we strive to become like the Lord, keep his commandments, want what he wants, and assume his work as our own, we will fully come to him, and then we will see him. The new heart that was given to us by the Lord, a heart resembling his heart, now bids us seek and cleave unto him.

The brother of Jared, in his wilderness experience, discovered that in every difficulty there is an opportunity to come to Christ. The challenge of lighting their vessels became the miracle of lighting a life.[373] Joseph Smith's dilemma of finding the true Church became the miracle of finding the true God. The famine that drove Abraham from Ur to Haran became the harvest of blessings known as the Abrahamic covenant, which the Lord gave to the patriarch in a face-to-face encounter. That event culminated a long wilderness search that caused Abraham to say in his heart, "Thy servant has sought thee earnestly; now I have found thee."[374]

The Lord's wilderness is intended to prepare us to find the Lord. The "keys" for such a discovery are given to us in the temple: "And this greater priesthood administereth the gospel and holdeth the key of the mysteries of the kingdom, even the key of the knowledge of God. Therefore, in the ordinances thereof, the power of godliness is manifest. And without the ordinances thereof, and the authority of the priesthood, the

---

370 Thomas, "Benjamin and the Mysteries of God," 292.
371 Thomas, "Benjamin and the Mysteries of God," 277.
372 Smith, *History of the Church*, 4:227.
373 Ether 3:1–16.
374 Abraham 2:12.

power of godliness is not manifest unto men in the flesh; for without this no man can see the face of God, even the Father, and live."[375] Blaine Yorgason explained:

> The temple is the doorway through which all wilderness travelers must pass to reenter the presence of the Lord. Having lost that presence through birth and our own carnal ways of living, still we yearn after the perfect love we once felt. Thus we are drawn to the temple, where by sacred ordinances the Lord seals His children to Himself and brings them back into His presence. Adam, cast out into the lone and dreary world, searched relentlessly until he found the keys that would open the narrow doorway behind which the Lord was waiting. Abraham, seeking all the blessings of the fathers, embarked on the same quest. . . .
>
> Isaac and Jacob at their sacred altars, Moses on Mount Horeb, Lehi at the Tree, Nephi on the mountaintop, Moriancumer on the mount Shelem—all these wilderness travelers conducted the search that is outlined and empowered for each of us in the temple, gradually increasing the hold, the seal, between themselves and their Lord, until in reality they were brought back into His presence. That was the very quest for which they had sought and obtained a remission of their sins and for which they had entered the Lord's wilderness—to rend the veil of unbelief, stand in the Lord's presence (see JST Genesis 14:30–31; D&C 84:19; 107:19), and be encircled eternally in the arms of His love (see D&C 6:20; 2 Nephi 1:15).[376]

Nephi's wilderness experience often beckoned him "into the mount," where he "did pray oft unto the Lord," who showed him "great things."[377] Speaking of Nephi and others who went into the mount to find and commune with God, Blaine Yorgason commented: "And what sorts of 'great things' were shown these ancient sojourners in their lofty, cloud-shrouded temples? The exact things we can see and learn today."[378] Elder John A. Widtsoe said, "The Temple endowment relates the story of man's eternal journey; sets forth the conditions upon which progress in the eternal journey depends; requires covenants or agreements of those participating, to accept and use the laws of progress; gives tests by which our willingness and fitness for righteousness may be known, and finally points out the ultimate destiny of those who love truth and live by it."[379]

375 D&C 84:19–22.
376 Yorgason, *Spiritual Progression in the Last Days*, 193–94.
377 1 Nephi 18:3.
378 Yorgason, *I Need Thee Every Hour*, 358.
379 Widtsoe, *Priesthood and Church Government*, 333.

From the days of Adam to the present, faithful wilderness travelers have come face-to-face with their God in a temple setting that is most holy. Blaine Yorgason continued by saying, "All this is much more real than most of us realize. As the scripture says of the brother of Jared, 'The Lord showed himself unto him, and said: Because thou knowest these things ye are redeemed from the fall; therefore ye are brought back into my presence; therefore I show myself unto you' (Ether 3:13). Therefore, what Mahonri Moriancumer had beheld for so long with the eye of faith was now visually confirmed. He had rent 'the veil of unbelief' (Ether 4:15) with his persistent efforts, and now he had beheld the face of the Lord. Rather than seeing in order to believe, which is the way of the world, he had believed in order to see, and so on the mountain of the Lord's temple, God rewarded his righteous faith and efforts."[380]

The end goal of the Lord's wilderness is to enter his presence and experience his ultimate deliverance. The Lord's promises are sure: "Verily, thus saith the Lord: It shall come to pass that every soul who forsaketh his sins and cometh unto me, and calleth on my name, and obeyeth my voice, and keepeth my commandments, shall see my face and know that I am."[381]

Deliverance

The Lord's wilderness provides us ample opportunities of deliverance. As we have mentioned, each deliverance event is meant to increase our faith and prepare us for our ultimate deliverance. As with the Israelites who wandered in the wilderness for forty years, every aspect of our own journey points to our becoming something new and holy, which is an important goal of deliverance. Once we are refined and sanctified, we are ready for the Lord to come to us, defeat our enemies, and establish Zion in our lives.

Looking back, we will realize that everything about our wilderness experience has prepared us for deliverance.

- We separated from Babylon and put off the natural man.
- We learned to live by faith and to trust God.
- We made the sacrifice of all things.
- We confronted and overcame Satan.
- We fully took upon ourselves the name of Christ.
- We fully came to him.

Now we are ready to "cross over," as did the Israelites, Jaredites, and Nephites, and inherit our own promised land. *This is deliverance!*

We take with us other lessons we have learned in the Lord's wilderness. For example, the wilderness experience has shaped us so that we are now much more like Jesus, who has guided us through his wilderness. From the outset of our journey, he invited us to yoke ourselves to him and stride alongside him—with the promise that he would help

380 Yorgason, *I Need Thee Every Hour,* 360; Joseph Smith revealed that Mahonri Moriancumr was the name of the brother of Jared (see Reynolds, "The Jaredites," 282).
381 D&C 93:1.

us shoulder the weight. We discovered that his is an "easy" yoke.[382] Along the way, he and we have conversed and shared bonding experiences; for our part, we became acquainted with his character, attributes, and perfections. Now, when he speaks, we recognize his voice, and because we have been delivered by him multiple times, we recognize that he has power to deliver us again. These are just a few of the discoveries and the level of righteousness that we have gained.

The people of Enoch, Melchizedek, Nephi, and others achieved this level of righteousness, which allowed the Lord to establish Zion among them. Then the Lord raised up these Zion people, both literally and figuratively, and took them into his bosom.[383] They had qualified for these blessings by enduring to the end of their wilderness experiences in faithfulness and, having been true to their covenants, became eligible for the Lord's deliverance.

What we learn from their accounts is that ultimate deliverance is often preceded by the most difficult test of faith. Both Nephi and the brother of Jared had to build boats, leave behind beautiful environs, cast off into the stormy sea, and commit themselves into the hands of the Lord. Sarah was required to wait ninety years to bear a son. Abraham was required to be willing to sacrifice Isaac. The ancient Israelites were required to walk into the overflowing Jordan River with faith that the Lord would part the waters. The scriptures record the result. The waters rolled back "and the priests that bare the ark of the covenant of the Lord stood firm on dry ground in the midst of Jordan, and all the Israelites passed over on dry ground, until all the people were passed clean over Jordan."[384] Likewise, when the moment of our deliverance is at hand, the Lord will part the waters so we can "cross over," and we will do so, as it were, on dry ground.

Ultimately, deliverance comes after all we can do. Limhi's people tried and tried to deliver themselves but could not.[385] That is not the way it works in the Lord's wilderness. Only God can deliver us. After we have tried repeatedly, we finally come to the conclusion that we are helpless without him. It is usually then that we cease looking to ourselves or to others for solutions and we urgently look to God. It is usually then that we begin to pray another way—we pray in faith. That is, we move from simply listing our requests to truly communing with and crying unto the Lord. We supplicate, plead, beg, beseech, implore, appeal, and importune. Why? Evidently so that we can cement in our souls the lessons of the wilderness and solidify our relationship with the Lord; now it is second nature to know that his deliverance is forthcoming. That instinct of faith seems to be essential to deliverance.

Perhaps deliverance is delayed to allow us to persevere in mighty supplication so that we can completely internalize the concept that there is power and safety in the Covenant. We need to know—*really know*—that the Lord interacts with and delivers us by the pure motivation of compassion and love. Maybe deliverance is postponed to give us the opportunity to develop the essential virtues of mighty faith and unwavering

382 Matthew 11:29–30.
383 D&C 38:4; Moses 7:31, 69.
384 Joshua 3:17.
385 Mosiah 21:1–15.

trust in the Lord, which are developed only by waiting in humble anticipation. Thus, to allow us time to learn valuable lessons, the Lord often withholds deliverance or waits until the very last minute. But the education is worth the wait. Moroni tells us that "the Lord did hear the brother of Jared, and had compassion upon him, and said unto him: . . . I will go before thee into a land which is choice above all the lands of the earth. And there will I bless thee and thy seed, and raise up unto me of thy seed, and of the seed of thy brother, and they who shall go with thee, a great nation. And there shall be none greater than the nation which I will raise up unto me of thy seed, upon all the face of the earth. *And this I will do unto thee because this long time ye have cried unto me*."[386]

Giving Ourselves Free

Interestingly, ultimate deliverance seems to pivot on our willingness to shed selfishness and summon the courage to give and extend charity. The people of Limhi tried every conceivable way to deliver themselves and could not. It appears that it was only when they began to take care of the widows and orphans that the Lord's deliverance came.[387]

This powerful principle—that charity opens the door to deliverance—is so simple we often miss it. As we have mentioned, giving time, talents, and resources can be manifested telestially, terrestrially, and celestially. A telestial person might not give unless he is forced to or unless he can receive something in return. A terrestrial person will give if he already has something to give. A celestial person gives, not because he is forced to or expects something in return or because he has wherewithal to give, but because he loves God and his children more than he considers his inconvenience. A celestial person gives despite his present circumstances because he knows that the Lord will compensate him "an hundredfold,"[388] which will provide him more so that he can give again. This level and attitude of charitable giving has the power to break the bonds of captivity. Armed only with the unselfish motivation of pure love, we can literally *give* ourselves into freedom!

We recall that despite a lifetime of extending charity,[389] Job was required to give yet one more time in the darkest hour of his life; he extended charity to his accusatory friends and the result liberated him: "And the Lord turned the captivity of Job, when he prayed for his friends."[390] Most certainly, Job's past acts of giving contributed to his deliverance, but they did not carry as much weight as the present opportunity to give. Hence, after all Job had suffered, the single thing that stood between him and deliverance was one last charitable act. Then, when Job was able to reach deeply within himself and find the strength to give one more time, he was set free.

When the widow chose to give to Elijah rather than to give to her son and herself, she obtained deliverance from the famine, and later she experienced another type of deliver-

386 Ether 1:40–43; emphasis added.
387 Mosiah 21:17.
388 Matthew 19:29.
389 Job 31:6, 16–23.
390 Job 42:10.

ance when the Lord mercifully restored her son from the jaws of death.[391] Likewise, we are set free when we choose to give one last time or to place another's needs before our own.

Mortality provides us ample opportunities to go to the Lord and plead for deliverance. But, according to Amulek, prayer without giving charitable service is hypocritical; moreover, such a prayer is powerless to yield blessings: "And now behold, my beloved brethren, I say unto you, do not suppose that this is all; for after ye have done all these things, if ye turn away the needy, and the naked, and visit not the sick and afflicted, and impart of your substance, if ye have, to those who stand in need—I say unto you, if ye do not any of these things, behold, your prayer is vain, and availeth you nothing, and ye are as hypocrites who do deny the faith. Therefore, if ye do not remember to be charitable, ye are as dross, which the refiners do cast out."[392] Prayer without extending charity is just words.

In addition, we often fast to obtain deliverance. We should fast to "loose the bands of wickedness, to undo the heavy burdens, and to let the oppressed go free, and that ye break every yoke." According to Isaiah, our fast counts for nothing more than going hungry unless we "deal [our] bread to the hungry, and . . . bring the poor that are cast out to [our] house," and when we see "the naked, that [we] cover him." It is only *after* we give charitable service that deliverance comes. Notice that Isaiah's promises begin with the word *then*:

> *Then* shall thy light break forth as the morning, and thine health shall spring forth speedily: and thy righteousness shall go before thee; the glory of the Lord shall be thy rereward [protector]. *Then* shalt thou call, and the Lord shall answer; thou shalt cry, and he shall say, Here I am. . . . And if thou draw out thy soul to the hungry, and satisfy the afflicted soul; *then* shall thy light rise in obscurity, and thy darkness be as the noonday: And the Lord shall guide thee continually, and satisfy thy soul in drought, and make fat thy bones: and thou shalt be like a watered garden, and like a spring of water, whose waters fail not. And they that shall be of thee [your family] shall build the old waste places: thou shalt raise up the foundations of many generations; and thou shalt be called, The repairer of the breach, The restorer of paths to dwell in.[393]

Clearly, prayer and fasting, without charity, is powerless to deliver .

Throughout our wilderness journey with the Lord, we have learned to love him by emulating him, and in the process we have become what he is: love.[394] If the pure love of Christ is called charity, then we, like Christ whom we love, are charity. Charity is not

391 1 Kings 17:10–24.
392 Alma 34:28–29.
393 Isaiah 58:5–12; emphasis added.
394 1 John 4:8.

an act but what we become.[395] And what we have now become holds sufficient power to deliver us. When people learn to extend charity, they become Zion. While the world seeks safety with armies and treaties, while it looks for security in rising markets and fat portfolios, and while it tries untold numbers of options to obtain deliverance, Zion people simply keep God's commandments and apply acts of charity. As easy as it was for the Israelites to look upon Moses' brazen serpent to obtain healing, it is likewise easy for us to invoke the simple principle of giving to experience the Lord's safety, security, and deliverance.

Restoration and Exaltation

The land of promise—Zion—is a place or condition where or in which the Lord dwells with his people in righteousness.[396] When we arrive in our promised land, we will have come full circle, back to our beginning and our heritage. This process of falling, being snatched out of the world, traveling through the Lord's wilderness, being delivered, and crossing over into the land of promise is accomplished both by individuals and groups of people. For example, the Latter-day Saints, collectively, will be delivered from the wilderness and return to their first Zion home, Adam-ondi-Ahman.[397] Then they will return to the place of the earth's first Zion, Jackson County, Missouri, the location of the Garden of Eden.[398]

Just so, we, individually, must fall, experience being snatched out of the world, travel the Lord's wilderness, exit by the Lord's intervention, and enter our personal lands of promise. These "promised lands" can take any number of forms: restoration of health, a healed marriage, a child rescued from certain ruin, a return to financial stability, or even moving to a new location. But in one way or another, we are restored, healed, rescued, and stabilized, and we feel as though we have returned home.

Collectively and individually, we are restored to Zion in a similar manner. This restoration will be played out in dramatic fashion after the Saints have completed their collective wilderness experience. Then select righteous individuals will gather at Adam-ondi-Ahman, and there, those people will witness the crowning of their King.[399] At that point, the King, having taken the reins of government, will accelerate the process of redeeming Zion by commissioning the building of a temple and a holy temple city. When these are completed, the King will visit his people in his temple.[400] Afterward, the city of Enoch will descend and join with the earthly Zion, and heaven and earth will literally meet and become one.[401] Then the King will overthrow the wicked, cleanse the earth, and restore this planet to its original paradisiacal glory.[402] We will enter a time of unimaginable joy. This will be our collective restoration to Zion.

395 Oaks, "The Challenge to Become," 32–33.
396 Moses 7:17.
397 D&C 116:1.
398 McConkie, *Mormon Doctrine,* 20; see also Kimball, *Journal of Discourses,* 10:235; Cannon, *Journal of Discourses,* 11:336–37.
399 McConkie, *A New Witness for the Articles of Faith,* 640.
400 McConkie, *A New Witness for the Articles of Faith,* 601.
401 McConkie, *A New Witness for the Articles of Faith,* 588.
402 McConkie, *A New Witness for the Articles of Faith,* 563–64.

Individually, after we are delivered from the wilderness, the Lord judges us worthy of a crown.[403] Essentially, our day of judgment is advanced.[404] Keep in mind that these events are always described as taking place in connection with a temple. Significantly, the Lord commands us individually to purify and sanctify ourselves so that we might become a holy temple,[405] and, as we have learned, it is in the temple where we receive the coronation rites and ordinances. Deliverance from the wilderness launches us into a land of promise, which is symbolic of Zion and also means membership in the Church of the Firstborn, the heavenly church.[406] Deliverance renders us *one* with the members of that church. Now we rise to a level of righteousness enjoyed by former Zion peoples whose existence was paradisiacal,[407] a level of increased power and joy. Now we enter a time of extended happiness.

Our deliverance lands us in new surroundings or conditions that do not resemble the wilderness. Whereas we once were required to walk by faith, we now enjoy ready access to the Lord.[408] We recall that Zion, whether it is a place or a condition, is the Lord's habitation.[409] Zion is a place or situation of beauty and holiness.[410] There, we are no longer separated from God, but, rather, *at one* with him through the *at-one-ment* of Jesus Christ. Being at one is the condition of unity that leads to "one heart," which all Zion people achieve.[411] As much as the lands of promise of the brother of Jared, the Israelites, Lehi, Alma, and the Anti-Nephi-Lehies were different from their wilderness environments, so the city of New Jerusalem and its Zion stakes will be different from the collective wilderness experience of the Latter-day Saints. Equally important, and on an individual basis, every promised land for each wilderness traveler is a vastly different environment from their former experiences.

The elect of God qualify for this quality of deliverance that results in complete restoration and exaltation. Elder McConkie explained:

> The elect of God comprise a very select group, an inner circle of faithful members of The Church of Jesus Christ of Latter-day Saints. They are the portion of church members who are striving with all their hearts to keep the fulness of the gospel law in this life so that they can become inheritors of the fulness of gospel rewards in the life to come. . . . To gain this elect status they must be endowed in the temple of the Lord (D&C 95:8), enter into that "order of the priesthood" named "the new and everlasting covenant of marriage" (D&C 131:1–4),

403 McConkie, *Mormon Doctrine*, 173.
404 McConkie, *Mormon Doctrine*, 109–10.
405 1 Corinthians 6:19.
406 McConkie, *A New Witness for the Articles of Faith*, 337.
407 Young, *Discourses of Brigham Young*, 438.
408 Moses 7:16.
409 Psalm 132:13.
410 D&C 82:14; Psalm 50:2.
411 Moses 7:18.

> and overcome by faith until, as the sons of God, they merit membership in the Church of the Firstborn. (D&C 76:50–70, 94–96.) The elect of God are the chosen of God; and he has said: "There are many who have been ordained among you, whom I have called but few of them are chosen." (D&C 95:5; 121:34–40).[412]

May we strive to become the elect of God, the restored and exalted of Zion.

Sent Back as an Emissary of Zion

Now delivered, restored, and, to a degree, exalted in their Zion, the elect of God are commissioned by the Lord to return (1) to the wilderness of sin to call people out, and (2) to the Lord's wilderness to help others until the Lord also delivers them. This is Zion at its finest: imparting of our "substance to the poor, . . . feeding the hungry, clothing the naked, visiting the sick and administering to their relief, both spiritually and temporally, according to their wants."[413] That is not to say that we should not have been living this way all along, but now, for a heightened purpose, the Lord sends us back as his emissaries of Zion.

We recall that when Jesus pronounced his Apostles separate from the world,[414] he then sent them back to bring out others: "Then said Jesus to them again, Peace be unto you: as my Father hath sent me, even so send I you."[415] Blaine Yorgason explained:

> The Lord invariably expects His successfully graduated wilderness students to carry the things they have learned back to others. That is as it should be, for the closer the wilderness travelers draw to the Lord, the more filled with charity or pure love they become, and the more anxious they are to share their joyous knowledge. Of the repentant sons of Mosiah the record states: "They were desirous that salvation should be declared to every creature, for they could not bear that any human soul should perish; yea, even the very thoughts that any soul should endure endless torment did cause them to quake and tremble. And thus did the Spirit of the Lord work upon them" (Mosiah 28:3–4).
>
> Both Jesus and Moses eagerly returned to teach the very people they were originally led away from, and Enos and Alma left vivid descriptions of their lifelong efforts to bring the message of Christ to the people

412 McConkie, *Mormon Doctrine,* 217.
413 Mosiah 4:26.
414 John 17:6–16.
415 John 17:6–16.

> they called enemies—those they loved who had chosen the things of Babylon over the things of God. Alma declared concerning the success of his life's work: "The Lord doth give me exceedingly great joy in the fruit of my labors; for because of the word which he has imparted unto me, behold, many have been born of God, and have tasted as I have tasted, and have seen eye to eye as I have seen; therefore they do know of these things of which I have spoken, as I do know; and the knowledge which I have is of God. And I have been supported under trials and troubles of every kind, yea, and in all manner of afflictions; yea, God has delivered me from prison, and from bonds, and from death; yea, and I do put my trust in him, and he will still deliver me. And I know that he will raise me up at the last day, to dwell with him in glory; yea, and I will praise him forever" (Alma 36:25–28).[416]

Summary and Conclusion

This, then, forms the pattern of our universal journey to Zion, our origin, heritage, and destiny.

To become like God necessitated our experiencing the highs and lows of mortal life. That is, we had to fall; we had to descend below all things, as did the Savior, and this to gain the ability to ascend above all things.

Our fall from Zion landed us in a "dark and dreary waste," which inevitably led us into the wilderness of sin. Because we were created for the purpose of becoming consummately happy, and finally realizing that wickedness never could result in happiness, we awoke to our awful situation and cried out for the Lord's deliverance.

The process of deliverance required that we make a covenant with the Lord by which he agreed to rescue us on the condition that we would change—not just stop sinning, but actually change—our natural disposition to want to sin. Upon attempting such a feat, we immediately understood that our desire to change would fall short of our ability to effect such a transformation. Therefore, we called upon the Lord to help us; we placed our lives in his hands and agreed to abide with him in the Covenant while he guided us through the difficult process of purification and sanctification. Only by our submitting to this process could we place ourselves in a position for the Lord to one day perform the ultimate deliverance and take us into our own personal land of promise—our Zion. Now, with the new and everlasting covenant in place, we fled, or were delivered from, the wilderness of sin, rendering us safe in the Lord from that situation, and forever after, we agreed to remain separate from the world, which is Babylon.

416 Yorgason, *I Need Thee Every Hour*, 249–50.

The place or condition in which our covenantal transformation took place was another wilderness—the Lord's wilderness. Having been baptized and blessed with the Holy Ghost, we could now discern between good and evil; therefore, we began to judge and choose between telestial and celestial things. Consequently, we began to feel like strangers and pilgrims in a foreign land. The Lord's wilderness was not home; it was simply *the way* home.

To accelerate and punctuate our progress in the wilderness, we encountered extremely difficult periods called crucibles. Their purposes were to weld us to the Lord through the Covenant, teach us to have faith and to trust him, and prove us trustworthy of the blessings of eternity. In the face of these trying times, our challenge was to avoid murmuring against the Lord and to find joy in the journey. Significantly, our achieving cheerfulness in the face of adversity actually empowered us to endure to the end.

We soon discovered that the conditions of the Lord's wilderness involved hard work, traveling by revelation, and journeying exactly as the Lord directed. We also discovered that angels attended us. Despite the odds, we realized that we had always enjoyed the Lord's safety and security. We realized something else that was important: To prepare us for the ultimate day of deliverance, the Lord had delivered us multiple times from seemingly impossible situations.

Somewhere along the way, we were confronted by Satan. This necessary experience forced us to choose once and for all between Satan and God. In some cases, this confrontation was also coupled with the equally necessary Abrahamic test. Armed with little information and in the face of irony, we were required to climb our own Mount Moriahs, build altars of faith, cry our allegiance to God, and sacrifice all things. Overcoming Satan and sacrificing all things brought us to the point where we fully took upon ourselves the name of Jesus Christ, the ultimate manifestation of being born again. Then we were ushered into the presence of the Lord.

We learned invaluable lessons in the Lord's wilderness, lessons that prepared us to live the higher law. Little by little, we felt our "natural man" give way to the Saint that wanted to emerge. Occasionally, the Lord brought us to our own Bountifuls, or places of reprieve. We used these reprieves as Sabbaths: to commune with the Lord, to enter into his rest, and to prepare us for the final and most difficult part of our journey, which became our ultimate test of faith. By miraculous means, the Lord delivered us from his wilderness and returned us home to Zion, our promised land.

This wilderness journey is how we come to Zion and to Christ. The wilderness journey is the "adventure of discipleship, [the] trek of treks,"[417] the path called the "strait and narrow."

417 Maxwell, *The Promise of Discipleship*, i.

Section 2
The Pure in Heart

In the final analysis, Zion people are defined by a single phrase: "the pure in heart."[418] This simple but powerful statement carries with it the further definition that the pure in heart are those who see God.[419] Joseph Smith corrected the promise in the gospel of Matthew to read: "And blessed are *all* the pure in heart; for they *shall* see God."[420] It stands to reason, then, that the pure in heart are all those who seek to qualify to see God and who are working toward that future privilege. Until then, the promise stands: "They *shall* see God."

This event differs from the global viewing of the Savior when he comes again in glory. The pure in heart qualify to see Christ personally, *as he is*, because they have become like him. What, therefore, is the determining factor that makes a person pure in heart? Moroni gave the answer: Charity. He taught, "Wherefore, my beloved brethren, pray unto the Father with all the energy of heart, that ye may be filled with *this love*, which he hath bestowed upon all who are true followers of his Son, Jesus Christ; that ye may become the sons of God; *that when he shall appear we shall be like him, for we shall see him as he is*; that we may have this hope; that we may be purified even as he is pure."[421] Charity, then, is the deciding virtue that leads to our becoming pure in heart, pure "even as he is pure."

Where will the pure in heart see their God? The temple is the likely location: "Yea, and my presence shall be there [in the temple], for I will come into it, and all the pure in heart that shall come into it shall see God."[422] "My name shall be here [in the temple]; and I will manifest myself to my people in mercy in this house. Yea, I will appear unto my servants, and speak unto them with mine own voice, if my people will keep my commandments."[423]

---

418 D&C 97:21.
419 Matthew 5:8; 3 Nephi 12:8.
420 JST, Matthew 5:10; emphasis added.
421 Moroni 7:48; emphasis added.
422 D&C 97:16.
423 D&C 110:7–8.

Blessings for the Pure in Heart

The Book of Mormon prophet Jacob offered counsel to the pure in heart: "But behold, I, Jacob, would speak unto you that are pure in heart. Look unto God with firmness of mind, and pray unto him with exceeding faith. . . . O all ye that are pure in heart, lift up your heads and receive the pleasing word of God, and feast upon his love." His counsel was coupled with promises: "And he will console you in your afflictions, and he will plead your cause, and send down justice upon those who seek your destruction." And then came the ultimate promise: "For ye may [receive the pleasing word of God and feast upon his love], if your minds are firm, forever."

On the other hand, Jacob pronounced woes upon those who are not pure in heart: "But, wo, wo, unto you that are not pure in heart, that are filthy this day before God; for except ye repent the land is cursed for your sakes; and [your enemies] . . . shall scourge you even unto destruction."[424]

The Lord further defines the pure in heart as those who have broken hearts and contrite spirits. The Lord promises these people deliverance and abundance: "But blessed are the poor who are pure in heart, whose hearts are broken, and whose spirits are contrite, for they shall see the kingdom of God coming in power and great glory unto their deliverance; for the fatness of the earth shall be theirs."[425]

The pure in heart experience life in a vastly different manner than do the people of Babylon. As Babylon self-destructs, Zion rises from the ashes: "Therefore, verily, thus saith the Lord, let Zion rejoice, for this is Zion—THE PURE IN HEART; therefore, let Zion rejoice, while all the wicked shall mourn."[426] We would venture that all the pure in heart will spiritually survive the destructions of the last days and that many will temporally and physically survive. Then, with their families who are sealed to them, they will go forth and help to lay the foundation of latter-day Zion, where they will receive an eternal inheritance in the celestial kingdom of God: "They that remain, and are pure in heart, shall return, and come to their inheritances, they and their children, with songs of everlasting joy, to build up the waste places of Zion."[427]

Commanded to Seek the Lord's Face

Elder Jeffrey R. Holland said, "My desire today is for *all* of us—not just those who are 'poor in spirit' but *all* of us—to have more straightforward personal experience with the Savior's example. Sometimes we seek heaven too obliquely, focusing on programs or history or the experience of others. Those are important but not as important as personal experience, true discipleship, and the strength that comes from experiencing firsthand the majesty of His touch."[428]

424 Jacob 3:1–3.
425 D&C 56:18.
426 D&C 97:21.
427 D&C 101:18.
428 Holland, "Broken Things to Mend," 69–71.

Something dire happens when we fail to obey the Lord's commands and live up to our privileges. Consider the Israelites, who lost the Melchizedek Priesthood and its blessings when they rejected Moses' offer to bring them into the presence of the Lord: "Now *this* [meaning the Melchizedek Priesthood and its ordinances, which are the power to see God] Moses plainly taught to the children of Israel in the wilderness, and sought diligently to sanctify his people that they might behold the face of God; but they hardened their hearts and could not endure his presence; therefore, the Lord in his wrath, for his anger was kindled against them, swore that they should not enter into his rest while in the wilderness, which rest is the fulness of his glory. Therefore, he took Moses out of their midst, and the Holy Priesthood also; and the lesser priesthood continued."[429] That the Melchizedek Priesthood has been restored carries the injunction to apply that power and earnestly seek the face of God.

The Lord extends the invitation to all the pure in heart: "Call upon me while I am near—Draw near unto me and I will draw near unto you; seek me diligently and ye shall find me; ask, and ye shall receive; knock, and it shall be opened unto you."[430] Commenting on this passage, Elder McConkie wrote: "Surely, this is what we must do if we ever expect to see his face. He is there waiting our call, anxious to have us seek his face, awaiting our importuning pleas to rend the veil so that we can see the things of the Spirit."[431]

Purification

We are commanded most literally to seek the Lord's face *while in the flesh* by loving God and purifying ourselves. Purification, as we recall, is to draw out contaminations whereas sanctification is to change the purpose of something after it has been purified. Combined, purification and sanctification form the process of becoming like God.

Concerning purification as a requirement to see God, the Lord said, "But great and marvelous are the works of the Lord, and the mysteries of his kingdom which he showed unto us, which surpass all understanding in glory, and in might, and in dominion; . . . they are only to be seen and understood by the power of the Holy Spirit, which God bestows on those who love him, and *purify themselves* before him; to whom he grants this privilege of seeing and knowing for themselves; that through the power and manifestation of the Spirit, *while in the flesh*, they may be able to bear his presence in the world of glory."[432] Elder McConkie wrote:

> There is a true doctrine on these points, a doctrine unknown to many and unbelieved by more, a doctrine that is spelled out as specifically and extensively in the revealed word as are any of the other great revealed truths. There is no need for uncertainty or misunderstanding; and surely, if the Lord reveals a doctrine, we should seek to learn

429 D&C 84:23–26; emphasis added.
430 D&C 88:62.
431 McConkie, *The Promised Messiah*, 582.
432 D&C 76:114–18; emphasis added.

> its principles and strive to apply them in our lives. This doctrine is that mortal man, *while in the flesh*, has it in his power to see the Lord, to stand in his presence, to feel the nail marks in his hands and feet, and to receive from him such blessings as are reserved for those only who keep all his commandments and who are qualified for that eternal life which includes being in his presence forever.[433]

Sanctification

The Lord is ever beckoning us to sanctify ourselves so that we might return to his presence and see him. Again, to sanctify is to make holy, to change the purpose of, to set apart for another use; for example, we bless common bread by the authority of the priesthood and thereby change its purpose so that the common bread now becomes a sanctified sacramental emblem.[434] In a similar manner, the Lord bids us to sanctify ourselves and change our purpose (to experience the mighty change of heart) by fully taking upon ourselves his name so that we might enter into his presence:

> Behold, that which you hear is as the voice of one crying in the wilderness—in the wilderness, because you cannot see him—my voice, because my voice is Spirit; my Spirit is truth; truth abideth and hath no end; and if it be in you it shall abound. And if your eye be single to my glory, your whole bodies shall be filled with light, and there shall be no darkness in you; and that body which is filled with light comprehendeth all things.
>
> Therefore, *sanctify yourselves* that your minds become single to God, and the days will come that you shall see him; for he will unveil his face unto you, and it shall be in his own time, and in his own way, and according to his own will.

Then he pleads: "Remember the great and last promise which I have made unto you."[435] The great and last promise is his vow to reveal himself to us.

Who May Seek the Lord's Face?

The Lord gave the following instructions to those who would be pure in heart and seek his face: "Verily, thus saith the Lord: It shall come to pass that every soul who forsaketh his sins and cometh unto me, and calleth on my name, and obeyeth my voice, and keep-

433 McConkie, *A New Witness for the Articles of Faith*, 492.
434 D&C 20:77.
435 D&C 88:67–69; emphasis added.

eth my commandments, shall see my face and know that I am."[436] Notice the inclusive language: "every soul." Jesus offered his disciples the same universal promise, stating that anyone who exercises obedience and loves him qualifies to enjoy the presence of the Father and the Son: "If a man love me, he will keep my words: and my Father will love him, and we will come unto him, and make our abode with him."[437] Of that all-encompassing promise, Elder McConkie commented:

> After the true saints receive and enjoy the gift of the Holy Ghost; after they know how to attune themselves to the voice of the Spirit; after they mature spiritually so that they see visions, work miracles, and entertain angels; after they make their calling and election sure and prove themselves worthy of every trust—after all this and more—it becomes their right and privilege to see the Lord and commune with him face to face. Revelations, visions, angelic visitations, the rending of the heavens, and appearances among men of the Lord himself—all these things are for all of the faithful. They are not reserved for apostles and prophets only. God is no respecter of persons. They are not reserved for one age only, or for a select lineage or people. We are all our Father's children. All men are welcome. "And he inviteth them all to come unto him and partake of his goodness; and he denieth none that come unto him, black and white, bond and free, male and female; and he remembereth the heathen; and all are alike unto God, both Jew and Gentile" (2 Ne. 26:33).[438]

Brigham Young taught, "We live far beneath our privileges."[439] The pure in heart must raise their sights and pursue with vigor the promised blessings ever within their reach.

How Do We Come into the Presence of the Lord?

In Doctrine and Covenants 88, which the Prophet Joseph Smith called the "olive leaf . . . plucked from the Tree of Paradise, the Lord's message of peace to us,"[440] the Lord gave a parable that reveals his management of and personal attention to all of the lesser kingdoms that comprise his universal kingdom.[441] Of significance, he indicated that "each man," like each of the individual kingdoms, shall have his hour with the Lord: "And thus they all received

436 D&C 93:1.
437 John 14:23.
438 McConkie, *The Promised Messiah*, 575.
439 Young, *Discourses of Brigham Young*, 32.
440 Smith, *Teachings of the Prophet Joseph Smith*, 18.
441 D&C 88:46–61.

the light of the countenance of their lord, every man in his hour, and in his time, and in his season."[442] Unmistakably, each individual who is pure in heart may expect this special one-on-one experience with the Lord. Of that event and the various ways it might happen, Nephi prophesied that the Lord "shall manifest himself unto [us] in word, and also in power, in very deed."[443]

We do not rush into the presence of the Lord. We must work our way there by continually purifying and sanctifying ourselves. For example, we must continually exercise faith in Jesus Christ, repent, make and recommit to our covenants, and constantly follow the voice of the Holy Ghost. This is the process of progression that leads to perfection: "Therefore, *not* leaving the principles of the doctrine of Christ, let us go on unto perfection."[444]

There are three requirements to become pure in heart so that we might see God: (1) Know and live the correct process, (2) know and live the higher law and its principles of progression, and (3) receive power from on high.

Knowing and Living the Correct Process

In 2 Nephi 31, we learn the process of coming into God's presence: faith, repentance, baptism, receiving the Holy Ghost, feasting on the word of Christ, and enduring to the end. Nephi declared, "This is the way; and there is none other way . . . , behold, this is the doctrine of Christ."[445] The doctrine of Christ, which is synonymous with the process of coming into God's presence, is described and verified in the "words of Christ," which are delivered to us by the Holy Ghost, who "will show unto [us] all things what [we] should do."[446] Thus, the Holy Ghost imparts to us the words of Christ, which reveal the process of coming into the presence of the Lord. That process is a continuous cycle of faith in Jesus Christ, repentance, making and recommitting to covenants, feasting on the word of Christ, and enduring to the end.

The inclusive language in the above scriptures is impressive. Without exception, the process, the words of Christ, and the Holy Ghost will lead us to every truth, law, principle, and perfection, and, ultimately, into the presence of the Lord.

Knowing and Living the Higher Law and Its Principles of Progression

Revealed in the Sermon on the Mount and the sermon at the Nephite temple are the higher law and its principles of progression and perfection.[447] President Harold B. Lee called these teachings (the Beatitudes) the "constitution for a perfect life."[448] These two sermons provide us a description of the personality and celestial lifestyle of God, and, by living the laws and principles contained therein, we become ready to see the face of the Lord. Both sermons state definitively, "Blessed are all the pure in heart, for they shall see God."[449]

442 D&C 88:58.
443 1 Nephi 14:1.
444 JST, Hebrews 6:1; emphasis added.
445 2 Nephi 31:21.
446 2 Nephi 32:3, 5.
447 Matthew 5–7; 3 Nephi 12–14.
448 Lee, *Stand Ye in Holy Places*, 342–43.
449 Matthew 5:8; 3 Nephi 12:8.

Receiving Power from on High

Finally, the temple covenants and ordinances endow us with "power from on high."[450] This power is necessary so that we can transcend this fallen existence and literally come into the presence of Jesus Christ.

The account of the Savior's appearance in 3 Nephi is proof that following the correct process, accepting and internalizing the higher law, and being endowed with power from on high are sufficient to usher us into the presence of the Lord. This account also proves that once we are face-to-face with the Lord, we will receive incredible blessings, greater knowledge, doctrine, understanding, and even higher commandments.

Receiving More Doctrine

Nephi declared that faith, repentance, baptism, receiving the Holy Ghost, feasting on the word of Christ, and enduring to the end are "the doctrine of Christ." Then he made an intriguing statement: "And there will be no more doctrine given until after he shall manifest himself unto you in the flesh."[451] At first glance, we would interpret this scripture as meaning that Christ would reveal doctrine beyond the first principles of the gospel, and that would certainly serve as an accurate interpretation. But perhaps there is a deeper meaning. We have learned that these principles lead us to perfection,[452] so what doctrine could be greater?

For a possible answer, we refer to Abraham, who was not content with living the gospel superficially but desired to be "a greater follower of righteousness, desiring also to be one who possessed great knowledge, and to be a greater follower of righteousness, and to possess a greater knowledge, and to be a father of many nations, a prince of peace, and desiring to receive [greater] instructions, and to keep the [greater] commandments of God."[453] We are commanded to "do the works of Abraham."[454] So what did he do? He entered into the law of Christ,[455] the new and everlasting covenant,[456] which culminates with the new and everlasting covenant of marriage.[457] Thereafter, he abode in the Covenant in faithfulness and diligently sought the face of the Lord. Then, after Abraham had *found* the Lord, who manifested himself unto Abraham[458] "in the flesh,"[459] Abraham received more doctrine and commandments, as the book of Abraham testifies. The fact does not escape us that all of this plays out in a temple setting. The greater doctrine and commandments are temple doctrine and commandments, which lead us to see him, whereupon we receive more doctrine and commandments.

---

450 D&C 95:8; 105:11.
451 2 Nephi 32:6.
452 JST, Hebrews 6:1.
453 Abraham 1:2.
454 D&C 132:32
455 D&C 132:32.
456 D&C 132:4–7.
457 D&C 131:2.
458 Abraham 2:12.
459 2 Nephi 32:6.

When we consider that commandments are really revelations of the pattern of the divine lifestyle, and when we further remember that obedience to commandments unlocks the door to blessings, we realize that it is no wonder Abraham and other noble people actively sought to receive greater commandments and more doctrine. Such revelations are events of great joy. Ammon exulted, "I know that which the Lord hath commanded me, and I glory in it. I do not glory of myself, but *I glory in that which the Lord hath commanded me*; yea, and this is my glory, that perhaps I may be an instrument in the hands of God to bring some soul to repentance; and this is my joy."[460] Zion people are they who qualify to receive more doctrine and greater commandments: "Yea, blessed are they whose feet stand upon the land of Zion, who have obeyed my gospel; for they shall receive for their reward the good things of the earth, and it shall bring forth in its strength. And they shall also be crowned with blessings from above, *yea, and with commandments not a few,* and with revelations in their time—they that are faithful and diligent before me."[461]

Nephi revealed what will happen when the Lord manifests himself unto us in the flesh: "And when he shall manifest himself unto you in the flesh, *the things which he shall say unto you* shall ye observe to do."[462] On that occasion, Jesus will reveal to us much more of his doctrine, and he will ask us to do some things for him that will stretch us and bless us. Until then, he will work with us, and when he knows that we will do everything he will command and that we will not retreat from the things he will tell us, he will manifest himself unto us "in the flesh."

Receiving More Doctrine by Choice

The pure in heart begin their quest to seek the face of the Lord by first making a choice; that choice is to abandon the telestial and embrace the celestial, even when the celestial does not make immediate sense. The choice is formalized at an altar in a temple setting where covenants are made, ordinances are given, and tokens are exchanged. Altars are the only place where legitimizing our choice can take place. Altars are where we make sacrifices and exchange gifts—the more the better. Such sacrifices and gifts are intended to be the best we have to give.

At the altar we sacrifice the life of our natural man (the wild, untamed part of us) to the Lord, and, in return, the Lord sacrifices his life for us. At the altar we give him the gift of our heart and he gives us the gift of his Atonement. From that point forward, our covenant relationship with the Lord is defined by a broken heart: "not my will"; and a contrite spirit: "but thine be done."[463]

Brigham Young taught that our choice to become Zion-like and to seek the face of the Lord colors everything in our lives: "If you want to make Zion in your families and be happy in your homes, you must retain the Spirit of the Lord in your own hearts; and let it be the first and the last, the Alpha and Omega of your lives. *Then you will have Zion*; and

460 Alma 29:9; emphasis added.
461 D&C 59:3–4; emphasis added.
462 2 Nephi 32:6; emphasis added.
463 Luke 22:42.

the little difficulties, losses, crosses, and changing scenes of this mortal life will not disturb the equanimity of your lives; but they will appear frivolous things of no moment."[464]

Receiving More Doctrine by Desire

Our choice to seek the Lord's face emerges from our desire. Alma noted that our longing summons the Lord's "unalterable decree," his absolute promise that we shall obtain our wish: "For I know that he granteth unto men according to their desire, . . . yea, I know that he allotteth unto men, yea, *decreeth unto them decrees which are unalterable, according to their wills*."[465]

Receiving More Doctrine by Faith

Our desire motivates us to obey the Lord and follow him on faith alone. This attitude is essential to our progress because in this telestial world we usually do not comprehend celestial laws and their principles immediately . President Boyd K. Packer wrote, "Somewhere in your quest for spiritual knowledge, there is that 'leap of faith,' as the philosophers call it. It is the moment when you have gone to the edge of the light and step into the darkness to discover that the way is lighted ahead for just a footstep or two."[466] The process of faith is also the process of receiving more doctrine. We are required to travel the path to the presence of the Lord by conviction and trust and by allowing him "from time to time . . . to unfold the mysteries of the kingdom,"[467] as if he were carefully opening up the petals of a beautiful flower until it is fully displayed.

Receiving More Doctrine by Persistence and Improvement

Our experiment with faith in the word of God always yields a harvest of blessings. The evidence of growth encourages us to persevere. Blaine Yorgason wrote:

> To obtain the ultimate blessing of seeing the face of Christ and partaking of His divine love and approbation, righteous individuals must progress steadily forward in the spirit, clinging steadfastly to every word that proceeds forth from the mouth of God, and fulfilling the other requirements outlined by the Lord: "Strip yourselves from jealousies and fears, and humble yourselves before me, . . . let[ting] not your minds turn back" (D&C 67:10, 14); "seek the face of the Lord always, that in patience ye may possess your souls, and ye shall have eternal life" (D&C 101:38). Then, "in mine own due time, . . . " the Lord promises, "the veil shall be rent and you shall see me and know that I am" (D&C 64:114, 10).[468]

464 Young, *Millennial Star* 16:674–75; emphasis added.
465 Alma 29:4; emphasis added.
466 Packer, *That All May Be Edified*, 340.
467 D&C 90:14.
468 Yorgason, *I Need Thee Every Hour*, 431.

Receiving More Doctrine by Service

Joseph Smith asked, "How do men obtain a knowledge of the glory of God, his perfections and attributes?" Then, answering the question, he said, "By devoting themselves to his service, through prayer and supplication incessantly strengthening their faith in him, until, like Enoch, the brother of Jared, and Moses, they obtain a manifestation of God to themselves."[469] Without service, we have learned, prayers are just words,[470] and fasting is just going hungry.[471]

Receiving More Doctrine by Seeking

Blaine Yorgason wrote, "Diligent seeking . . . permits qualified, pure-hearted men and women to 'have the privilege of receiving the mysteries of the kingdom of heaven, to have the heavens opened unto them, to commune with the general assembly and church of the Firstborn, and to enjoy the communion and presence of God the Father, and Jesus the mediator of the new covenant' (D&C 107:19)."[472]

Elder McConkie taught similarly: "The attainment of such a state of righteousness and perfection is the object and end toward which all of the Lord's people are striving. We seek to see the face of the Lord while we yet dwell in mortality, and we seek to dwell with him everlastingly in the eternal kingdoms that are prepared."[473] Of these and other promises, we might apply the Lord's counsel: "Treasure up these words in thy heart."[474]

Receiving More Doctrine by Treasuring Up

The Lord has repeatedly commanded that we "treasure up in [our] minds continually the words of life."[475] "Wherefore, ye shall treasure up the things which ye have seen and heard."[476] To treasure up is like finding something valuable and placing it in a safe and secure place so that we never lose it.

In this world, we "enjoy the words of eternal life" and treasure them so that one day we might achieve "eternal life in the world to come, even immortal glory."[477] For now, we are to treasure and "give diligent heed to the words of eternal life."[478]

When a great division came among the disciples of Jesus, and many who had once believed now abandoned him, he turned to His apostles and poignantly asked, "Will ye also go away? Then Simon Peter answered him, Lord, to whom shall we go? thou hast the words of eternal life. And we believe and are sure that thou art that Christ, the Son of the living God."[479] Peter answered for all of us: there is nowhere else to go. Only through the Word of God can we receive the words of God; and only

469 Smith, *Lectures on Faith*, 2:55.
470 Alma 34:28.
471 Isaiah 58:7, 10.
472 Yorgason, *I Need Thee Every Hour*, 432.
473 McConkie, *The Promised Messiah*, 578.
474 D&C 6:20.
475 D&C 84:85.
476 Ether 3:21.
477 Moses 6:59.
478 D&C 84:43.
479 John 6:67–69.

by treasuring them up can we obtain eternal life. "Therefore treasure up these words in thy heart."[480]

So much depends on our desiring, seeking, and treasuring up more doctrine. The Lord piqued our interest when he revealed, "Now, as touching the law of the priesthood, there are many things pertaining thereunto."[481] Upon the foundation of the Atonement stands the doctrine of Zion, which comprises the three pillars: (1) The New and Everlasting Covenant; (2) The Oath and Covenant of the Priesthood; and (3) The Law of Consecration.[482] Beyond receiving these covenants, we must seek to understand the doctrine so that we might better live it. Therein lies our opportunity to become Zion people.

The Significance of the Temple Recommend

How do we know we are on track? President Gordon B. Hinckley suggested that our temple recommend is a good indicator. If the temple represents heaven on earth and most literally the house and presence of God, if it is in the temple that we are taught how to come into the presence of the Lord, and if it is in the temple that the pure in heart at last see God, then our temple recommend should be tangible proof—if our lives are absolutely square with the temple recommend questions—that we are living up to the basic requirements of the gospel and doing what the Lord expects of us.[483]

Where do our efforts to live up to our covenants and to the requirements of the temple recommend lead us? If our hearts are right, if our private devotions, devotedness, yearnings, and consecrations are right before God, the day will come when we will see him. Could there be a greater blessing than finally beholding the face of the Lord? Elder McConkie exclaimed: "What greater personal revelation could anyone receive than to see the face of his Maker? Is not this the crowning blessing of life? Can all the wealth of the earth, all of the powers of the world, and all of the honors of men compare with it? And is it an unseemly or unrighteous desire on man's part to hope and live and pray, all in such a way as to qualify for so great a manifestation?"[484]

Such are the promised blessings for the pure in heart.

By What Power Might We Seek the Lord's Face?

No man casually approaches the Lord and suddenly finds himself face-to-face with Deity. The common aim of fallen men who seek to become pure in heart is to return to their God and stand again in his presence. But by what means might we attain to such a lofty goal? The Lord himself gave the answer: "And this greater priesthood administereth the gospel and holdeth the key of the mysteries of the kingdom, *even the key of the knowledge of God*. Therefore, in the ordinances thereof, the power of godliness is manifest. And

480 D&C 6:20.
481 D&C 132:58.
482 D&C 42:67.
483 Hinckley, speech given at the BYU Center for Near Eastern Studies in Jerusalem, Mar. 21, 1999.
484 McConkie, *A New Witness for the Articles of Faith*, 492.

without the ordinances thereof, and the authority of the priesthood, the power of godliness is not manifest unto men in the flesh; *for without this no man can see the face of God, even the Father, and live.*"[485]

Thus, it is this "power of godliness"—which flows from the Melchizedek Priesthood and its ordinances—that provides us the capacity to "see the face of God."

According to Joseph Smith, the "key of the knowledge of God"[486] is synonymous with "the keys of this [Melchizedek] priesthood," which resulted in Noah "obtaining the voice of Jehovah that He talked with him [Noah] in a familiar and friendly manner, that He continued to him the keys, the covenants, the power and the glory, with which He blessed Adam at the beginning."[487] That is, the Melchizedek Priesthood keys have always been the source of power righteous individuals have employed to see and talk with God. (Note: The word *key*(s) in this instance does not mean administrative powers but rather revelatory powers.[488])

The power to see God has always resided in the revelatory keys of the Melchizedek Priesthood. What are the priesthood keys that yield such a magnificent revelation? According to the scripture above, the "key to the knowledge of God" is synonymous with the "ordinances thereof," meaning the ordinances of the Melchizedek Priesthood. Thus, these keys are the temple ordinances that comprise the endowment of "power from on high."[489] The Prophet explained, "Now the great and grand secret of the whole matter, and the *summum bonum* of the whole subject that is lying before us, consists in obtaining the powers of the Holy Priesthood. For him to whom these keys are given there is no difficulty in obtaining a knowledge of facts in relation to the salvation of the children of men, both as well for the dead as for the living."[490]

What "facts" and whose "salvation"?

Obviously, these are the facts of eternal life relevant to our salvation related to us by the Lord. Elder McConkie explained:

> The priesthood is the power, authority, and means that prepares men to see their Lord; also, . . . in the priesthood is found everything that is needed to bring this consummation to pass. Accordingly, it is written: "The power and authority of the higher, or Melchizedek Priesthood, is to hold the keys of all the spiritual blessings of the church—To have the privilege of receiving the mysteries of the kingdom of heaven, to have the heavens opened unto them, to commune with the general assembly and church of the Firstborn,

485 D&C 84:19–22; emphasis added.
486 D&C 84:19.
487 Smith, *Teachings of the Prophet Joseph Smith*, 172.
488 D&C 142:27–28, 34; see Smith, *History of the Church*, 4:608; 5:1–2; Smith, *Teachings of the Prophet Joseph Smith*, 226.
489 D&C 38:32, 38; 95:8; 105:11.
490 D&C 128:11.

> and to enjoy the communion and presence of God the Father, and Jesus the mediator of the new covenant" (D&C 107:18–19).[491]

Only when the priesthood operates fully in our lives—ordination for men and the endowment for men and women—can we qualify for the supernal event of standing in the presence of God. Elder McConkie wrote: "Thus, through the priesthood the door may be opened and the way provided for men to see the Father and the Son. From all of this it follows, automatically and axiomatically, that if and when the holy priesthood operates to the full in the life of any man [or woman], he will receive its great and full blessings, which are that rending of the heavens and that parting of the veil of which we now speak. . . . *The purpose of the endowment in the house of the Lord is to prepare and sanctify his saints so they will be able to see his face, here and now, as well as to bear the glory of his presence in the eternal worlds.*"[492]

How does the priesthood operate fully in our lives? The Lord says, "Sanctify yourselves; yea, purify your hearts, and cleanse your hands and your feet before me, that I may make you clean; that I may testify unto your Father, and your God, and my God, that you are clean from the blood of this wicked generation."[493]

Then comes the Lord's "great and last promise"— "the days will come that you shall see him; for he will unveil his face unto you, and it shall be in his own time, and in his own way, and according to his own will."[494]

Andrew Ehat and Lyndon Cook commented, "These keys of access to God (D&C 128:10–11), held in all their fulness by the President of the Church, enable the 'least member' in the Church to have power in his priesthood (see *Teachings of the Prophet Joseph Smith*, p. 137). It was not enough to Joseph Smith to be a king and a priest unto the Most High, but he insisted that his people be a society of priests 'as in Paul's day, as in Enoch's day' through the ordinances of the temple. . . . Throughout the remainder of his Nauvoo experience, Joseph Smith taught and emphasized the importance of the temple ordinances, ordinances that would bestow upon members of the Church the knowledge and power he foreshadows in this discourse [on the priesthood]."[495]

Blaine Yorgason expounded, "This experience, of course, is true worship, and according to Moses, it occurs when calling upon God through the name of His Only Begotten in mighty prayer (Moses 1:17), which for the pure in heart is accomplished with greatest effectiveness through worship in God's holy temples."[496] As Paul said, "Eye hath not seen, nor ear heard, neither have entered into the heart of man, the things which God hath prepared for them that love him."[497]

491 McConkie, *The Promised Messiah*, 587.
492 McConkie, *The Promised Messiah*, 588; emphasis added.
493 D&C 88:74–75.
494 D&C 88:68.
495 Smith, *The Words of Joseph Smith*, 54–55.
496 Yorgason, *I Need Thee Every Hour*, 433.
497 1 Corinthians 2:9.

Holiness to the Lord

Why must Zion people actively seek to purify and sanctify themselves so that they might see the face of the Lord? One of the reasons is that the priesthood society of Zion is described as a place where God dwells with his people.[498] Ultimately, the ideal of Zion and seeing the Lord are synonymous. Of course, that level of purification and sanctification occurs line upon line and step by step—growing from one "grace" to another by giving "grace for grace."[499]

We become Zion-like by degrees. At times, we might not even perceive that we are progressing. Imagine a man who stands up in an airplane and begins to stride toward the stewardess. From his point of view, each step covers only a few feet; but from an outsider's point of view, because of the movement of the airplane, the man has spanned thousands of feet. Just so, from our point of view we may perceive our progress as minuscule whereas God may perceive our advancement as extensive. Small, consistent efforts to purify the heart, a characteristic of Zion people, transform a life. These concerted daily efforts include seeking out and gathering in the elect of God, genealogical work, temple worship and service, covenant renewal, welfare and compassionate service, and striving better to live the law of consecration by the generous payment of fast offerings, donations, and by giving our time, talents, and means to help the less fortunate.[500] Each of these may appear to us as small steps, but they, in fact, cover enormous ground toward the goal of holiness.

A marvelous transformation takes place in the lives of those who strive to become pure in heart. As the prophet Zachariah said, "Holiness to the Lord" is written in their hearts and in all aspects of their lives.[501] This attitude is so prevalent in Zion that "even upon the bells of the horses shall be written *Holiness to the Lord*."[502]

Of Zion as a pervasive theme, Brigham Young said, "Let there be an hallowed influence go from us over all things over which we have any power; over the soil we cultivate, over the houses we build, and over everything we possess." Such is the condition of Zion. Continuing, he said,

> I have Zion in my view constantly. We are not going to wait for angels, or for Enoch and his company to come and build up Zion, but we are going to build it. We will raise our wheat, build our houses, fence our farms, plant our vineyards and orchards, and produce everything that will make our bodies comfortable and happy, and in this manner we intend to build up Zion on the earth and purify it and cleanse it from all pollutions. . . . If we cease to hold fellowship with that which is corrupt

498 Moses 7:16, 21.
499 D&C 93:12, 20; Helaman 12:24.
500 Gardner, "Becoming a Zion Society," 31.
501 Zechariah 14:20.
502 Smith, *History of the Church*, 2:357–58.

> and establish the Zion of God in our hearts, in our own houses, in our cities, and throughout our country, we shall ultimately overcome the earth, for we are the lords of the earth; and, instead of thorns and thistles, every useful plant that is good for the food of man and to beautify and adorn will spring from its bosom.[503]

This condition would truly be holiness to the Lord.

On a personal level, holiness to the Lord requires a mighty change of heart,[504] the conversion experience or experiences that transform a natural man into a Zion person. President James E. Faust connected holiness to spiritual strength. Becoming holy, he said, is a process that involves receiving the covenants and ordinances, then trusting God as he purifies and purges our hearts.[505] The resulting mighty change is common to Zion people. As we are purified and cleansed from sin, we progressively receive more light. Holiness is achieved by humbling ourselves, seeking the priesthood and its blessings, and persistently desiring to bring people to Christ. Moreover, holiness comes by our doggedly trying to rise above the telestial world and seeking for the celestial in all things. Holiness transforms priesthood authority into priesthood power. Holiness increases our confidence to ask for and receive blessings in the name of Jesus Christ.[506] Ultimately, holiness allows us to literally stand in the presence of the Father and the Son and enjoy their association.[507]

The ability to become holy is within our reach. Absolutely everything we need to achieve a mighty change of heart and attain holiness to the Lord—every principle, truth, power, covenant, and ordinance—has been revealed in the latter days. We need only understand what we have and live it.

A New Commitment

To become Zion people, we must make a decision. Once and for all, we must commit to both believe and live what we have received. It is not enough to go through the motions of being a Latter-day Saint. We must thoroughly study and understand the new and everlasting covenant, which is the offspring of the Atonement. Receiving, committing to, studying, and living the Covenant are the vehicles that allow us to *become* Zion people. In the final analysis, it is what we have become that will determine our eternal possibilities.[508]

If we are to become Zion people, what will be our characteristics?

- Above all, pure in heart
- Separate from Babylon
- Of one heart and mind—unified with God and our fellowmen

503 Young, *Discourses of Brigham Young,* 443.
504 Alma 5:13.
505 Faust, "Standing in Holy Places," 62.
506 D&C 50:24–29.
507 John 14:15–23.
508 Oaks, "The Challenge to Become," 32–34.

- Equal in opportunity for and access to God's blessings
- Stewards, not owners, who are accountable to God
- Having chosen God over mammon
- Striving to labor for Zion and not to amass personal wealth
- Having completely consecrated ourselves: our time, talents, and all that we have and are for the upbuilding of the kingdom of God and the establishment of Zion

If Zion is our aspiration, this description is what we must become. And it all starts with making a commitment. Well did Elijah challenge his contemporaries: "How long halt ye between two opinions? if the Lord be God, follow him: but if Baal, then follow him."[509] As long as our commitment waits, Zion's blessings remain unclaimed.

In a conference address entitled "Becoming the Pure in Heart," President Spencer W. Kimball taught that we should keep uppermost in our minds the vision of who we are and what we are about. He said, "For many years we have been taught that one important end result of our labors, hopes, and aspirations in this work is the building of a latter-day Zion, a Zion characterized by love, harmony, and peace—a Zion in which the Lord's children are as one." Then he quoted Doctrine and Covenants 48, in which the Lord gives us a glimpse of the latter-day Zion:

> Ye cannot behold with your natural eyes, for the present time, the design of your God concerning those things which shall come hereafter, and the glory which shall follow after much tribulation. For after much tribulation come the blessings. Wherefore the day cometh that ye shall be crowned with much glory; the hour is not yet, but is nigh at hand. . . .
>
> Behold, verily I say unto you, for this cause I have sent you—that you might be obedient, and that your hearts might be prepared to bear testimony of the things which are to come; and also that you might be honored in laying the foundation, and in bearing record of the land upon which the Zion of God shall stand.
>
> And after that cometh the day of my power; then shall the poor, the lame, and the blind, and the deaf, come in unto the marriage of the Lamb, and partake of the supper of the Lord, prepared for the great day to come. Behold, I, the Lord, have spoken it.[510]

With the gift of seership, President Kimball proclaimed that this scripture will be fulfilled. The day of Zion will surely come, and it is our destiny to cause it to happen. Then

509 1 Kings 18:21.
510 D&C 58:3–12.

he asked if these promises do not inspire us to lengthen our stride and quicken our pace to do our part in this marvelous latter-day work. At that point he mourned that many of us are still mired in Babylon, uncommitted and floundering between two divergent philosophies. He said,

> Unfortunately we live in a world that largely rejects the values of Zion. Babylon has not and never will comprehend Zion. . . . Zion can be built up only among those who are the pure in heart, not a people torn by covetousness or greed, but a pure and selfless people. Not a people who are pure in appearance, rather a people who are pure in heart. Zion is to be in the world and not of the world, not dulled by a sense of carnal security, nor paralyzed by materialism. No, Zion is not things of the lower, but of the higher order, things that exalt the mind and sanctify the heart. Zion is "every man seeking the interest of his neighbor, and doing all things with an eye single to the glory of God." (D&C 82:19.) As I understand these matters, Zion can be established only by those who are pure in heart, and who labor for Zion, for "the laborer in Zion shall labor for Zion; for if they labor for money they shall perish." (2 Nephi 26:31).[511]

Our duty and our opportunity are clear. We need only to commit.

"It Is High Time to Establish Zion"

In an address given to the Saints on May 2, 1842, Joseph Smith rejoiced in the coming day of Zion, which assumes that some individuals within the Church will have prepared themselves to become the pure in heart: "The building up of Zion is a cause that has interested the people of God in every age; it is a theme upon which prophets, priests and kings have dwelt with peculiar delight; they have looked forward with joyful anticipation to the day in which we live; and fired with heavenly and joyful anticipations they have sung and written and prophesied of this our day; but they died without the sight; we are the favored people that God has made choice of to bring about the latter-day glory; it is left for us to see, participate in and help to roll forward the latter-day glory."

Continuing, the Prophet announced that three great gatherings will take place in "the dispensation of the fulness of times." First, "the Saints of God will be gathered in one from every nation, and kindred, and people, and tongue." Second, "the Jews will be gathered together into one." And third, "the wicked will also be gathered together to be destroyed." The polarization that will result from these gatherings will be felt by all

511 Kimball, *The Teachings of Spencer W. Kimball*, 362–63.

people: "The Spirit of God will also dwell with His people, and be withdrawn from the rest of the nations."

Joseph taught that the effects of the outpouring of the Spirit of God and the gathering will result in an astounding oneness among the people of God, a oneness which is unique to the dispensation of the fulness of times. He said, "[The Lord will draw together] all things whether in heaven or on earth, [and all things] will be in one, even in Christ." Moreover, "the heavenly Priesthood will unite with the earthly, to bring about those great purposes." Being "thus united in one common cause, to roll forth the kingdom of God, the heavenly Priesthood [will not be] idle spectators." Rather, "the Spirit of God will be showered down from above, and it will dwell in our midst. The blessings of the Most High will rest upon our tabernacles, and our name will be handed down to future ages; our children will rise up and call us blessed; and generations yet unborn will dwell with peculiar delight upon the scenes that we have passed through, the privations that we have endured; the untiring zeal that we have manifested; the all but insurmountable difficulties that we have overcome in laying the foundation of a work that brought about the glory and blessing which they will realize." Clearly, we will enjoy the ministering of angels as we go forth in our individual missions and stewardships.

Finally, the Prophet taught that the establishment of Zion is "a work that God and angels have contemplated with delight for generations past; that fired the souls of the ancient patriarchs and prophets; a work that is destined to bring about the destruction of the powers of darkness, the renovation of the earth, the glory of God, and the salvation of the human family."[512]

To establish Zion, whether in the heart of an individual, a marriage, a family, or in a priesthood community of Saints, President Lorenzo Snow admonished us to cease the destructive practice of competition and the selfish building up of our own kingdoms. We must resolve now, he said, to center our efforts on the building of God's kingdom for the establishment of Zion: "It is high time to establish Zion. Let us try to build up Zion. Zion is the pure in heart. Zion cannot be built up except on the principles of union required by the celestial law. It is high time for us to enter into these things. It is more pleasant and agreeable for the Latter-day Saints to enter into this work and build up Zion, than to build up ourselves and have this great competition which is destroying us." Again calling for us to prepare for the establishment of Zion today and simultaneously denouncing the competitive practices that prohibit Zion, President Snow said, "What a lovely thing it would be if there was a Zion now, as in the days of Enoch, that there would be peace in our midst and no necessity for a man to contend and tread upon the toes of another to attain a better position, and advance himself ahead of his neighbor! And there should be no unjust competition in matters that belong to the Latter-day Saints. That which creates division among us pertaining to our temporal interests should not be."[513]

Let us state here that Zion, meaning the ideal of Zion, is the perfection of sanctification. That is our aim and the reason we submit to the transforming process of being

512 Smith, *Teachings of the Prophet Joseph Smith*, 231.
513 Snow, *The Teachings of Lorenzo Snow*, 181.

sanctified by the Holy Ghost. If Zion is the pure in heart, then we must become pure—that is to say, unalloyed, unmixed, uncontaminated, uncorrupted, unsullied—if we truly desire to qualify for the ultimate blessings of Zion. President Snow ended with this definitive statement: "So long as unrighteous acts are suffered in the Church, it cannot be sanctified, neither can Zion be redeemed."[514] Our call to become Zion people is a call to act now and begin to embrace the principles of Zion, "or else," the Lord warns, our "faith is vain."[515]

An editorial written by Bishop Newel K. Whitney and his counselors in the *Messenger and Advocate* sums up the urgency to become Zion people now: "Whatever is glorious. Whatever is desirable—Whatever pertains to salvation, either temporal or spiritual. Our hopes, our expectations, our glory and our reward, all depend on our building up Zion according to the testimony of the prophets. For unless Zion is built: our hopes perish, our expectations fail, our prospects are blasted, our salvation withers, and God will come and smite the whole earth with a curse."[516]

Priesthood Holders Must Set the Example

Although all members of the Church are called to become Zion people, President Snow pointed to priesthood holders specifically as those who are called to promote the cause of Zion: "We are told that the priesthood is not called to work for money, but to establish Zion."[517] President Snow further stipulated that priesthood brethren must decide once and for all to embrace the principles of Zion by setting a proper example and by living the law of consecration: "I will assure you, my brethren, that you and I will never be selected and called to go to Jackson County until it is evident that we are willing to abide that law [consecration]. It is a perfect law. Had the people in Jackson County observed it, it would have united them together, made them immensely rich, and they could have accomplished all that the Lord desired."[518]

Elders have the specific responsibility to call people out of Babylon and into Zion by extending Christlike service that exemplifies Zion. By fulfilling their responsibility, Joseph Smith taught, priesthood holders can rid their garments of the blood and sins of this generation: "Every Elder that can, after providing for his family (if he has any) and paying his debts, must go forth and clear his skirts from the blood of this generation. . . . Let every one labor to prepare himself for the vineyard, sparing a little time to comfort the mourners, to bind up the broken-hearted, to reclaim the backslider, to bring back the wanderer, to re-invite into the kingdom such as have been cut off, by encouraging them to lay to while the day lasts, and work righteousness, and, with one heart and one mind, prepare to help to redeem Zion, that goodly land of promise, where the willing and obedient shall be blessed."[519]

514 Smith, *History of the Church,* 2:146.
515 D&C 104:54–55.
516 Whitney, Cahoon, and Knight, *Messenger and Advocate* 3 (Sept. 1837): 563.
517 Snow, *The Teachings of Lorenzo Snow,* 181.
518 Snow, *The Teachings of Lorenzo Snow,* 183.
519 Smith, *History of the Church,* 2:228–29.

According to our several abilities and standing in our callings, we must all do our part, said the Prophet: "The advancement of the cause of God and the building up of Zion is as much one man's business as another's. The only difference is, that one is called to fulfill one duty, and another duty; 'but if one member suffers, all the members suffer with it, and if one member is honored all the rest rejoice with it, and the eye cannot say to the ear, I have no need of thee, nor the head to the foot, I have no need of thee;' party feelings, separate interests, exclusive designs should be lost sight of in the one common cause, in the interest of the whole."[520]

The duty of the priesthood is to gather "the elect of the Lord out of every nation on earth, and [bring] them to the place of the Lord of Hosts, when the city of righteousness shall be built, and where the people shall be of one heart and one mind, when the Savior comes: yea, where the people shall walk with God like Enoch, and be free from sin."[521] According to the Prophet, this work is described in the scriptures as "righteousness and truth sweeping the earth as with a flood."[522] "And now, I ask, how righteousness and truth are going to sweep the earth as with a flood? I will answer. *Men and angels are to be co-workers in bringing to pass this great work,* and Zion is to be prepared, even a new Jerusalem, for the elect that are to be gathered from the four quarters of the earth, and to be established an holy city, for the tabernacle of the Lord shall be with them."[523] To accomplish an endeavor that involves heavenly partnering, elders must truly be pure in heart.

A Few Could Form the Foundation of Zion

If we accept the Book of Mormon to be our latter-day guide, we also accept the account in 3 Nephi to be our model for the latter-day establishment of Zion. In surveying that account, we are immediately struck by the fact that even a few pure-in-heart people could anchor the principles of Zion to the earth. Mormon makes the point that only twenty-five hundred Nephites made up the initial group of Zion people. According to the 3 Nephi model, the small group of the pure-in-heart people act as leaven by setting an example and encouraging others to become pure in heart and join with them under the organizational leadership of the priesthood. We note with interest that within a few years, the entire Nephite population had become pure in heart and was assimilated into Zion.[524]

Are we willing to be counted among the few who have the courage to embrace the principles of Zion in our lives? Hugh Nibley quoted Brigham Young, who issued the following warning: "If we are not faithful, others will take our place." Zion is our opportunity, but we can lose it through apathy or carelessness. President Young said that though individuals might fail, nevertheless the Church will succeed: "We may fail, if we are not faithful; but God will not fail in accomplishing his work, whether we abide it or

520 Smith, *Teachings of the Prophet Joseph Smith,* 231.
521 Smith, *Teachings of the Prophet Joseph Smith,* 93.
522 Moses 7:62.
523 Smith, *Teachings of the Prophet Joseph Smith,* 84; emphasis added.
524 3 Nephi 17:25; 19:1–5; 4 Nephi 1:2.

not." Obviously, our individual inaction will have little impact on the Lord's global plans for Zion. His purposes will roll forth, and the prophecies and promises concerning Zion will all be fulfilled: "If we do not wake up and cease to long after the things of this earth, we will find that we as individuals will go down to hell, although the Lord will preserve a people unto himself."

Then President Young asked, "Shall we do this in our present condition as a people? No; for we must be pure and holy." Continuing, he said, "If my brethren and sisters do not walk up to the principles of the holy Gospel . . . they will be removed out of their places, and others will be called to occupy them." To the uncommitted, he stated that the unifying principles of Zion can be divisive and troublesome: "Of the great many who have been baptized into this Church, but few have been able to abide the word of the Lord; they have fallen out on the right and on the left . . . and a few have gathered together."

Joseph Smith also lamented about the Saints' lack of commitment to the cause of Zion: "I have tried for a number of years to get the minds of the Saints prepared to receive the things of God; but we frequently see some of them, after suffering all they have for the work of God, will fly to pieces like glass as soon as anything comes that is contrary to their traditions: they cannot stand the fire at all. How many will be able to abide a celestial law, and go through and receive their exaltation, I am unable to say, as many are called, but few are chosen."[525]

The first latter-day opportunity to build up Zion evaporated with the contentions and jealousies of the early Saints. That will not happen again. Most certainly, the Lord, through his prophet, will call a "select" few, "who are worthy to be called" to form the foundation of latter-day Zion, and when that happens, Babylon's fate is sealed. Elder McConkie wrote:

> "There has been a day of calling," a day in which all the elders of the kingdom were invited to come forward and build the New Jerusalem, "but the time has come for a day of choosing." The response of his early Latter-day Saints having been inadequate, the Lord will now choose, when he will, those who are to accomplish the great work. "And let those be chosen that are worthy." When the day comes, none but those who qualify by obedience and righteousness will participate in the work. "And it shall be manifest unto my servant"—the President of the Church who then governs the kingdom—"by the voice of the Spirit, those that are chosen; and they shall be sanctified; and inasmuch as they follow the counsel which they receive, they shall have power after many days to accomplish all things per-

525 Nibley, "Educating the Saints—a Brigham Young Mosaic," 85, quoting Young in *Journal of Discourses*, 8:144, 183; 18:304; 8:144; 16:26; 11:324; Smith, *Teachings of the Prophet Joseph Smith*, 331.

> taining to Zion." (D&C 105:14–37.) After many days, a designated period in which we still live, those who are called, chosen, selected, appointed, and sent forth by the voice of the Spirit, as it speaks to the President of the Church, shall build the New Jerusalem and the holy temple to which the Lord Jesus Christ shall come in power and glory as the great Millennium is ushered in. In the meantime, our work as a people is to keep the commandments and sanctify ourselves so that if the call comes in our day, we shall be worthy to respond.[526]

If we are waiting to become Zion people when we hear the announcement of the priesthood society of Zion, we will be sorely disappointed. Zion is a condition of the heart. Hence, we no more wait for an announcement to become Zion-like than we wait for an announcement to live the law of consecration. When it comes to living the laws and principles of Zion in our individual lives, nothing waits. We have covenanted and we are expected to strive to become Zion people today.

According to Revelation

Regarding the future priesthood society of Zion, we cannot overemphasize the fact that we must not step in front of the Lord or his authorized servants. Zion is "the highest order of priesthood society";[527] therefore, Zion must be established under the direction of the priesthood and not by some alternative movement or individual initiative. Joseph Smith taught:

> In regard to the building up of Zion, it has to be done by the counsel of Jehovah, by the revelations of heaven; and we should feel to say, "If the Lord go not with us, carry us not up hence." We would say to the Saints that come here, we have laid the foundation for the gathering of God's people to this place, and they expect that when the Saints do come, they will be under the counsel that God has appointed. The Twelve are set apart to counsel the Saints pertaining to this matter; and we expect that those who come here will send before them their wise men according to revelation; or if not practicable, be subject to the counsel that God has given, or they cannot receive an inheritance among the Saints, or be considered as God's people, and they will be dealt

526 McConkie, *A New Witness for the Articles of Faith*, 619.
527 Kimball, *The Teachings of Spencer W. Kimball*, 125.

> with as transgressors of the laws of God. We are trying here to gird up our loins, and purge from our midst the workers of iniquity; and we hope that when our brethren arrive from abroad, they will assist us to roll forth this good work, and to accomplish this great design, that "Zion may be built up in righteousness; and all nations flock to her standard;" that as God's people, under His direction, and obedient to His law, we may grow up in righteousness and truth; that when His purposes shall be accomplished, we may receive an inheritance among those that are sanctified.[528]

While the priesthood society of Zion can be established only under the direction of the President of the Church, Zion people are most definitely established by their own initiative, facilitated by their priesthood leaders. Zion people, of course, are those who will one day make up the priesthood society of Zion.

We are assured that the Lord, who sees the "end from the beginning,"[529] has a master plan for the establishment of the priesthood society of Zion. He knows both the timing and how that holy society will be established. Robert Millet wrote:

> As Zion has grown, so has our understanding of Zion. And a part of that understanding is an appreciation for the patient maturity required for the regeneration of a people and the renovation of a society, an awareness that Zion is established "in process of time." (Moses 7:21.) Neither spiritual marathons nor excessive zeal are required; rather, the peaceful plodding that characterizes those who have a "steadfastness in Christ" (2 Nephi 31:20) will result in purity of heart and achievement of the prophetic ideal. "Let our anxiety be centred [sic] upon this one thing," President Brigham Young counseled, "the sanctification of our own hearts, the purifying of our own affections, the preparing of ourselves for the approach of the events that are hastening upon us." And then in a manner that has particular relevance to those of us who grow impatient with the Lord's timetable, President Young added: "Be satisfied to let the Lord have his own time and way, and be patient. Seek to have the Spirit of Christ, that we may . . . prepare ourselves for the times that are coming. This is our duty."[530]

528 Smith, *Teachings of the Prophet Joseph Smith*, 254.
529 Abraham 2:8.
530 Millet, *Quest for the City of God*, 169–70.

Our Duty to Individually Become Zion

Our preparation for "the upbuilding of an 'holy city' which shall be called Zion" is plainly an individual effort that centers on our attempts to purify our hearts. Joseph Smith said, "All who build thereon [the foundation of Zion] are to worship the true and living God, and all believe in one doctrine, even the doctrine of our Lord and Savior Jesus Christ."[531] To this end, President Lorenzo Snow counseled, "Then let us practice honesty and diligence in our various callings, seeking unity and to cultivate the spirit of brotherhood financially as well as spiritually, that we may be in readiness, upon call, to go forth and build up the center stake of Zion and prepare a house in which to meet the Lord our Savior and Redeemer."[532] Until the prophetic call to Zion comes, said Joseph Smith, "the Lord wants the wheat and tares to grow together; for Zion must be redeemed with judgment, and her converts with righteousness."[533]

What, then, must we be about? The Prophet Joseph Smith answered, "We ought to have the building up of Zion as our greatest object."[534] The Lord has repeatedly commanded us to "seek to bring forth and establish the cause of Zion."[535] Therefore, we are to "arise and shine forth, that [our] light may be a standard for the nations." Our safety and the safety of other good-hearted people is at stake. Only in Zion will there be temporal and spiritual protection: "And that the gathering together upon the land of Zion, and upon her stakes, may be for a defense, and for a refuge from the storm, and from wrath when it shall be poured out without mixture upon the whole earth."[536] Our unique latter-day calling is to prepare the earth for the coming of Christ, the great Millennium, and the vanquishing of Satan.[537]

How shall we begin to become individual Zion persons? President Kimball outlined three steps: "First, we must eliminate the individual tendency to selfishness that snares the soul, shrinks the heart, and darkens the mind. . . . Second, we must cooperate completely and work in harmony one with the other. . . . Third, we must lay on the altar and sacrifice whatever is required by the Lord."[538] The result of living these steps, he said, is charity. Everything about Zion comes down to love. If we are filled with charity, we will be selfless, cooperative, and willing to sacrifice all that we have and are; we truly will be Zion people. It is interesting to note that Enoch established a city called Zion *after* his people had been denominated *Zion* by the Lord.[539] The society *of* Zion is comprised of people who have first qualified *as* Zion in their hearts.

531 Smith, *Teachings of the Prophet Joseph Smith*, 79.
532 Snow, *The Teachings of Lorenzo Snow*, 185.
533 Smith, *History of the Church*, 2:228.
534 Smith, *Teachings of the Prophet Joseph Smith*, 160.
535 D&C 6:6; 11:6; 12:6; 14:6.
536 D&C 115:5–6.
537 Moses 7:60–65; D&C 43:28–35.
538 Kimball, *The Teachings of Spencer W. Kimball*, 364.
539 Moses 7:18–19.

3 Nephi—Latter-day Guide to Establishing Zion

The Lord renewed with Noah the same promise he had made with Enoch, Noah's great-grandfather. That promise concerned the advent of latter-day Zion. The Lord vowed, "When men should keep all my commandments, Zion should again come on the earth."[540] Understanding the process, Brigham Young said, "[Zion] commences in the heart of each person."[541] He prefaced this statement by saying, "The length of time required 'to accomplish all things pertaining to Zion' is strictly up to us and how we live."[542] At another time President Young suggested an intriguing time frame for the establishment of Zion in our lives: "which we might have received in one year."[543]

If it were not for the account in 3 Nephi, we might discount President Young's preparatory "year" as optimistically short. Nevertheless, as we shall see, the Nephites, who were very much like us, qualified in about a year to become pure in heart so they could see God and achieve Zion. The account in 3 Nephi, then, becomes our model for how individuals and a people prepare to become Zion and to enter into the presence of the Lord. But let us first examine the parallels between the Nephites and ourselves as conditions and events lead to the destruction of the wicked and the establishment of Zion.

The book of 3 Nephi begins with a spectacular sign of the Savior's birth. This sign served to save the believers from certain death. We are struck with the fact that the Savior was saving his people from the moment of his birth! We read that as the sun set, the sky remained as bright as at noonday—a phenomenon that had never before occurred. The people responded with a combination of fear and awe that pierced every heart. The prophet Mormon recounted that "*all* the people upon the face of the *whole* earth from the west to the east, both in the land north and the land south, were so exceedingly astonished that they fell to the earth."[544] This powerful heavenly display was given to the people as a sign of the Savior's coming. Likewise, we are told that the Lord's *Second* Coming will be announced by celestial manifestations: "The stars shall fall from heaven, and there shall be greater signs in heaven above."[545]

In the case of the Nephites, the signs fell on many who were weak in faith and could not retain the impact of the miracle in their hearts. Therefore, when Satan sent forth "lyings and deceivings" among the people to harden their hearts,[546] "the people began to forget those signs and wonders which they had heard, and began to be less and less astonished at a sign or a wonder from heaven, insomuch that they began to be hard in their hearts, and blind in their minds, and began to disbelieve all which they had heard and seen—imagining up some vain thing in their hearts, that it was wrought by men and by the power of the devil, to lead away and deceive the hearts of the people; and thus did Satan get possession of the hearts of the people again, inso-

540 JST, Gen. 9:21Genesis 9:21.
541 Young, *Journal of Discourses*, 9:284.
542 Young, *Journal of Discourses*, 9:283.
543 Young, *Journal of Discourses*, 11:300.
544 3 Nephi 1:17; emphasis added.
545 D&C 29:14.
546 3 Nephi 1:22.

much that he did blind their eyes and lead them away to believe that the doctrine of Christ was a foolish and a vain thing."[547]

In the last days, we might expect that we will experience a variety of signs of the imminent coming of the Lord. We might also expect that as astonishing as these signs might be, they will be widely dismissed. To the wicked or the weak in faith, signs do not carry conversion power; only the Holy Ghost can convert. Rather, signs are designed to warn the wicked and call them to repentance and to confirm the faith of the righteous, not produce it: "Faith cometh not by signs, but signs follow those that believe."[548]

We learn from the Nephite account that if people do not respond to the signs and persist in their evil ways, they will become vulnerable to Satan's attacks, and soon they will explain away the signs with their own version of the truth. Then, horrifyingly, their wickedness becomes worse than it was before, causing an ever-widening rift between themselves and the righteous. Thus Mormon reported, "And it came to pass that the people began to wax strong in wickedness and abominations; and they did not believe that there should be any more signs or wonders given; and Satan did go about, leading away the hearts of the people, tempting them and causing them that they should do great wickedness in the land."[549]

We need only review the modern-day response to signs and catastrophic events to note that people initially reach out to God when they are frightened, but after they catch their breath they are quick to return to wickedness, which results in greater evil and further decline.

Although the Nephite prophets made a concerted effort to reclaim the people with "much preaching and prophesying which was sent among them," their effort made little difference. "The people did still remain in wickedness." Then the society began to deteriorate rapidly: "There began to be wars and contentions throughout all the land." We will shortly discuss contention, which Jesus says is a major deterrent to the establishment of Zion. Contention can evolve until it spawns secret combinations such as the ancient terrorists that gained a foothold in the Nephite society. They soon became "so numerous" that they "did slay so many of the people, and did lay waste so many cities, and did spread so much death and carnage throughout the land, that it became expedient that *all* the people . . . should take up arms against them." Interestingly, during this time when the Nephite Babylon was crumbling, missionary work flourished, and the people who were converted "did unite with their brethren." Nevertheless, the people as a whole were threatened with the loss of rights, freedom, and liberty, including the ability to worship God. Soon war erupted in their own land and became "exceedingly sore." Now the entire Nephite people "were threatened with utter destruction."[550]

It requires little imagination to see the parallels between the Nephite civilization and ours today. From the moment that the signs were given, only nine years elapsed before the Nephites found themselves awash in wickedness and caught in a life-and-death

547 3 Nephi 2:1–2.
548 D&C 63:9.
549 3 Nephi 2:3.
550 3 Nephi 2:10–13.

struggle.[551] Within seventeen years, the Nephites had surrendered their lands to the terrorists and supporters of secret combinations, and finally they were obligated to gather into one body to preserve themselves.[552] Do we not have similar prophecies of rapid decline, threats to freedoms, external and internal wars, polarization of the righteous and the wicked, and the necessity of gathering for safety? And do we not have prophecies of astounding missionary success in the midst of worldwide chaos?[553]

When God delivered the embattled Nephites from their enemies, the people repented, and peace and prosperity abounded for about twelve years. Mormon told us straight out: "And now there was nothing in all the land to hinder the people from prospering continually, except they should fall into transgression." But peace was not to last. Once again, contention became the culprit: "There began to be some disputings among the people." Suddenly, we hear "the bells of Hades" tolling. From the over four hundred pages in the Book of Mormon, we know what contention and pride can do to crush a people. We should be so versed in the subject at this point that we can predict where the downward cycle of destruction will lead. Anytime we encounter statements such as, "some were lifted up unto pride and boastings because of their exceedingly great riches, yea, even unto great persecutions,"[554] we know that we soon will be reading about another war.

Why would Mormon have included these accounts if they were not important? No one in his generation benefitted from reading his book. The Book of Mormon was written only for us. Mormon's task was not to recount history; it was to draw parallels from his history to warn and instruct us. With little doubt, our generation has been more anticipated and prepared for than any other. Ours is the generation that must prepare for the establishment of Zion and the Second Coming of the Lord. If we overlook the parallels and messages of the Book of Mormon, we dismiss the single most significant book that has the power to help us accomplish our mission; a book that can save and protect us.

Let us look at Mormon's deliberate mirroring language. He explained that the Nephite nation, at the time of the first coming of Christ, was much like ours today: "There were many merchants in the land, and also many lawyers, and many officers." Then, with a voice of warning, he said that a terrible stratification began to occur, primarily because of affluence and the disparity of educational opportunities: "And the people began to be distinguished by ranks, according to their riches and their chances for learning; yea, some were ignorant because of their poverty, and others did receive great learning because of their riches. Some were lifted up in pride, and others were exceedingly humble; some did return railing for railing, while others would receive railing and persecution and all manner of afflictions, and would not turn and revile again, but were humble and penitent before God." We should pay particular attention to the fact that even the Saints were caught up in this insanity: "And thus there became a great inequal-

551 3 Nephi 2:8.
552 3 Nephi 3:22.
553 Hinckley, "The Stone Cut Out of the Mountain," 83–86.
554 3 Nephi 6:5, 10.

ity in all the land, insomuch that the church began to be broken up."[555] Mormon traced this sad state of affairs to wanton and deliberate wickedness:

> Now the cause of this iniquity of the people was this—Satan had great power, unto the stirring up of the people to do all manner of iniquity, and to the puffing them up with pride, tempting them to seek for power, and authority, and riches, and the vain things of the world. And thus Satan did lead away the hearts of the people to do all manner of iniquity; therefore they had enjoyed peace but a few years.
>
> And thus, in the commencement of the thirtieth year—the people having been delivered up for the space of a long time to be carried about by the temptations of the devil whithersoever he desired to carry them, and to do whatsoever iniquity he desired they should—and thus in the commencement of this, the thirtieth year, they were in a state of awful wickedness.
>
> *Now they did not sin ignorantly, for they knew the will of God concerning them, for it had been taught unto them; therefore they did wilfully rebel against God.*[556]

This last sentence is perhaps the most frightening. The only people who cannot sin ignorantly and who unmistakably know the will of God concerning them would be the members of the Church. Was Mormon sending us a warning?

Continuing, we read that when the Lord increased his efforts to recover the wayward Nephites, anger, contention's ugly sister, surfaced: "Now there were many of the people who were exceedingly angry. . . . And they did set at defiance the law and the rights of their country."[557] Note that a secret combination formed and became so powerful that it was able to infiltrate the inner circles of leadership and finally succeeded in murdering the chief judge and overthrowing the government.

Then the unthinkable happened, something that had never occurred in all the history of the Nephites: they divided into tribes. Mormon wrote: "And the people were divided one against another; and they did separate one from another into tribes, every man according to his family and his kindred and friends; and thus they did destroy the government of the land . . . *and all this iniquity had come upon the people because they did yield themselves unto the power of Satan.* And the regulations of the government were destroyed, because of the secret combination of the friends and kindreds of those who murdered the prophets. *And they did cause a great contention in the land,* insomuch that the more righteous part of the people had nearly all become wicked; yea, there were but few righteous men among them."

555 3 Nephi 6:11–14.
556 3 Nephi 6:15–18; emphasis added.
557 3 Nephi 6:21, 30.

Mormon could not contain his disgust: "And thus six years had not passed away since the more part of the people had turned from their righteousness, like the dog to his vomit, or like the sow to her wallowing in the mire."[558] Mormon noted that the current prophet, whose name was Nephi, had success in turning some people back to Christ, but the majority remained wicked.[559]

Reviewing this scene, do we not see a template emerge for the latter days? Knowing what happens next, we are left to wonder how the Lord was able to establish Zion in the midst of such wickedness.

"Which We Might Have Received in One Year"[560]

We recall that at the Crucifixion of Jesus Christ, the wicked Nephites and Lamanites were all destroyed. Such will be the case at the Lord's Second Coming: the wicked will be destroyed "with the brightness of his coming."[561] From the darkness and ashes of that cataclysmic event in their time, the surviving Nephites heard the voice of the Lord declaring that they who had been spared were alive only because they had been more righteous. There was little comfort in those words. The Lord told them that they still had a great spiritual distance to travel, and unless they repented and came to him with full purpose of heart, "the places of your dwellings shall become desolate." In other words, they would suffer the same fate as had the wicked. Then the Lord reminded the Nephites of his long-term effort to gather them into the Covenant, but "ye would not."[562] This scathing rebuke is something we ought to take to heart. How many times has the Lord tried to gather us to him with the hope that we will learn of and embrace the Covenant, and we will not?

Mormon made the point that the destruction and the three days of darkness happened at the beginning of the Nephite year, "in the thirty and fourth year, in the first month, on the fourth day of the month."[563] Later, Mormon stated that he was going to leap ahead and pick up his narrative at "the ending of the thirty and fourth year"[564]—nearly *one year* later. At that point, he said that he would give us an account of the coming of the resurrected Lord, who would show his glorified body to a group of Nephites, minister unto them, and bless them with great favors and blessings.[565]

By carefully following the chronology of events, we discover the astonishing fact that Jesus was able to establish Zion among a people who only one year earlier had been rebuked by the Lord, even though they had been righteous enough to avoid destruction. These were the same people whom the Savior had tried repeatedly to gather without success. These were the ones whom he had told to repent and come to him with full pur-

558 3 Nephi 7:2–8; emphasis added.
559 3 Nephi 7:21–26; emphasis added.
560 Young, *Journal of Discourses,* 11:300.
561 2 Thessalonians 2:8.
562 3 Nephi 9:13; 10:4–7.
563 3 Nephi 8:4, 23; emphasis added.
564 3 Nephi 10:18.
565 3 Nephi 10:18–19.

pose of heart or else they would suffer the same fate as the wicked. We are left to wonder what miraculous transformation happened in these people's lives during that pivotal year. What had taken place in twelve months that qualified them for such supernal blessings as coming into the presence of the Lord, having the individual experience of touching the nail marks in his hands and feet, thrusting their hands into the spear wound in his side, and being healed from every infirmity? The scriptures are silent as to what happened during that preparatory year, but Mormon has given us a few hints.

In the first place, we suspect that the Nephites took to heart Jesus' admonition to repent—really repent—and come to him with full—not partial—purpose of heart. Alma described this process as being "born of the spirit."[566] King Benjamin's people called it the "mighty change" in which they had "no more disposition to do evil, but to do good continually."[567] In examining various scriptural accounts of those who attempted to describe the transformation that had occurred in their hearts—often within a short period of time—Blaine Yorgason listed ten significant aspects of this mighty change:

1. The birth of the Spirit, being born again, most often occurs after we have been stirred up to complete repentance of all our sins, usually through uncomfortable circumstances of some sort. . . .

2. We must be taught of Christ's Atonement prior to the experience and have a sincere desire to believe in it.

3. We must show godly sorrow for our sins, manifested as a broken heart and a contrite spirit.

4. The birth of the spirit occurs only after crying out to God for mercy in mighty prayer, which is exercising faith in Christ unto repentance.

5. As the experience concludes, we feel our guilt swept away as we receive a remission of sins through the power of the Holy Ghost. This is the baptism of fire, which some in modern times have described as a sensation of warmth that sweeps over their body in a cleansing action that is otherwise indescribable. Others describe it as being filled with an overwhelming feeling of love, which lingers for an indeterminate period of time and is absolutely indescribable. This is certainly a manifestation of Christ's charity or Christ's pure love.

6. Knowing that our sins have been remitted, we feel complete peace of conscience for all our past sins. This feeling is so wonderful that all sin becomes abhorrent to us, we have no more disposition to do evil, and we resolve to never sin intentionally again. However, this does not mean that we will never sin again—

566 Mosiah 27:24.
567 Mosiah 5:2.

only that we will do everything in our power to avoid sinning intentionally. Nor does it mean that we will forget our sins; it seems that memory is left until the resurrection so that learning will occur. . . . However, with guilt swept away through the Atonement of Christ, the memory is no longer painful, and it will ever after be useful for instruction of self and others. That is why Benjamin said to "remember and perish not" (Mosiah 4:30).

7. Once the experience is over, we are filled with an amazing heightened sense of love for our fellow beings, which is a further manifestation of charity, or the pure love of Christ. This love will be manifested by long-suffering, kindness, lack of envy, loss of pride, selflessness, being not easily provoked to anger, thinking only good rather than evil, rejoicing not in iniquity but only in the truth, and being perfectly willing to bear all things, believe all things, hope all things, and endure all things (Moroni 7:45).

8. Consumed with this love, we are also filled with the burning desire to acquaint all others with what we have discovered concerning Christ and His power to deliver from sin—this that they might enjoy the same peace and happiness we have found.

9. From this time forward, we will strive for a closer relationship with God and His Son. We will do this through intense study, humble living, constant repentance, earnest keeping of the commandments, and diligent service to those around us. With the light of heaven resting upon us, the course we are to pursue is now lighted plainly. In exactly following this course, we will be manifesting the image of Christ in our countenances.

10. Through this process, we have received a witness from the Father that Christ's suffering and dying have been gifts of God and that those gifts have wrought an at-one-ment in our lives, making us one with, or bringing us into the family of, the Lord Jesus Christ.[568]

Another thing the Nephites must have done during their year of preparation was to rid themselves of contention and disputations. When the Savior appeared to them, he said, "And there shall be no disputations among you, *as there have hitherto been;* neither shall there be disputations among you concerning the points of my doctrine, *as there have hitherto been.* For verily, verily I say unto you, he that hath the spirit of contention is not of me, but is of the devil, who is the father of contention, and he stirreth up the hearts of men to contend with anger, one with another. Behold, this is not my doctrine, to stir up the hearts of men with anger, one against another; but this is my doctrine, that such things should be done away."[569]

568 Yorgason, *I Need Thee Every Hour,* 171–74.
569 3 Nephi 11:28–30; emphasis added.

Contentions and disputations had always been the common denominator of Nephite decline, apostasy, and war.[570] Contentions had also brought down the Jaredite civilization,[571] and later contention nearly destroyed the Nephites after the birth of Christ.[572] Jesus seemed to be reminding and warning them about contentions and disputations with the commandment to abandon such behavior once and for all. His teaching against contention was a central theme of the Sermon on the Plain.[573] Joseph Smith translated a key passage from that sermon to read, "And unto him who smiteth thee on the cheek, offer also the other; *or in other words, it is better to offer the other, than to revile again.* And him who taketh away thy cloak, forbid not to take thy coat also. *For it is better that thou suffer thine enemy to take these things, than to contend with him.* Verily I say unto you, Your heavenly Father who seeth in secret, shall bring that wicked one into judgment."[574] Evidently contention is so dangerous and so damning that it must be avoided with extraordinary actions and care. Contention is the specific evil that Mormon names as standing between us and the establishment of Zion.[575]

A curse is pronounced upon those who contend,[576] and prophets and great leaders have sought to teach equalizing and unifying principles to help us avoid contention.[577] King Benjamin warned, "But, O my people, beware lest there shall arise contentions among you, and ye list to obey the evil spirit. . . . For behold, there is a wo pronounced upon him who listeth to obey that spirit; for if he listeth to obey him, and remaineth and dieth in his sins, the same drinketh damnation to his own soul; for he receiveth for his wages an everlasting punishment, having transgressed the law of God contrary to his own knowledge."[578] Later, Alma commanded the members of the Church "that there should be no contention one with another, but that . . . their hearts [should be] knit together in unity and in love one towards another."[579] Looking out across the generations of his children, Nephi sadly prophesied that contention would define his people's history and eventually cause their downfall: "For behold, I say unto you that I have beheld that many generations shall pass away, and there shall be great wars and contentions among my people."[580]

When the resurrected Jesus appeared to the Nephites, he commanded them never again to contend or dispute with each other. If they would obey this command, he said, they would also, to a great degree, eliminate envy, strife, tumult, sexual sin, lying, murder, lasciviousness, secret combinations, and economic and social distinctions.[581] We know that the people obeyed the Lord, because the next time we read about them, we discover that "there was no contention in the land, because of the love of God which

570 1 Nephi 9:4; 12:3; 19:4; 2 Nephi 26:2, 32; 28:4; Omni 1:17; Words of Mormon 1:12; Mosiah 9:13; Alma 2:5; 4:9; 50:25; 51:9; Helaman 16:22; 3 Nephi 2:11.
571 Ether 11:7.
572 3 Nephi 2:11.
573 "Sermon Given to Different People," *LDS Church News*, Feb. 18, 1995.
574 JST, Luke 6:29–30; emphasis added.
575 3 Nephi 11:28–30.
576 Ether 4:8.
577 Mosiah 29:7.
578 Mosiah 2:32–33.
579 Mosiah 18:21.
580 2 Nephi 26:2.
581 4 Nephi 1:24–25.

did dwell in the hearts of the people. . . . And surely there could not be a happier people among all the people who had been created by the hand of God."[582] What a difference a year of intense preparation can make!

Perhaps the greatest change the Nephites made during that preparatory year was developing faith—true and vibrant faith—in Christ. Moroni indicated as much: "For it was by faith that Christ showed himself unto our fathers, after he had risen from the dead; and he showed not himself unto them until after they had faith in him." Evidently, not everyone was able to immediately achieve the faith necessary to enter into the presence of the Lord. For the time being, the nation would need to rely on the initial twenty-five hundred chosen few to anchor Zion to the earth: "Wherefore, it must needs be that *some* had faith in him, for he showed himself not unto the world." Then Moroni offered us the same privilege if we would strive to develop faith in Christ: "Wherefore, ye may also have hope, and be partakers of the gift, if ye will but have faith." However, this miracle, as with all miracles, will lie forever outside our reach "until after [our] faith. Wherefore," Moroni said of the Nephites, "they first believed in the Son of God." From the days of Adam to the present day, this promise is universal to every Zion seeker: "And there were many whose faith was so exceedingly strong, even before Christ came, who could not be kept from within the veil, but truly saw with their eyes the things which they had beheld with an eye of faith, and they were glad."[583]

Therefore, we might conjecture that if we will diligently strive to exercise an elevated level of faith in Christ, repent, and come to him with full purpose of heart, and rid our lives of contentions and disputations, we too might qualify in a short period of time, even in as little as one year, as the Nephite record and Brigham Young suggest, for the Lord to come to us and establish us as individual Zion people.

The Pure in Heart *Shall* See God

The account in 3 Nephi describes the ultimate reward for the pure in heart. Diligent striving to sanctify ourselves carries the promise that one day we—all of us—will return to the presence of the Lord and behold him: "And blessed are *all* the pure in heart, for they *shall* see God."[584]

Once again, we pause to note that the Book of Mormon was written as a guide for our day. From the outset of his record, Nephi counsels us to liken the scriptures to our individual lives and circumstances.[585] If we were not to keep in mind this "likening," we might peruse the account of the Savior's appearance to the Nephite believers and miss the point that we are reading about a universal experience that will happen to each of us who endeavors to become pure in heart. Therefore, by likening the account in 3 Nephi to ourselves, we can extract a list of events and blessings each of us can expect during our eventual face-to-face encounter with the Lord.

582 4 Nephi 1:15–18; emphasis added.
583 Ether 12:7, 9, 18–19; emphasis added.
584 3 Nephi 12:8; emphasis added.
585 1 Nephi 19:23.

The Father's Testimony

First, we are told that the Father himself introduced his Son and commanded the people that they should hear and obey Jesus: "Behold my Beloved Son, in whom I am well pleased, in whom I have glorified my name—hear ye him."[586] This is the ultimate testimony of Jesus Christ—and once we hear it we must obey.

Failure to hear has always characterized the disobedient: "They hear thy words, but they will not do them."[587] On the other hand, hearing with the intent of acting on that which is said summons great blessings: "Unto you that hear shall more be given."[588] The Ten Commandments begin with the mandate to hear and obey: "Hear, O Israel: The Lord our God is one Lord."[589] We must live so as to anticipate and merit the Father's testimony: "If [the Lord] call thee, that thou shalt say, Speak, Lord; for thy servant heareth."[590] Therefore, to the end that we might warrant the experience of seeing and hearing for ourselves, Jesus instructs, "He that hath ears to hear let him hear."[591] The greatest message we will ever hear is the Father's testimony of his Son.

The Savior's Testimony

After Jesus appeared to the Nephites, he declared his true identity: "Behold, I am Jesus Christ, whom the prophets testified shall come into the world. And behold, I am the light and the life of the world; and I have drunk out of that bitter cup which the Father hath given me, and have glorified the Father in taking upon me the sins of the world, in the which I have suffered the will of the Father in all things from the beginning."[592]

Again, we must remember that Jesus' appearance to the Nephites is a model of his appearance to each of us individually. We might expect the Savior to bear similar testimony to us. A survey of the scriptural revelation verifies that Jesus often bears testimony of his identity and mission. For example: "Thus saith the Lord your God, even Jesus Christ, the Great I AM, Alpha and Omega, the beginning and the end, the same which looked upon the wide expanse of eternity, and all the seraphic hosts of heaven, before the world was made; the same which knoweth all things, for all things are present before mine eyes; I am the same which spake, and the world was made, and all things came by me."[593]

The Father's testimony of the Son and the Son's testimony of himself fulfill the law of witnesses.[594] These two testimonies establish the truth concerning the identity of the Savior and his mission as it pertains to each person who receives these testimonies. But there are other testimonies borne either at the moment of visitation or previously with the purpose of bringing us to this experience; these are the testimonies of the Holy

586 3 Nephi 11:7.
587 Ezekiel 33:31.
588 Mark 4:24.
589 Deuteronomy 6:4.
590 1 Samuel 3:9.
591 Mark 4:9.
592 3 Nephi 11:10–11.
593 D&C 38:1–3.
594 Deuteronomy 19:15.

Ghost and the prophets. Notice the voices of the testifiers (the Holy Ghost who bore witness to the prophets, who then bear witness to us) in the following verses: "And now, after the many testimonies which have been given of him, this is the testimony, last of all, which we give of him: That he lives! For we saw him, even on the right hand of God; and we heard the voice bearing record that he is the Only Begotten of the Father—That by him, and through him, and of him, the worlds are and were created, and the inhabitants thereof are begotten sons and daughters unto God."[595]

As we shall see, these testimonies summon from us our own personal declaration of the reality of the Savior.

Coming Forth to See and Know

We read that the Lord beckoned the Nephites to come to him *one by one* and experience for themselves the reality of the Atonement and the sacrifice that the Savior had made in *each* person's behalf:

> Arise and come forth unto me, that ye may thrust your hands into my side, and also that ye may feel the prints of the nails in my hands and in my feet, that ye may know that I am the God of Israel, and the God of the whole earth, and have been slain for the sins of the world. And it came to pass that the multitude went forth, and thrust their hands into his side, and did feel the prints of the nails in his hands and in his feet; and this they did do, going forth one by one until they had all gone forth, and did see with their eyes and did feel with their hands, and did know of a surety and did bear record, that it was he, of whom it was written by the prophets, that should come.[596]

That each individual was invited to touch the Savior's wounds reminds us of the Lord's promise that each of us will have our "hour" with the Lord.[597] Could there be a greater evidence of the reality of the price he paid for our individual redemption than to come to the Lord and touch his wounds?

When that happens to us, we are placed in a position to bear testimony with greater surety. This is evidenced by the fact that every Nephite "witnessed for themselves."[598] Now we add our testimony to that of the Father, the Son, the Holy Ghost, and the prophets.

595 D&C 76:22–24.
596 3 Nephi 11:14–15.
597 D&C 88:58.
598 3 Nephi 11:16.

Rejoicing, Worshipping, and Bearing Testimony

Our testimony is accompanied by worshipping and rejoicing. "With one accord," the people, both as a group and as individuals, rejoiced in their salvation, worshipped the Savior, and testified of him in his presence: "Hosanna! Blessed be the name of the Most High God! And they did fall down at the feet of Jesus, and did worship him."[599] *Hosanna* means: "Save now!" Or "Save I pray thee."[600] This is a fitting exclamation in that it simultaneously recognizes Jesus as the Savior and bears testimony of him.

We remember that others have testified of Christ in his presence. For example, Nathanael, upon first meeting the Lord, declared, "Thou art the Son of God; thou art the King of Israel."[601] Also, when Jesus calmed the sea and saved his frightened disciples, they cried, "Of a truth thou art the Son of God."[602] And to the Lord's question, "But whom say ye that I am? . . . Simon Peter answered and said, Thou art the Christ, the Son of the living God."[603] Hence, we might expect our interaction with the Lord to evoke from us a shout of praise and an expression of testimony.

Receiving an Endowment of Knowledge

When the Lord appeared to the Nephites, he gave them a new revelation, or an endowment of knowledge.[604] We recall that Abraham began his journey into the Lord's presence by desiring "greater knowledge."[605] When Enoch and Moses stood before the Lord, they were endowed with great knowledge concerning God's creations and their place among them.[606] Likewise, the brother of Jared, John the Revelator, Nephi, Mormon, Moroni, Joseph Smith, and a host of other righteous people received "greater knowledge" when they stood in the presence of the Lord. In the case of the Nephites, they received the higher law of the gospel. This expanded their vision of the things of eternity and gave them additional tools to continue on and achieve celestial glory.

In our case, the "greater knowledge" we might receive could include anything recorded in the visions of the prophets or anything Lord deems to tell us during our "hour" with him. We cannot overemphasize that this experience is highly personalized, both in the method and the content of the manifestation. Nevertheless, we might expect this model of similarities to be followed.

599 3 Nephi 11:17.
600 *Easton Illustrated Bible Dictionary*, s.v. "Hosanna."
601 John 1:49.
602 Matthew 14:33.
603 Matthew 16:15–16.
604 3 Nephi 12–16.
605 Abraham 1:2.
606 Moses 1–8.

Healing

The Nephites next received a tender gift, a gift that speaks of the Savior's individual concern for each of us. That gift was the blessing of healing. A scan of the scriptures shows that whenever the Savior is among his people, he heals them. Healing is a sign of his divinity and his ability to save us from anything, including death and sin. As mentioned previously, healing is also a condition of the ideal of Zion. The Lord promised ancient Israel: "Thou shalt be blessed above all people: there shall not be male or female barren among you, or among your cattle. *And the Lord will take away from thee all sickness*."[607] We recall that, in addition to overcoming sin and death, the Lord's Atonement involved "suffering pains and afflictions and temptations of every kind; and this that the word might be fulfilled which saith he will take upon him the pains and the sicknesses of his people."[608] We might conclude, therefore, that unless the Savior had a reason that we should continue with an affliction, our face-to-face interview with him would include the blessing of healing.

We look to the experience of the Nephites as an example:

> And he said unto them: Behold, my bowels are filled with compassion towards you. Have ye any that are sick among you? Bring them hither. Have ye any that are lame, or blind, or halt, or maimed, or leprous, or that are withered, or that are deaf, or that are afflicted in any manner? Bring them hither and I will heal them, for I have compassion upon you; my bowels are filled with mercy. For I perceive that ye desire that I should show unto you what I have done unto your brethren at Jerusalem, for I see that your faith is sufficient that I should heal you.
>
> And it came to pass that when he had thus spoken, all the multitude, with one accord, did go forth with their sick and their afflicted, and their lame, and with their blind, and with their dumb, and with all them that were afflicted in any manner; and he did heal them every one as they were brought forth unto him. And they did all, both they who had been healed and they who were whole, bow down at his feet, and did worship him; and as many as could come for the multitude did kiss his feet, insomuch that they did bathe his feet with their tears.[609]

607 Deuteronomy 7:14–15; emphasis added

608 Alma 7:11.

609 3 Nephi 17:6–10.

The Savior's Prayer for Us and Our Prayer to Him

Another tender blessing we might expect in our experience with the Lord is to have him pray for us while we are in his presence. Imagine how the Nephites felt when the Savior prayed for them, when they discovered firsthand what actually happens when the Savior pleads our case to the Father and advocates for mercy in our behalf:

> And it came to pass that when they had all been brought, and Jesus stood in the midst, he commanded the multitude that they should kneel down upon the ground. And it came to pass that when they had knelt upon the ground, Jesus groaned within himself, and said: Father, I am troubled because of the wickedness of the people of the house of Israel. And when he had said these words, he himself also knelt upon the earth; and behold he prayed unto the Father, and the things which he prayed cannot be written, and the multitude did bear record who heard him.
>
> And after this manner do they bear record: The eye hath never seen, neither hath the ear heard, before, so great and marvelous things as we saw and heard Jesus speak unto the Father; and no tongue can speak, neither can there be written by any man, neither can the hearts of men conceive so great and marvelous things as we both saw and heard Jesus speak; and no one can conceive of the joy which filled our souls at the time we heard him pray for us unto the Father.[610]

From these verses, we gain a glimpse into what the Savior might ask the Father in our behalf. Undoubtedly, he would be troubled by the wickedness that surrounds us and he would seek to protect us as much as we would be willing to accept.

Notice that when the Savior once again prayed for the Nephite people, he spoke of choosing them out and separating them from the world: "It is because of their belief in me that I have chosen them out of the world."[611] The word *chosen* reminds us of the chosen few who are among the many called to eternal life. These chosen few are the truly pure in heart, they who are "full of charity towards all men, and to the household of faith." It is to such people that the Lord commanded, "Let virtue garnish thy thoughts unceasingly." They mature spiritually to the point that their "confidence [waxes] strong in the presence of God; and the doctrine of the priesthood distil[s] upon [their] souls as the dews from heaven." These chosen few enjoy the Holy Ghost as their "constant

610 3 Nephi 17:13–17.
611 3 Nephi 19:20.

companion." They are promised that their "scepter" shall be "an unchanging scepter of righteousness and truth; and [their] dominion shall be an everlasting dominion, and without compulsory means it shall flow unto [them] forever and ever."[612]

We might expect that after the Lord defines us as one of the "chosen few," he would send us back into the world, as he sent out his initial Nephite disciples,[613] to become his emissaries, that is, to invite people out of the world and to bring them to Christ. A result of this gathering is to achieve oneness between the pure in heart and the Father and the Son: "Father, I pray thee that thou wilt give the Holy Ghost unto all them that shall believe in their words. . . . And now Father, I pray unto thee for them, and also for all those who shall believe on their words, that they may believe in me, that I may be in them as thou, Father, art in me, *that we may be one*."[614]

Notice that when we are in the presence of the Savior, it is proper to pray to him as he prays for us: "They did pray unto Jesus, calling him their Lord and their God." Then Jesus prayed, "Father, . . . they pray unto me because I am with them."[615] Standing before the Lord, our prayers become intensified as they are guided by the Holy Ghost. Our confidence waxes strong in his presence,[616] and we are consumed with desire: "Behold, they did still continue, without ceasing, to pray unto him; and they did not multiply many words, for it was given unto them what they should pray, and they were filled with desire." Then came the Lord's blessing: "And it came to pass that Jesus blessed them as they did pray unto him."[617]

At this point, something remarkable happened: "His countenance did smile upon them."[618] That is, Jesus was *pleased*. This is an understatement, of course. Human vocabulary fails when we attempt to explain what occurs when we merit divine approval. Somehow, in the way that Heavenly Father is "well pleased"[619] with his Beloved Son, the Beloved Son is also well pleased with us,[620] and thus the Lord's countenance smiles upon us. We are filled with light, power, and glory: "And the light of his countenance did shine upon them, and behold they were as white as the countenance and also the garments of Jesus; and behold the whiteness thereof did exceed all the whiteness, yea, even there could be nothing upon earth so white as the whiteness thereof."[621] We become more than we were. We are transformed into the image of his countenance.[622]

When we stand in the presence of the Lord, we, too, will experience this transformation that the Savior has prayed for in our behalf. What will happen is summed up in two words: (1) *purification*, which indicates that all impurities have been separated from our souls, and (2) *sanctification*, which signifies that our purpose has changed to that of

612 D&C 121:45–46.
613 3 Nephi 19:2–3.
614 3 Nephi 19:20–21, 23.
615 3 Nephi 19:18, 22.
616 D&C 121:45.
617 3 Nephi 19:24–25.
618 3 Nephi 19:25.
619 Matthew 3:17; 3 Nephi 11:7.
620 D&C 1:30; 38:10; 50:37; 51:3; 61:35; 84:3; 97:3; 124:1, 12.
621 3 Nephi 19:25.
622 Alma 5:14.

the Savior's. Notice that Jesus prayed, "Father, I thank thee that thou hast purified those whom I have chosen." Then he indicated that their purification had led to their sanctification; their purpose had changed, and now they had become saviors on Mount Zion, who would continue the Savior's work: "Because of their faith, . . . I pray for them, and also for them who shall believe on their words, that they [the people of the world] may be purified in me, through faith on their [my disciples'] words, even as they [my disciples] are purified in me."[623]

It is through this process—divine approval, purification, and sanctification—that we fully assume the work of God[624] and become one with him: "Father, I pray . . . for those whom thou hast given me out of the world, because of their faith, that they may be purified in me, that I may be in them as thou, Father, art in me, that we may be one, that I may be glorified in them."[625]

Elements of the prayer that the Savior would offer for us while we are in his presence would most likely be beyond our ability to comprehend, let alone record: "And tongue cannot speak the words which he prayed, neither can be written by man the words which he prayed. And the multitude did hear and do bear record; and their hearts were open and they did understand in their hearts the words which he prayed. Nevertheless, so great and marvelous were the words which he prayed that they cannot be written, neither can they be uttered by man."[626]

Encircled About by Angels

We are taught that the pure in heart who receive and keep the oath and covenant of the priesthood are entitled to the ministering of angels: "I have given the heavenly hosts and mine angels charge concerning you."[627] Because every faithful man and woman receives the Melchizedek Priesthood ordinances in the house of the Lord, and because the oath and covenant of the priesthood "is renewed when the recipient enters the order of eternal marriage,"[628] the ministration of angels is available to each worthy individual. This promise is articulated in section 107 of the Doctrine and Covenants, where we learn that righteousness, coupled with the Melchizedek Priesthood and its ordinances, qualifies both men and women "to hold the keys of all the spiritual blessings of the church—To have the privilege of receiving the mysteries of the kingdom of heaven, to have the heavens opened unto them, to commune with the general assembly and church of the Firstborn, and to enjoy the communion and presence of God the Father, and Jesus the mediator of the new covenant."[629]

Like the Nephite children who beheld the Savior's face and who were surrounded and blessed by angels, we too will be encircled about and ministered to by angels, which

---

623 3 Nephi 19:28–29.
624 Moses 1:39.
625 3 Nephi 19:29.
626 3 Nephi 19:32–24.
627 D&C 84:42.
628 McConkie, *A New Witness for the Articles of Faith*, 313.
629 D&C 107:18–19.

will likely include our loved ones, friends, and co-workers in the heavenly Church of the Firstborn: "And as they looked to behold they cast their eyes towards heaven, and they saw the heavens open, and they saw angels descending out of heaven as it were in the midst of fire; and they came down and encircled those little ones about, and they were encircled about with fire; and the angels did minister unto them."[630] Standing in the presence of the Lord, we might also expect to enjoy the ministering of angels and commune with heavenly hosts.

Partaking of the Lord's Supper in His Presence

Both Jesus' disciples in Jerusalem and in America partook of the sacrament while the Lord was in attendance (and saw him actually administer it).[631] At some point, in the presence of the Lord, each person who is pure in heart, who strives to lay the foundation of Zion in his life, will be invited to "a supper of the house of the Lord."[632] This "supper" corresponds with "the marriage of the Lamb," when he will receive his bride: *us*![633] On that beautiful occasion, we will "partake of the supper of the Lord, prepared for the great day to come."[634] As we then literally "internalize"—take into our own bodies—the Atonement, we will understand, perhaps better than we ever have, the significance of the emblems, the personal nature of Christ's sacrifice for us, and why he holds us as dear as a husband holds his bride.

Receiving a Greater Endowment of the Holy Ghost

It is interesting that even though the Nephites were in the presence of the Lord, they longed for the Holy Ghost. Thus we read that they prayed "for that which they most desired"—the Holy Ghost.[635] Remarkably, of all the things they might have wanted, the Holy Ghost was preeminent. Once bestowed, that supernal gift unlocked amazing blessings: "The Holy Ghost did fall upon them, and they were filled with the Holy Ghost and with fire. And behold, they were encircled about as if it were by fire; and it came down from heaven, and the multitude did witness it, and did bear record; and angels did come down out of heaven and did minister unto them. And it came to pass that while the angels were ministering unto the disciples, behold, Jesus came and stood in the midst and ministered unto them."[636]

The command to receive the Holy Ghost is given at the time of baptism and confirmation, but the fulness of this gift is not automatic. The enjoyment of the gift of the Holy Ghost comes to us incrementally by asking and by righteous living. Nephi said that

630 3 Nephi 17:24.
631 Matthew 26:26–28; 3 Nephi 18:1–10.
632 D&C 58:9.
633 Revelation 21:2, 9; Isaiah 62:5.
634 D&C 58:7–11.
635 3 Nephi 19:9.
636 3 Nephi 19:13–15.

the Holy Ghost "is the gift of God unto all those who diligently seek him."[637] Thus, we might expect that when we become the pure in heart who see the Lord, we will desire a greater endowment of the Holy Ghost, as did the Nephites, and we will desire that gift so that our knowledge, power, affections, and perfections might approach those of God. The Holy Ghost is the only way to obtain these supernal blessings.[638]

The Hundredfold Law

Essential to and indicative of Zion is the principle of abundance. To both the disciples in Jerusalem and the Nephites, the Lord demonstrated this principle of abundance, the hundredfold law, by multiplying a small resource so that it fed a multitude.[639]

In each of our lives, we experience this principle of returned abundance when we pay tithes and offerings or when we give service. When we are in the presence of the Lord, we might expect him to multiply our blessings in proportion to our sacrifices and service and to compensate us for our sufferings, sorrows, and pain[640] "an hundredfold."[641]

Revelations, Prophecies, and Explanations

Some of the most remarkable blessings the Savior gave the Nephites while they were in his presence were new revelations, doctrines, principles, laws, and prophecies regarding them personally and their children.[642] These revelations had profound implications. For example, the sermon at the temple,[643] which is the Book of Mormon equivalent of the Sermon on the Mount,[644] prepared the Nephite faithful to enter the Father's presence by teaching them how they should live to become pure in heart and by revealing the celestial laws that make the Father who he is.

To the Nephites who stood in the Lord's presence, Jesus, the consummate prophet, seer, and revelator, became the perfect teacher. He expounded all things pertaining to the gospel; he paid close attention to detail so that the people would not misunderstand the new revelations, doctrines, principles, laws, and prophecies: "And now it came to pass that when Jesus had told these things he expounded them unto the multitude; and he did expound all things unto them, both great and small. . . . And now there cannot be written in this book even a hundredth part of the things which Jesus did truly teach unto the people."[645]

When we stand before Christ, we might expect him to expand our minds, too, with revelations, prophecies, and insights that we have not previously known. This level of teaching, explained by Joseph Smith, often involves the privilege of receiving the Second Comforter:

637 1 Nephi 10:17.
638 Moroni 10:5.
639 Mark 6:35–44; 8:1–9; 3 Nephi 20:6–9.
640 Revelation 21:4.
641 Genesis 26:12; 2 Samuel 24:3; Matthew 13:8–23; 19:29; Mark 10:30; Luke 8:8; D&C 98:25; 132:55.
642 3 Nephi 12–16, 18, 20–27.
643 3 Nephi 12–14.
644 Matthew 5–7.
645 3 Nephi 26:1, 6.

> Now what is this other Comforter? It is no more nor less than the Lord Jesus Christ Himself; and this is the sum and substance of the whole matter; that when any man obtains this last Comforter, he will have the personage of Jesus Christ to attend him, or appear unto him from time to time, and even He will manifest the Father unto him, and they will take up their abode with him, and the visions of the heavens will be opened unto him, and the Lord will teach him face to face, and he may have a perfect knowledge of the mysteries of the Kingdom of God; and this is the state and place the ancient Saints arrived at when they had such glorious visions—Isaiah, Ezekiel, John upon the Isle of Patmos, St. Paul in the three heavens, and all the Saints who held communion with the general assembly and Church of the Firstborn.[646]

The caveat the Lord held out to the Nephites was this: If they were willing to receive the "lesser part of the things which [Jesus] taught," they would qualify to receive "greater things." Likewise, Mormon promised the pure in heart of the latter days: "And when they shall have received this, which is expedient that they should have first, to try their faith, and if it shall so be that they shall believe these things then shall the greater things be made manifest unto them."[647]

Of immediate interest, the "greater things" would include the writings of the brother of Jared—"they reveal all things from the foundation of the world unto the end thereof."[648] The Lord told Moroni: "There never were greater things made manifest than those which were made manifest unto the brother of Jared. . . . And in that day [the latter days] that they shall exercise faith in me, saith the Lord, even as the brother of Jared did, that they may become sanctified in me, then will I manifest unto them the things which the brother of Jared saw, even to the unfolding unto them all my revelations, saith Jesus Christ, the Son of God, the Father of the heavens and of the earth, and all things that in them are."[649]

We might speculate that one definition of the "day of faith" Moroni refers to is the day when we individually stand in the presence of the Lord and partake of his revelations, prophecies, and detailed explanations.

Greater Commandments

Greater commandments accompany greater revelations. We realize the importance of receiving greater commandments when we read that Elder Orson F. Whitney referred

646 Smith, *Teachings of the Prophet Joseph Smith,* 151.
647 3 Nephi 26:8–10.
648 2 Nephi 27:10; see verses 7–11.
649 Ether 4:4, 7.

to commandments as "sacred patterns,"[650] or, in other words, what we might call God's revelation of his celestial lifestyle. We recall that one of the crowning blessings of becoming Zion people is to receive "commandments not a few."[651] In the presence of Christ, the pure in heart seek and receive greater commandments that are calculated to align our lives with that of God and those who live in the celestial kingdom.

As we have learned, Abraham desired to become like God and to receive greater revelations and privileges. Therefore, to that end he sought for the higher commandments, which are associated with the Melchizedek Priesthood and which yield those results. These greater commandments helped to conduct Abraham, a "follower of righteousness," into the Lord's presence.[652] Likewise, when the Nephites stood in the presence of the Lord, they received greater commandments that had to do with celestial living.[653] Their account becomes our model.

The Greater Commandment to Pray Always

Of the many commandments the Lord gave to the Nephites on the occasion of his appearance, we will single out three that directly produce a Zion-like life. The first is the commandment to pray always. Jesus "commanded them that they should not cease to pray in their hearts."[654]

At a minimum, "praying always" would mean that we assume a reverent, prayerful attitude while we go about our daily activities. This would include continual communication, worship, awareness, gratitude, accountability to God for our actions, and recognizing our total dependence on the Lord. This prayerful attitude is the engine that drives humility and the purification of the heart; this attitude raises the antenna of revelation and demands we search for opportunities to serve.

Continual prayer forms a shield of protection against the adversary, whose attacks are as persistent as should be our prayers. To the Nephites, Jesus said, "Verily, verily, I say unto you, ye must watch and pray always, lest ye be tempted by the devil, and ye be led away captive by him. . . . Behold, verily, verily, I say unto you, ye must watch and pray always lest ye enter into temptation; for Satan desireth to have you, that he may sift you as wheat. Therefore ye must always pray unto the Father in my name."[655]

Then Jesus raised the issue of *light* as a reason to pray. As much as he was *the* Light and had set a bright example, so his disciples must become lights themselves for the purpose of drawing people to the Light by means of their prayers and actions: "Behold I am the light; I have set an example for you. . . . Therefore, hold up your light that it may shine unto the world. Behold I am the light which ye shall hold up—that which ye have seen me do. Behold ye see that I have prayed unto the Father, and ye all have witnessed. And ye see that I have commanded that none of you should go away, but rather have commanded

650 Whitney, *Saturday Night Thoughts*, 133–34; Whitney, *Gospel Themes*, 115.
651 D&C 59:4.
652 Abraham 1:2, 15–19.
653 See, for example, 3 Nephi 12–14.
654 3 Nephi 20:1.
655 3 Nephi 18:15, 18–19.

that ye should come unto me, that ye might feel and see; *even so shall ye do unto the world.*" We must personalize and live this commandment; but if we neglect to live it, we will lose the protection of prayer and become vulnerable to the attacks of Satan: "And whosoever breaketh this commandment suffereth himself to be led into temptation."[656]

Constant prayer helps us to retain *light.* As we know, light[657] is synonymous with truth,[658] spirit,[659] intelligence,[660] power,[661] law,[662] life,[663] agency,[664] and glory,[665] to name a few things. Whereas a celestially resurrected body "shall be filled with light, and there shall be no darkness in [it],"[666] a telestial body must receive ongoing transfusions of light in order to progress spiritually: That which is of God is light; and that light growth brighter and brighter until the perfect day."[667]

The Lord has told us how we can infuse light into our systems. A few transfusion methods include participating in scripture study, partaking of the sacrament, being anointed with oil, performing charitable service, participating in temple worship, and, of course, praying. The more our bodies are filled with light, the more we comprehend all things.[668] Therefore, we should pray always.

Continual prayer facilitates the creation of Zion people by offering them an avenue of communication with God. But there is more. Continual prayer provides Zion people access to God's protection and power of discernment. Continual prayer gives them a way to infuse light into their beings, thus increasing their capacity to assimilate or enjoy truth, spirit, intelligence, power, celestial law, spiritual life, glory, and agency. Once "lighted" through constant prayer, a Zion person is commanded to "light" others and bring them to *the* Light, even Jesus Christ.

Prayer fulfills the law of asking and receiving.[669] The simple act of praying is a powerful way to access God and draw upon his goodness, abilities, and resources. As we have discussed, asking the Father in the name of Jesus Christ for the things we need is central to the law of consecration. Once we have covenanted to live that law—and indeed are striving to live it—we are forevermore entitled to ask for those things that we need and want from the higher kingdom so that we might build ours. And what is the eternal kingdom we are striving to build by asking and receiving? *Our families.* Therefore, the Lord instructed, "Pray in your families unto the Father, always in my name, that your wives and your children may be blessed."[670] Continual prayer is the vehicle for asking and receiving, and sincere prayer carries the Lord's absolute promise: "And whatsoever ye

656 3 Nephi 18:16, 24–25; emphasis added.
657 D&C 88:7–13.
658 1 John 5:6; D&C 84:45; 88:66.
659 D&C 84:45.
660 D&C 93:29.
661 D&C 88:7–10, 13.
662 D&C 88:13.
663 John 1:4.
664 D&C 93:30–31.
665 D&C 93:36.
666 D&C 88:67.
667 D&C 50:23–24.
668 D&C 88:67.
669 John 16:24; 3 Nephi 27:29; D&C 4:7; 49:26; 88:63; 103:31.
670 3 Nephi 18:21.

shall ask the Father in my name, which is right, believing that ye shall receive, *behold it shall be given unto you.*"[671]

From all indications, it seems that once the Nephites—in their interaction with the resurrected Lord—experienced the power of prayer, they never returned to offering casual prayers. Surely they recognized prayer's inherent power to make them Zion people, and, obviously, they employed it. If we wish to become Zion people with the ability to ask for and receive blessings, we must follow this same pattern.

The Greater Commandment to Have All Things in Common

Almost as an aside, Mormon noted that after the Savior's visit, the Nephites experienced a cultural transformation as extraordinary as the mighty change they had experienced in their hearts. Mormon wrote: "And they taught, and did minister one to another; and they had all things common among them, every man dealing justly, one with another."[672]

It is difficult to overstate the significance of this occurrence. The cultural change that had happened among the converted Nephites was the polar opposite to life as they had known it. Once they had made a covenant to assume this new way of life, they determined to live that new way without external legislation. That is, they managed to live a new way by individual *choice.* Because of the new condition of their hearts, they were determined to become stewards who were accountable to God; no longer would they see themselves as owners of the Lord's property. Forevermore, they would labor to build up the Church and their Zion instead of selfishly pursuing individual wealth-building enterprises. They would fully embrace the royal law of the gospel: "Thou shalt love the Lord thy God with all thy heart, and with all thy soul, and with all thy mind. This is the first and great commandment. And the second is like unto it, Thou shalt love thy neighbour as thyself."[673] The result of their transformation was that they became one and had all things in common.

Their faith in living this new cultural experiment paid off with unbelievable and unanticipated blessings. Mormon recorded that contentions and disputations ceased; "and every man did deal justly one with another;" poverty, servitude, and social stratification were eradicated; the people became equal; peace prevailed; and great and marvelous miracles became the norm. Moreover, the people experienced unequalled prosperity. Now unified, they built great cities, and "did wax strong, and did multiply exceedingly fast, and became an exceedingly fair and delightsome people." They married within the Covenant, "and were blessed according to the multitude of the promises which the Lord had made unto them." They became strictly obedient and "did walk after the commandments which they had received from their Lord and their God, continuing in fasting and prayer, and in meeting together oft both to pray and to hear the word of the Lord." The love of God dwelt in the hearts of the people. "And there were no envyings, nor strifes, nor tumults, nor whoredoms, nor lyings, nor murders, nor any manner of lasciviousness; and surely there

671 3 Nephi 18:20; emphasis added.
672 3 Nephi 26:19.
673 Matthew 22:37–39.

could not be a happier people among all the people who had been created by the hand of God. There were no robbers, nor murderers, neither were there Lamanites, nor any manner of -ites; but they were in one, the children of Christ, and heirs to the kingdom of God. And how blessed were they! For the Lord did bless them in all their doings."[674]

We might expect that our initial attempts to implement the law of Zion so that commonality could prevail would feel like a temporary cultural shock, causing us to rethink our priorities. But if we can summon courage and push through the learning curve, incredible blessings await us, which will more than compensate for the effort.

The Greater Commandment to Be "Even As the Lord Is"

For the commandments to pray always and have all things in common, Jesus is our exemplar. When he prayed for the Nephites he focused their attention on his example: "Behold ye see that I have prayed unto the Father, and ye have all witnessed."[675] Jesus is our model of a celestial lifestyle: "I have set an example for you."[676] Pertaining to the law of consecration, which produces commonality among all people, the Lord said that this law is "even as I am." If we were to choose one word to describe Jesus' relationship with the Father and the relationship to which we must aspire if we hope to become even as he is, that word would be *oneness*: "I say unto you, be one; and if ye are not one ye are not mine."[677]

If we are commanded to become like him, we might ask ourselves, What are the Father and the Son like? Perhaps Joseph Smith offered the best description: "God is the only supreme governor and independent being in whom all fullness and perfection dwell; who is omnipotent, omnipresent, and omniscient; without beginning of days or end of life; and that in him every good gift and every good principle dwell; and that he is the Father of lights; in him the principle of faith dwells independently."[678] Of course, at this stage of our existence, we can only appreciate these divine traits; for now, these traits are beyond our reach. Therefore, our efforts should be centered on developing these divine traits. As we continue to progress, we rely on the Lord's promise that our journey will lead us to inheriting all that God has and becoming all that he is.[679]

As we strive to become even as the Father and the Son are, we remember that we have in common with them our co-eternalness; that is, our origin is the same. Because we are literal children of God, our potential destiny can be the same. Our challenge, therefore, is to become co-equal with the Father and the Son,[680] and that is accomplished by following their example and developing their traits and their level of oneness.

To become like God is to internalize his lifestyle so completely that we will not depart from it. Describing God, Joseph Smith said that he was the same before the creation as he is today: "He changes not, neither is there variableness with him; but that he is the

674 4 Nephi 1:3–18.
675 3 Nephi 18:24.
676 3 Nephi 18:16.
677 D&C 38:27.
678 Smith, *Lectures on Faith*, 2:2.
679 D&C 84:35–39; 132:19–24.
680 Smith, *Teachings of the Prophet Joseph Smith*, 395.

same from everlasting to everlasting, being the same yesterday, to-day, and for ever; and that his course is one eternal round, without variation." For us to become even as the Father and the Son are, we must strive for a consistency of righteousness.

The Prophet continued to list a set of characteristics and attributes that the Father and the Son possess in perfection. We must develop these traits if we are to become like them. The Prophet began with the characteristics of mercy and graciousness ("indulgent, generous, displaying divine grace and compassion"). Continuing, the Prophet said that God is "slow to anger" and "abundant in goodness." Moreover, "He is a God of truth and cannot lie"; "He is no respecter of persons"; that is, if we work righteousness, he is obliged to accept and bless us, just as he accepted and blessed Adam, Enoch, Noah, Abraham, Joseph Smith, and all who sought his face—and if we do wickedly, he is obliged to send consequences, regardless of our previous favor. Finally, "he is love."[681]

The Prophet went on to say that God's character is a set of perfect attributes; that is, he possesses the following qualities in totality. These are:

Knowledge—He knows all things past, present, and future.

Faith or power—He is all powerful.

Justice—He is completely fair and equitable.

Judgment—He is perfect in both his reasoning and his rulings.

Mercy—His grace, compassion, long-suffering, pity, clemency, forgiveness, kindness, sympathy, understanding, leniency, and benevolence are infinite and unending.

Truth—Beyond being incapable of lying, he deals with things as they really are; he is accurate, genuine, precise; he is honest, loyal, devoted, and sincere; his integrity is impeccable; he deals with unimpeachable facts and certainties.[682]

When the Lord commands us to become like him, he expects us to strive to attain these characteristics and attributes. Our eventual goal is to become like him: that is, celestial governors in our own right; independent beings in whom all fulness and perfection dwell; gods like the supreme God who is omnipotent, omnipresent, and omniscient, without beginning of days or end of life; beings who possess every good gift and in whom every good principle dwells; celestial fathers and mothers of lights, in whom the principles of faith dwell independently.[683]

These are samples of greater commandments—to pray always, to have all things in common, and to be even as Jesus Christ is—that have power to help us become the pure in heart and to qualify to stand in the presence of God.

681 Smith, *Lectures on Faith*, 3:13–18.
682 Smith, *Lectures on Faith*, 4:5–10.
683 Smith, *Lectures on Faith*, 2:2.

Receiving a Special Gift

Face-to-face with the Savior, the pure in heart are apparently offered the privilege of asking for or receiving a special, individualized gift—an *endowment* of some kind. Three of the Nephite disciples asked for the gift of being translated,[684] as did the Apostle John.[685] Enoch received the promise that the earth would be saved both temporally and spiritually through his great-grandson, Noah, through whose descendants the Savior would be born.[686] The Lord also promised Enoch that his city would return in the last days to join with the latter-day Zion and become the Lord's eternal abode. The Lord renewed that promise with Noah and established the rainbow as a token of that covenant.[687] Abraham received the gift of the rights to the gospel and the priesthood through his posterity.

Likewise, our hoped-for conversation with the Lord, which might precede our receiving a special gift, could resemble the conversation Jesus had with his Nephite disciples *individually*:

> And it came to pass when Jesus had said these words, he spake unto his disciples, *one by one*, saying unto them: What is it that ye desire of me, after that I am gone to the Father?
>
> And they all spake, save it were three, saying: We desire that after we have lived unto the age of man, that our ministry, wherein thou hast called us, may have an end, that we may speedily come unto thee in thy kingdom.
>
> And he said unto them: Blessed are ye because ye desired this thing of me; therefore, after that ye are seventy and two years old ye shall come unto me in my kingdom; and with me ye shall find rest.
>
> And when he had spoken unto them, he turned himself unto the three, and said unto them: What will ye that I should do unto you, when I am gone unto the Father?
>
> And they sorrowed in their hearts, for they durst not speak unto him the thing which they desired.
>
> And he said unto them: Behold, I know your thoughts, and ye have desired the thing which John, my beloved, who was with me in my ministry, before that I was lifted up by the Jews, desired of me. Therefore, more blessed are ye, for ye shall never taste of death;

---

684 3 Nephi 28:2.
685 John 21:21–23; D&C 7:1–8.
686 Moses 7:21, 42–47; JST, Genesis 9:21.
687 Moses 7:62–64.

> but ye shall live to behold all the doings of the Father unto the children of men, even until all things shall be fulfilled according to the will of the Father, when I shall come in my glory with the powers of heaven.[688]

Because Jesus Christ, like his Father, is no respecter of persons, we might expect that when we stand in his presence, he will grant us the privilege of asking for and receiving a special gift from him. The endowment we might receive from him is prefigured in the temple endowment—which is our guide to understanding the steps for such an experience. Propriety does not allow us to discuss these sacred proceedings in detail, the General Authorities have given us appropriate language to describe these things, .[689]

Suffice it to say that we might expect to receive, like prophets of old, a vision of that which we will eventually inherit; this vision could include a view of the vastness of God's creations.[690] We might expect to be shown our genesis, that is, our individual creation.[691] Then we might expect to be shown our unique placement on the earth and the realities of our fallen situation,[692] or, as Joseph Smith said, "a comprehensive view of our condition and true relation to God."[693] Now, fully understanding that we are in a telestial state, and desiring to receive from the Lord intelligence to transcend this sphere and to return home to celestial glory, we might expect to be tutored in the plan of salvation and our place in it.[694]

Our temple experience will have prepared us to receive this ultimate endowment when we at last stand in the presence of the Lord. We will have received the essential covenants and ordinances, which will have prepared us to "obtain every needful thing,"[695] prevented us from being "overcome by . . . evils,"[696] prepared us for our "missions in the world,"[697] helped us to seek "the fulness of the Holy Ghost,"[698] and secured for us "the blessings which have been prepared for the Church of the Firstborn,"[699] which would have empowered us with "power from on high"[700] so that we might approach the Lord with greater efficacy.

It is in the temple that we see in clear detail the end purpose of the priesthood: to come into the presence of the Lord and receive "all that [the] Father hath."[701] Now we see the various levels of ministry that have prepared us for this consummate event. The ministry of the priesthood is to bring us to the Holy Ghost. The ministry of the Holy

688 3 Nephi 28:1–7; emphasis added.
689 See, for example, Talmage, *The House of the Lord*, 99–101; *Encyclopedia of Mormonism*, 454–56; McConkie, *Mormon Doctrine*, 226–28.
690 D&C 84:38; Moses 1:27–38; Abraham 3:21.
691 Abraham 3:22–23.
692 Moses 1:6–10; 4:1–31.
693 Smith, *Teachings of the Prophet Joseph Smith*, 237.
694 Moses 5:6–12; Talmage, *The House of the Lord*, 83–84.
695 D&C 109:15.
696 Smith, *Teachings of the Prophet Joseph Smith*, 259.
697 Smith, *Teachings of the Prophet Joseph Smith*, 274.
698 D&C 109:15.
699 Smith, *Teachings of the Prophet Joseph Smith*, 237.
700 D&C 105:11.
701 D&C 84:38.

Ghost is to mentor, purify, justify, sanctify, and bring us to Christ. The ministry of Christ is to bring us to the Father, who endows us with all that he has. The endowment that we will receive when we at last stand worthily in the presence of God will certainly include the promise of all that the Father has. But, additionally, we might be invited, as were the Jerusalem Twelve and the Nephite Twelve, to request a gift or endowment of a special nature, perhaps a special mission to bring people to Christ. We recall that after such an experience, Enoch, Abraham, Moses, Joseph Smith, and others were sent back into the world by the Lord to perform a significant mission.

Considering the beautiful promises foreshadowed by our temple worship experience, we might ask ourselves: Is it worth the effort? Should we not pay the price to become pure in heart so that we might qualify to return to God and see him as he is? Are we willing to work diligently so that we might be transformed in as little as one year, as Brigham Young suggested, to qualify for our hour with the Lord and for an eternity with the Father?

Beautiful Zion

We sing of Zion's beauty in the beloved hymn:

> Zion, Zion, lovely Zion;
> Beautiful Zion;
> Zion, city of our God![702]

What we could say of Zion, the priesthood society, we could say of Zion, the people: *Zion is beautiful!* Whether Zion is an individual, a marriage, a family, or a priesthood community, Zion is "the perfection of beauty," where "God hath shined."[703]

An example of irony in the Book of Mormon is the account of Abinadi, who, with his life hanging in the balance, was questioned by King Noah's wicked priests concerning, of all things, the identity of those whom the Lord had called *beautiful,* or those whose beautiful feet bring the gospel message. This, of course, was a satanic trick, an effort to trap and convict him. A similar ploy was later attempted by the lawyer who tempted Jesus with a supposedly unanswerable question: "Which is the great commandment in the law?" Jesus' answer—to love God and to love your neighbor—put to rest the issue once and for all.[704] In the case of Abinadi, the wicked priests challenged the prophet to interpret Isaiah's scripture: "How beautiful upon the mountains are the feet of him that bringeth good tidings."[705] The interpretation had been hotly debated for centuries.[706] Who were the beautiful ones? So-called scriptural scholars had never agreed; so to pose the question to this supposed madman seemed an easy way to gain a quick indict-

702 Gill, "Beautiful Zion, Built Above," *Hymns,* no. 44.
703 Psalm 50:2.
704 Matthew 22:36–40.
705 Isaiah 52:7–10.
706 Ludlow, *A Companion to Your Study of the Book of Mormon,* 186.

ment. But Abinadi's powerful answer, like the Savior's, silenced his critics. In the end, the wicked accusers on both continents had no evidence to indict their captors, so they executed them for their testimonies. Abinadi testified that "God himself should come down among the children of men,"[707] and Jesus testified that he was "the Son of God."[708]

To the question, Who are the beautiful ones? Abinadi offered an answer that helped convert a future prophet, Alma; set the doctrinal foundation for the Nephite church; and eventually changed a nation.[709] Abinadi gave his life, in part, for the testimony of the beautiful ones.

That Mormon would place such weight on this incident should signal to us its significance as it pertains to Zion. Consider Mormon's account of Abinadi's experience:

> And it came to pass that one of them said unto him: What meaneth the words which are written, and which have been taught by our fathers, saying:
>
> How beautiful upon the mountains are the feet of him that bringeth good tidings; that publisheth peace; that bringeth good tidings of good; that publisheth salvation; that saith unto Zion, Thy God reigneth;
>
> Thy watchmen shall lift up the voice; with the voice together shall they sing; for they shall see eye to eye when the Lord shall bring again Zion;
>
> Break forth into joy; sing together ye waste places of Jerusalem; for the Lord hath comforted his people, he hath redeemed Jerusalem;
>
> The Lord hath made bare his holy arm in the eyes of all the nations, and all the ends of the earth shall see the salvation of our God?[710]

Kent P. Jackson explained, "Abinadi did not answer the question immediately, but after his scathing rebuke of the priests for their wickedness, he taught them about the coming of the Savior as the Suffering Servant, reading them Isaiah 53 in its entirety. He interpreted chapter 53 that 'God himself should come down among the children of men' (Mosiah 17:8)—the teaching for which Abinadi would be put to death."[711] All of the preceding was building like a grand crescendo toward the answer.

Suddenly, Abinadi turned the tables and asked the wicked priests the question that Isaiah had once posed, the question of questions, the question each of us must answer as a testimony, the question that helps to define the beautiful ones: "And now I say unto you, who shall declare his generation?"[712] That is to say, Who is capable of discovering

707 Mosiah 17:8.
708 John 19:7.
709 Mosiah 17–18.
710 Mosiah 12:20–24.
711 Jackson, *Studies in Scripture*, 4:150.
712 Mosiah 15:10; Isaiah 53:8.

the origin of Jesus? Is he really the Son of God, *generated* by the Father himself, or was Jesus simply a great teacher and religious leader? Elder Bruce R. McConkie wrote:

> It is a true principle that 'no man can say [or, rather, know—see JST 1 Corinthians 12:3] that Jesus is the Lord, but by the Holy Ghost.' (1 Cor. 12:3.) The testimony of Jesus, which is also the spirit of prophecy, is to know by personal revelation that Jesus Christ is the Son of the living God. In the full and complete sense of the word no one ever knows that Jesus is Lord of all except by personal revelation; and all persons to whom that testimony or revelation comes are then able to declare His generation, to assert from a standpoint of personal knowledge that they know that Mary is his mother and God is his Father. And so, in the final analysis it is the faithful saints, those who have testimonies of the truth and divinity of this great latter-day work, who declare our Lord's generation to the world. Their testimony is that Mary's son is God's Son; that he was conceived and begotten in the normal way; that he took upon himself mortality by the natural birth processes; that he inherited the power of mortality from his mother and the power of immortality from his Father—in consequence of all of which he was able to work out the infinite and eternal Atonement. This is their testimony as to his generation and mission.[713]

Do we believe in Jesus Christ and who he really is, or do we not? Believers are the "beautiful ones," they who keep his commandments, give heed to his prophets, and follow his testator, the Holy Ghost. Beyond being called "beautiful," such people are called "his seed."

Who, therefore, can declare the reality of Jesus Christ, the mission of Joseph Smith, the truthfulness of the Book of Mormon, the actuality of the Restoration of the Church of Jesus Christ, or any other essential doctrine? Only those who receive this knowledge by revelation from the Holy Ghost. Who are they? Abinadi said that Christ's "seed" are they who receive this witness. These are they whom the Savior saw and suffered for, both the righteous whom he saw in the spirit world after the Atonement and the righteous whom he saw and sees from his heavenly vantage point.

Clearly, Jesus saw us and atoned for us. How might we come to know this? By the witness of the Holy Ghost. Then, we, "his seed," having received this witness, become the ones who bear record that Jesus is indeed the Christ, our adopted spiritual Father and personal Savior, and the Redeemer of the entire world.

713 McConkie, *The Promised Messiah*, 472.

Building toward the answer concerning the beautiful ones, Abinadi continued, "And who shall be his seed?" Then, responding to his own question, he said, "Behold I say unto you, that whosoever has heard the words of the prophets, yea, all the holy prophets who have prophesied concerning the coming of the Lord—I say unto you, that all those who have hearkened unto their words, and believed that the Lord would redeem his people, and have looked forward to that day for a remission of their sins, I say unto you, that these are his seed, or they are the heirs of the kingdom of God. For these are they whose sins he has borne; these are they for whom he has died, to redeem them from their transgressions. And now, are they not his seed?"[714]

That is, in obtaining the testimony that Jesus is the Christ, we are numbered among his seed; and if we bear that testimony to others, in one sense we are numbered among the prophets, "for the testimony of Jesus is the spirit of prophecy."[715] The holy prophets are also numbered among the seed of Christ. In the words of Abinadi: "Are not the prophets, every one that has opened his mouth to prophesy, that has not fallen into transgression, I mean all the holy prophets ever since the world began? I say unto you that they are his seed."

And what do we do as prophets?

Abinadi answered, "And these are they who have published peace, who have brought good tidings of good, who have published salvation; and said unto Zion: Thy God reigneth!"[716] The seed of Christ—we, who to one degree or another might be among those whom Abinadi called "prophets"—are they who proclaim the peace of the Prince of Peace; we bring to the world the good news of the gospel; we testify of the Author and plan of salvation; and we rejoice with all the pure in heart that the God of heaven lives; he works among his children; and he controls the affairs of nations.

And then comes Abinadi's answer to the priests' question: "And O how beautiful upon the mountains were their feet! And again, how beautiful upon the mountains are the feet of those that are still publishing peace! And again, how beautiful upon the mountains are the feet of those who shall hereafter publish peace, yea, from this time henceforth and forever!"[717] Anyone who qualifies as the seed of Christ and as a prophet by their publishing peace and testifying of Christ—that person is a beautiful one. That person is a true Zion person. *We* can be those whose feet are beautiful upon the mountains!

Blessings for the Beautiful Ones

What are the blessings for the beautiful ones? President Charles W. Penrose of the First Presidency prophesied:

> And the time will come when the Lord shall have established his Church perfectly upon the earth, and all things move in their proper course, that God will find a

714 Mosiah 15:11–12.
715 Revelation 19:10.
716 Mosiah 15:14.
717 Mosiah 15:15–17.

> place adapted to every person, in which each will have more joy than in any other place and be able to do more good to the community than in any other. . . . Now, my brethren, there are privileges and powers pertaining to these callings [of the priesthood]. . . . The powers of the Aaronic priesthood reach out a great way, for we are told that that priesthood holds the keys of the ministration of angels. . . . But we read that the Melchisedec priesthood contains greater powers than that. It not only holds the keys of the ministration of angels, but of communion with the heavenly Jerusalem, the general assembly and church of the first-born with Jesus Christ the Mediator of the new covenant and God the highest and holiest of all. And the time will come when under this priesthood to those who hold this authority and calling, and have the spirit of it and minister in that spirit and obtain the power thereof, the Lord will unveil his face and they shall gaze upon his glory. That time will come, for there is no word of the Lord revealed but what will come to pass. . . . The time will come when the servants of the living God will purify themselves before him until they will be fit to receive these blessings. When that holy temple is built in Zion, God will take away the veil from the eyes of his servants; and the day is yet to dawn when the sons of Moses and Aaron, having become sanctified to the renewing of their bodies, will administer in that holy house, and the veil will be taken away, and they will gaze upon the glories of that world now unseen, and upon the faces of beings now to them invisible; but it will be when they have purified themselves from the evils of this world, and are really the servants of the living God, and temples of the Holy Ghost.[718]

President Lorenzo Snow likewise prophesied that in the Lord's time "many of you will be living in Jackson County, and there you will be assisting in building the temple; and if you will not have seen the Lord Jesus at that time you may expect Him very soon, to see Him, to eat and drink with Him, to shake hands with Him and to invite Him to your houses as He was invited when He was here before. I am saying things to you now of which I know something of the truth of them."[719]

718 Penrose, *Journal of Discourses*, 21:49–50.
719 Snow, *The Teachings of Lorenzo Snow*, 186.

Certainly, Zion and its people are beautiful. Nephi gloried, "And blessed are they who shall seek to bring forth my Zion at that day, for they shall have the gift and the power of the Holy Ghost; and if they endure unto the end they shall be lifted up at the last day, and shall be saved in the everlasting kingdom of the Lamb; and whoso shall publish peace, yea, tidings of great joy, how beautiful upon the mountains shall they be."[720]

Summary and Conclusion—The Three Pillars of Zion

The new and everlasting covenant is the greatest revelation God has ever proffered his children. It is the ultimate message of peace and the fulness of the gospel of Jesus Christ, which encompasses all the knowledge, rites, covenants, and ordinances necessary for salvation and exaltation. The Covenant simultaneously cleanses and removes us from the blood and sins of this world and sets us on a course that leads to the presence of God. The Covenant provides the way to become what God is, to know what he knows, to have what he has, and to possess his power, perfections, and attributes of character. By means of the Covenant, our belief gives way to knowledge, "for they shall all know me, from the least of them unto the greatest of them, saith the Lord."[721]

The Covenant is designed to usher us into the vast celestial kingdom of God and set us and our eternal companions in our personal kingdoms, where we together will become gods in our own right. There, we will be resurrected, immortal, celestial beings, who will inherit "thrones, kingdoms, principalities, and powers, dominions, all heights and depths . . . pass[ing] by the angels, and the gods, which are set there, to [our] exaltation and glory in all things, as hath been sealed upon [our] heads, which glory shall be a fulness and a continuation of the seeds forever and ever."[722]

The Covenant fastens us to the Father securely, "as a nail in a sure place," as Isaiah said.[723] That is, the Covenant binds us to God as surely as Christ was bound to the cross—a very sacred reference. The tokens of Christ's atoning experience—the marks that Jesus still carries in his body—are tokens that we may receive symbolically in our bodies that bind us to him and make us *one.* This is the purpose of the Covenant: to help us to fully take upon ourselves the name of Jesus Christ and to obtain his presence.

Is the Covenant not the most wonderful of all revelations? We should rejoice in it continually and write its precepts in our hearts! Jeremiah proclaimed, "But this shall be the covenant that I will make with the house of Israel; After those days, saith the Lord, I will put my law in their inward parts, and write it in their hearts; and will be their God, and they shall be my people."[724]

A few times in history, most notably during the eras of Enoch and the Nephites at the time of Christ, the people sanctified themselves so that their bodies truly became temples.[725] Having thus prepared themselves, the Lord engraved the Covenant upon

720 1 Nephi 13:37.
721 Jeremiah 31:34.
722 D&C 132:19.
723 Isaiah 22:23.
724 Jeremiah 31:33.
725 1 Corinthians 6:19.

the altars of their hearts. Paul described this as "the epistle of Christ ministered by us, written not with ink, but with the Spirit of the living God; not in tablets of stone, but in fleshy tables of the heart."[726] Thus, Zion people are they who take upon them the Covenant, follow it through to its perfect conclusion, and thus become pure in heart. Upon their hearts the Covenant is inscribed forever. Zion people are they who treasure up in their hearts the testimony of Jesus and the sacred covenants and ordinances that comprise the new and everlasting covenant. Zion people are they who have experienced a mighty change of heart and now have no disposition to do evil.[727]

The Covenant is a product of the Atonement. By means of the Covenant, Zion people receive a new identity, that is, a new name, even that of *Jesus Christ.* The covenant of baptism, the first of two primary covenants that make up the new and everlasting covenant, gives them this new name in the first instance, and the accompanying ordinance of confirmation legalizes their adoption into the Lord's family. Now, with Christ as their father, they have familial rights, including the right to have access to the Father, so that they might gain intelligence from him and progress to become like him.

Through the Covenant, Zion people have access to the Atonement and receive a remission of their sins, a remission that is so comprehensive that the Father and the Son "remember [our sins] no more."[728] That is, without violating their ability to know everything, they choose to file away the recollection of our sins in a nether region of their minds so that the events are as though they never happened and therefore have no power to carry a memory. The Atonement makes this possible. Thus, by the Covenant that emerges from the Atonement, Zion people can grow from life's experiences without being destroyed by them.

The Covenant provides us with the gift of the Holy Ghost, entitling us, through worthy living, to the constant companionship of this member of the Godhead. The Holy Ghost is essential to our obtaining all the benefits of the Covenant and is charged with leading us through all the steps that guide us back to God. The benefits are enormous. The Holy Ghost "witnesses of the Father and the Son."[729] He reveals and "teaches the truth of all things."[730] He "will show [us] all things what [we] should do."[731] He helps us remember all things that Christ has taught.[732] He blesses us with special and otherwise unattainable spiritual gifts.[733] As the Comforter, the Holy Ghost blesses us with divine peace, which calms our troubled hearts and displaces fear.[734] He fills us "with hope and perfect love"[735] and will "teach [us] the peaceable things of the kingdom."[736] He helps us discern good from evil.[737] He is the Sanctifier and Purifier who purges us of all sin so that we might be fit for

726 2 Corinthians 3:3.
727 Mosiah 5:2.
728 D&C 58:42.
729 2 Nephi 31:18.
730 Moroni 10:5.
731 2 Nephi 32:1–5.
732 John 14:26.
733 D&C 46:9–11.
734 John 14:26–27.
735 Moroni 8:26.
736 D&C 36:2.
737 Moroni 7:13–16.

exaltation in the celestial kingdom.[738] In his unique calling, he baptizes us "with fire"[739] to burn out paralyzing impurities. He is the Holy Spirit of Promise, who confirms and ratifies our sacred covenants and ordinances.[740] Without the Holy Ghost, the new and everlasting covenant could not be entered into, followed, verified, or ratified. There could be no justification for righteous deeds redounding to eternal blessings.

One brief statement located in the law of the Church delineates how Zion can be established in the life of an individual, a marriage, a family, or a group of those who would become pure in heart: "And ye shall hereafter receive church covenants, such as shall be sufficient to establish you, both here and in the New Jerusalem."[741] The references in the footnotes to Doctrine and Covenants 42:67 lead to: (1) The New and Everlasting Covenant,[742] (2) The Oath and Covenant of the Priesthood,[743] and (3) The Law of Consecration.[744] These three covenants—The Three Pillars of Zion—are sufficient to establish us as Zion people! We have everything necessary to become Zion people. We only need understand what we have been given and live up to our privileges.[745]

The New and Everlasting Covenant is the key to our becoming Zion people. As we have noted, the Covenant is comprised of two primary covenants. The first is the covenant of baptism, which sets us on the path to becoming Zion-like and thus to eternal life. The second covenant is the oath and covenant of the priesthood, which leads us to the other priesthood covenants and their associated ordinances, which are received in the temple. Combined, these covenants and ordinances cleanse, purify, sanctify, protect, endow us with "power from on high,"[746] and set us in our eternal kingdoms.

The Melchizedek Priesthood is received by ordination with an oath and a covenant. Thereby the Lord puts upon us his name[747] or authority. When this takes place, worthy men can act in the name of Jesus Christ, and Jesus Christ will confirm their actions as if they themselves were the Lord. For the priesthood covenant to become valid, we must magnify our calling, receive the Father, and live by every word that proceeds from the mouth of God. Although magnifying one's calling could have a variety of meanings, the ultimate meaning of "calling" is the call to eternal life. When we magnify *that* calling, we will achieve the calling's greatest blessings, and we will finally come into total compliance with that covenantal calling and fully "receive" the Father and "all that the Father hath."[748] Beyond all other priesthood callings that we must magnify, the call to eternal life should be preeminent.

The Oath and Covenant of the Priesthood is the covenant that draws Zion people—both men and women—to the temple, where their priesthood experience continues.

738 Mosiah 5:1–6; 3 Nephi 27:20; Moses 6:64–68.
739 D&C 33:11.
740 D&C 132:7, 18–19, 26.
741 D&C 42:67.
742 D&C 132:4–7.
743 D&C 84:39.
744 D&C 82:11–15.
745 Young, *Discourses of Brigham Young*, 32.
746 D&C 38:32, 38; 95:8; 105:11.
747 Abraham 1:18.
748 D&C 84:33–44.

There they are ceremonially washed and anointed,[749] and sanctified—or set apart—for a holy purpose. That purpose is to become "kings and queens, priests and priestesses"[750] to God forever. In what is obviously a coronation event, we are endowed with *keys* that give us access to the knowledge and power of God. It is in the temple, said President Hinckley, that we learn "the answers of eternity"; we also learn "the eternal principles to be used in solving life's dilemmas, [that] mark the way to become more Christlike and progressively qualify to live with God. There [in the temple], the laws of the new and everlasting covenant are taught—laws of obedience, sacrifice, order, love, chastity, and consecration. In the temple, one learns the sacred roles of men and women in the eternal plan of God the Father and toward each other."[751]

The Law of Consecration, given and received in the temple, grows out of the priesthood covenant. We learn that all preceding covenants lead us to the law of consecration. This covenant is the "law of the celestial kingdom,"[752] the law that makes the Lord who he is.[753] Now, having been introduced to this foundational law of the celestial kingdom—the kingdom we are to inherit—having been taught and empowered to have access to God, having been justified to approach him, and having heard his voice, received his gift, and been invited into his presence, we lack but one thing to fully receive the Father and become all that he is, to inherit all that he has, and to truly become Zion people. Now we must enter into his *order*—we must marry for eternity.

The New and Everlasting Covenant of Marriage[754] is the culminating covenant of the new and everlasting covenant and the end purpose of the oath and covenant of the priesthood. This crowning covenant sets husbands and wives in the patriarchal order of the priesthood,[755] that is, the order of the gods into whose patriarchal chain we are to be welded.[756] Like the covenant of baptism, the covenant of marriage is called the covenant of exaltation.[757] Only by entering into this covenant and worthily abiding in it can husbands and wives achieve the highest degree of the celestial kingdom.[758] Having done so, we are now ready to become like God and live his life—*eternal life.*[759]

Our eternal kingdoms begin at a most sacred place in the temple: an altar. There, husbands and wives kneel at that which is symbolically the throne of God.[760] Before God, angels, and witnesses, we enter into the new and everlasting covenant of marriage whereby we make eternal covenants with each other and with the Father. Then he who represents God seals us together for time and eternity. He seals upon us the blessings of a glorious resurrection filled with infinite power—God's power—and the possibility of

749 D&C 124:39.
750 McConkie, *Mormon Doctrine*, 424.
751 *Encyclopedia of Mormonism*, 1449, quoting Hinckley in "Why These Temples?" 37.
752 D&C 105:4–5.
753 D&C 38:27.
754 D&C 131:2.
755 Smith, *History of the Church*, 5:554–55; McConkie, *A New Witness for the Articles of Faith*, 312.
756 D&C 128:18.
757 Smith, *Doctrines of Salvation*, 2:58; McConkie, *Mormon Doctrine*, 13.
758 D&C 131:1–2.
759 D&C 132:34.
760 Clarke, *Clarke's Commentary on the Bible*, 1:133.

endless posterity.[761] He seals upon us—both the man and the woman[762]—the promise contained in the oath and covenant of the priesthood: "all that [the] Father hath."[763] This promise includes the blessings mentioned in Doctrine and Covenants 132:19: "thrones, kingdoms, principalities, powers, dominions, [and] exaltation." He further blesses us with "the promises made to the fathers,"[764] even the fulness of the new and everlasting covenant as given to our progenitors, Abraham, Isaac, and Jacob.[765]

By faithfully abiding in the new and everlasting covenant and living true to all of our covenants, the kingdom we establish here on earth will become part of God's vast kingdom, which functions and progresses upon the principles of the law of consecration. Therefore, these three covenants, or *pillars*—the New and Everlasting Covenant, the Oath and Covenant of the Priesthood, and the Law of Consecration—are sufficient to establish us now and in eternity as Zion people who qualify to live in a Zion condition. These three pillars are sufficient to instruct and empower us so that we might live with God, obtain his power, know what he knows, do what he does, inherit all that he has, and become like him.

Zion, then, should be the ultimate aim of human existence. Zion is our origin and our destiny! Before we entered this existence, we lived in Zion, and there we were prepared to establish it again, first in our hearts, and second among others who were also pure in heart. Lorenzo Snow said, "Establish the principles of Zion in your hearts, and then you will be worthy to receive Zion outside."[766]

Will we do it? Will we live up to our latter-day calling and privileges?

Joseph Smith taught, "We ought to have the building up of Zion as our greatest object."[767] Then, exhorting us to take courage, the Prophet reminded us that the prize is worth the price: "Let us realize that we are not to live to ourselves, but to God; by so doing the greatest blessings will rest upon us both in time and in eternity."[768]

Should his words not fan the fire of the Covenant in our souls? Consider the following account from Church history:

> By September 1846, most of the Saints had crossed Iowa at a terrible price and were preparing to winter at Winter Quarters. (Before that winter was over, about six hundred died at Winter Quarters.) On September 25, Brigham Young received word of the Battle of Nauvoo from a group who had just come from Nauvoo. The last ones still in the city were the poor, the widowed, and the orphans who had not been able to find a way to

761 D&C 132:19–20.
762 McConkie, *A New Witness for the Articles of Faith*, 313.
763 D&C 84:38.
764 D&C 2:2.
765 D&C 132:1–14, 19–24.
766 Snow, *The Teachings of Lorenzo Snow*, 181.
767 Smith, *Teachings of the Prophet Joseph Smith*, 160.
768 Smith, *Teachings of the Prophet Joseph Smith*, 179.

> leave. Mobs finally came in and drove them out, picking up the men and throwing them in the river, driving the women and children with bayonets, threatening to kill them if they crossed back over the river. When Brigham Young received word of that, even though the rest of the Saints were in the most destitute and terrible of conditions themselves, he gathered the brethren and said: "The poor brethren and sisters, widows and orphans, sick and destitute, are now lying on the west bank of the Mississippi, waiting for teams and wagons and means to remove them. Now is the time for labor. *Let the fire of the covenant, which you made in the house of the Lord, burn in your hearts like flame unquenchable.*"[769]

Commenting on this incident, Susan Easton Black and William G. Hartley wrote: "Brigham Young didn't talk to them [just] about the suffering of those poor people. He called to their minds the covenants they had made with God in the house of the Lord. He went on: '[I want every man who is able to] rise up with his teams and go straightway. . . . This is a day of action and not of argument.' Before too many days had passed, almost a hundred wagons were moving east to go and rescue the poor. I love that phrase, 'the fire of the covenant,' because that is what drove these people. That is why they did what they did."[770]

May we feel the fire of the Covenant in our souls. May we rise to our destiny and establish Zion in our lives upon the three pillars that stand on the foundation of the Atonement of Jesus Christ. "This is Zion: THE PURE IN HEART."[771] There could be no greater cause in time or eternity.

---

769 Anderson, Dalton, and Green, *Every Good Thing*, 275–76; emphasis added.

770 Young, *Journal History*, Sept. 28, 1846, as cited in Black and Hartley, *The Iowa Mormon Trail*, 163.

771 D&C 97:21.

Bibliography

American Heritage Dictionary. Boston, MA: Houghton Mifflin, 2000.

Anderson, Dawn Hall, Susette Fletcher Green, and Dlora Hall Dalton, eds. *Clothed with Charity: Talks from the 1996 Women's Conference.* Salt Lake City, UT: Deseret Book, 1997.

Asay, Carlos E. "The Oath and Covenant of the Priesthood," *Ensign*, November 1985.

—*Family Pecan Trees: Planting a Legacy of Faith at Home.* Salt Lake City, UT: Deseret Book, 1992.

—*The Seven M's of Missionary Service: Proclaiming the Gospel as a Member or Full-time Missionary*. Salt Lake City, UT: Bookcraft, 1996.

Ashton, Marvin J. "Be a Quality Person," *Ensign*, February 1993.

—"Love Takes Time," *Ensign*, November 1975.

Bednar, David A. "Pray Always," *Ensign*, November 2008.

Benson, Ezra Taft. "A Vision and a Hope for the Youth of Zion," *Devotional Speeches of the Year*. Provo, UT: Brigham Young University Press, 1978.

—*A Witness and a Warning: A Modern-Day Prophet Testifies of the Book of Mormon*. Salt Lake City, UT: Deseret Book, 1988.

—"Beware of Pride," *Ensign*, May 1989.

—*Devotional Speeches of the Year*. Provo, UT: Brigham Young University Press, 1978.

—*God, Family, Country: Our Three Great Loyalties*. Salt Lake City, UT: Deseret Book, 1975.

—"In His Steps," *Ensign*, September 1988.

—"Jesus Christ—Gifts and Expectations," *New Era*, May 1975.

—*The Teachings of Ezra Taft Benson. Salt Lake City, UT: Deseret Book, 1988.*

—"What I Hope You Will Teach Your Children about the Temple," *Ensign*, August 1985;

Bible Dictionary. Salt Lake City, UT: The Church of Jesus Christ of Latter-day Saints, 1989;

Black , Susan Easton, et al. Doctrines for Exaltation: The 1989 Sperry Symposium on the Doctrine and Covenants. Salt Lake City, UT: Deseret Book, *1989.*

—*The Iowa Mormon Trail: Legacy of Faith and Courage*. Orem, UT: Helix Publishing, 1997.

Bowen, Albert E. *The Church Welfare Plan*. Salt Lake City, UT: The Church of Jesus Christ of Latter-day Saints, 1946.

Brewster, Hoyt W. Jr. *Doctrine and Covenants Encyclopedia*. Salt Lake City, UT: Bookcraft, 1988.

Brown, Hugh B. *Continuing the Quest*. Salt Lake City, UT: Bookcraft, 1961.

Brown, Matthew B. *Prophecies: The Gate of Heaven*. American Fork, UT: Covenant Communications, 1999.

—*Signs of the Times, Second Coming, Millenium*. American Fork, UT: Covenant Communications, 2006.

Budge, Ernest A. Wallis. *Coptic Martyrdoms Discourse on Abbaton. London: British Museum,* 1914.

Burton, Alma P., ed. *Discourses of the Prophet Joseph Smith. Salt Lake City, UT: Deseret Book, 1956.*

Cannon, Donald Q. *Teachings of the Latter-day Prophets*. Salt Lake City, UT: Bookcraft, 1998.

Cannon, Elaine. "Agency and Accountability." Salt Lake City, *Ensign*, November 1983.

Cannon, George Q. "Beware Lest Ye Fall." Discourse delivered at the Morgan Utah Stake Conference, Sunday, February 16, 1896.

—*Gospel Truth: Discourses and Writings of President George Q. Cannon.* Salt Lake City, UT: Deseret Book, 1974.

Cannon, Joseph A. "Sanctification," *Mormon Times,* June 12, 2008, http://www.mormontimes.com.

Clark, E. Douglas. *The Blessings of Abraham—Becoming a Zion People.* American Fork, UT: Covenant Communications, 2005.

Clark, J. Reuben. *Church Welfare Plan: A Discussion. Salt Lake, City, UT* General Church Welfare Committee, 1939.

Clark, James R., comp., *Messages of the First Presidency of The Church of Jesus Christ of Latter-day Saints.* Salt Lake City: Bookcraft, 1965–75.

Clarke, Adam. *Clarke's Commentary on the Bible.* Grand Rapids, MI: Baker Book House, 1967.

Clarke, J. Richard. "Successful Welfare Stewardship," *Ensign,* November 1978.

Conference Report, 1897–2009, Salt Lake City, UT: The Church of Jesus Christ of Latter-day Saints.

Cook, Gene R. "Home and Family: A Divine Eternal Pattern," *Ensign,* May 1984.

—"The Seat Next to You," *New Era,* October 1983.

Cook, Lyndon. *Joseph Smith and the Law of Consecration.* Provo, UT: Keepsake Books, 1991.

Cowley, Matthew. *Matthew Cowley Speaks: Discourses of Elder Matthew Cowley of the Quorum of the Twelve of the Church of Jesus Christ of Latter-day Saints.* Salt Lake City, UT: Deseret Book Company, 1954.

Dalrymple, G. Brent. *The Age of the Earth.* Stanford, CA: Stanford University Press, 1991.

Dellenbach, Robert K. "Hour of Conversion," *New Era,* June 2002.

DeMille, Cecil B. *BYU Speeches of the Year. Provo, UT: Brigham Young University Press,* May 1957.

Durham, G. Homer, ed. *The Gospel Kingdom: Selections from the Writings and Discourses of John Taylor, Third President of The Church of Jesus Christ of Latter-day Saints. Salt Lake City, UT: Bookcraft, 1943.*

—*Gospel Ideals: Selections from the Discourses of David O. McKay. Salt Lake City, UT: Improvement Era, 1953.*

Dibble, Philo. "Recollections of the Prophet Joseph Smith," *Juvenile Instructor,* June 1892.

Duffin, James G. "A Character Test," *Improvement Era,* February 1911.

Easton, M. G. *Illustrated Bible Dictionary.* Nashville: TN: Thomas Nelson, 1897.

"The Bondage of Sin," *Improvement Era,* February 1923.

Ehat, Andrew F. and Lyndon W. Cook. *The Words of Joseph Smith: The Contemporary Accounts of the Nauvoo Discourses of the Prophet Joseph.* Provo, UT: Religious Studies Center Brigham Young University, 1980.

Encarta World English Dictionary. New York, NY: St. Martins Press, 1999.

Eyring, Henry B. "Faith and the Oath and Covenant of the Priesthood," *Ensign,* May 2008.

Farley, S. Brent. "The Oath and Covenant of the Priesthood." *Sperry Symposium on the Doctrine and Covenants.* Salt Lake City: Desert Book, 1989.

First Presidency, "What is the Doctrine of the Priesthood?" Salt Lake City, UT: *Improvement Era,* February 1961.
Faust, James E. "A Royal Priesthood," *Ensign,* May 2006.
—*In the Strength of the Lord: The Life and Teachings of James E. Faust.* Salt Lake City, UT: Deseret Book, 1999.
—"He Healeth the Broken Heart," *Ensign* July 2005.
—"Our Search for Happiness, *Ensign,* Oct. 2000.
—"Standing in Holy Places," *Ensign,* May 2005.
—"The Devil's Throat," *Ensign,* May 2003.
—"The Gift of the Holy Ghost—A Sure Compass," *Ensign,* April 1996.
—"The Shield of Faith," *Ensign,* May 2000.
"Galaxy Map." Washington D.C.: The National Geographic Society, June 1983.
Galbraith, David B., D. Kelly Ogden, and Andrew C. Skinner. *Jerusalem—The Eternal City.* Salt Lake City, UT: Deseret Book, 1996.
Gardner, R. Quinn. "Becoming a Zion Society," *Ensign,* February 1979.
—"I Have a Question," *Ensign,* March 1978.
Gibbons, Ted L. *Be Not Afraid,* Springville, UT: Cedar Fort, Inc., 2009.
Goddard, Wallace H. "Blessed by Angels." *MeridianMagazine.com,* July 27, 2009.
—*Drawing Heaven into Your Marriage.* Fairfax, VA: Meridian Publishing, 2007.
Grant, Heber J. *Teachings of Presidents of the Church. Salt Lake City, UT: The Church of Jesus Christ of Latter-day Saints,* 2002.
Guralnik, David B., ed. *Webster's New World Dictionary, 2nd College Edition.* New York City, NY: The New World Publishing Company, 1970.
Hafen, Bruce C. *The Broken Heart: Applying the Atonement to Life's Experiences.* Salt Lake City, UT: Deseret Book, 1989.
Haight, David B. "The Sacrament and the Sacrifice," *Ensign,* November 1989.
Hamilton, Edith. *Spokesman for God. New York, NY: Norton and Company, 1977.*
Hinckley, Gordon B. "Blessed Are the Merciful," *Ensign,* May 1990.
—*Faith: The Essence of True Religion. Salt Lake City, UT: Deseret Book, 1989.*
—"Our Mission of Saving," *Ensign,* November 1991.
—"Priesthood: The Power of Godliness," *Improvement Era,* December 1970.
—*Stand a Little Taller.* Salt Lake City, UT: Eagle Gate, 2000.
—*Standing for Something.* New York, NY: Three Rivers Press, 2000.
—*Teachings of Gordon B. Hinckley.* Salt Lake City, UT: Deseret Book, 2002.
—"The Dawning of a Brighter Day," *Ensign,* May 2004.
—"The Stone Cut Out of the Mountain," *Ensign,* 2007.
—"Till We Meet Again," *Ensign,* November 2001.
—"We Thank Thee for This Sacred Structure," *Church News,* 8 November 1997.
— "Your Greatest Challenge, Mother," *Ensign,* November 2000.
Holland, Jeffrey R. "Broken Things to Mend," *Ensign,* May 2006.
—"However Long and Hard the Road," *Ensign,* September 2002.
—*On Earth As It Is in Heaven.* Salt Lake City, UT: Deseret Book, 1989.

Holzapfel, Richard Neitzel and Thomas A. Wayment, eds., *The Life and Teachings of Jesus Christ: From the Transfiguration through the Triumphant Entry.* Salt Lake City, UT: Deseret Book, 2006.

Horton, George A. "Abraham's Act of Faith Reflects 'a Soul Like Unto Our Savior,'" *LDS Church News,* April 2, 1994.

"'Hymn of the Pearl': an Ancient Counterpart To 'O My Father.'" *BYU Studies,* vol. 36, 1996–97.

Hymns of the Church of Jesus Christ of Latter-day Saints. Salt Lake City, UT: The Church of Jesus Christ of Latter-day Saints, 1985.

Jackson, Kent P. and Robert L. Millet. eds. *Studies in Scripture.* Salt Lake City, UT: Deseret Book 1989.

Jensen, Marlin K. "Living after the Manner of Happiness," *Ensign,* December 2002.

Jenson, Andrew, *Historical Record: A Monthly Periodical.* Salt Lake City, UT: Deseret News, 1886—1890.

Jessee, Dean. "Joseph Knight's Recollection of Early Mormon History." Provo, UT: *BYU Studies,* vol. 17, no. 1, 1976.

Johnson, Clark V. *Doctrines for Exaltation: The 1989 Sperry Symposium on the Doctrine and Covenants. Salt Lake City, UT: Deseret Book, 1989.*

Josephus. *Complete Works.* William Whiston, trans., Grand Rapids, MI: Kregal Publications, 1960.

Kimball, Spencer W. "A Gift of Gratitude," *Tambuli,* December 1977.

—"Becoming the Pure in Heart," *Ensign,* May 1978.

—*Faith Precedes the Miracle: Based on Discourses of Spencer W. Kimball.* Salt Lake City, UT: Deseret Book, 1972.

—"The Fruit of Our Welfare Services Labors," *Ensign,* November 1978.

—"The Role of Righteous Women," *Ensign,* November 1979.

—*The Teachings of Spencer W. Kimball.* Salt Lake City, UT: Bookcraft, 1982.

—"Welfare Services: The Gospel in Action," *Ensign,* November 1977.

—"Young Women Fireside 1981—In Love and Power and without Fear," *New Era,* July 1981.

Kirchhoff, Frederick. "Reconstruction of Self in Wordsworth's 'Ode on Intimations of Immortality from Recollections of Early Childhood.'" *Narcissism and the Text.* New York, NY: New York University Press, 1986.

Kirtland Council Minute Book, eds. Fred Collier and William S. Hartwell, Salt Lake City, UT: Collier's Publishing, 1996.

Largey, Dennis L. *Book of Mormon Reference Companion.* Salt Lake City, UT: Deseret Book, 2003.

Larsen, Dean L. "A Royal Generation," *Ensign,* May 1983.

Larson, Stan "The King Follett Discourse: a Newly Amalgamated Text." Provo, UT: *BYU Studies,* Vol. 18, 1977–1978.

Layton, Lynne and Schapiro, Barbara A. *Narcissism and the Text: Studies in Literature and the Psychology of Self.* New York, NY: New York University Press, 1986.

Lee, Harold B. *Decisions for Successful Living.* Salt Lake City, UT: Deseret Book, 1973.

—"Stand Ye in Holy Places," *Ensign*, July 1973.
—*The Teachings of Harold B. Lee.* Salt Lake City, UT: Deseret Book, 1974.
Lightner, Mary. Address to Brigham Young University. *BYU Archives and Manuscripts, Writings of Early Latter-day Saints,* 1905.
Ludlow, Daniel H. A *Companion to Your Study of the Book of Mormon.* Salt Lake City, UT: Deseret Book, 1976.
—*Encyclopedia of Mormonism.* New York City, NY: Macmillan Publishing, 1992.
Lund, Gerald N. *Jesus Christ, Key to the Plan of Salvation. Salt Lake City, UT: Deseret Book, 1991.*
—"Old Testament Types and Symbols," *A Witness of Jesus Christ: The 1989 Sperry Symposium on the Old Testament.* ed. Richard D. Draper, Salt Lake City, UT: Deseret Book, 1990.
Lundquist, John M. and Stephen D. Ricks, eds. *By Study and Also by Faith: Essays in Honor of Hugh W. Nibley on the Occasion of His Eightieth Birthday. Provo, UT: Maxwell Institute, 1992.*
Lundwall, N. B. *Temples of the Most High.* Salt Lake City, UT: Bookcraft, 1965.
"Map: Old Testament Stories: Part Two," *Deseret News.* Jan. 8, 1994.
Maxwell, Cory H., ed. *The Neal A. Maxwell Quote Book.* Salt Lake City, UT: Bookcraft, 1997.
Maxwell, Neal A. A *Wonderful Flood of Light.* Salt Lake City, UT: Deseret Book, 1991.
—*But for a Small Moment.* Salt Lake City, UT: Bookcraft, 1987.
—"Consecrate Thy Performance." *Ensign*, May 2002.
—*Disposition of a Disciple.* Salt Lake City, UT: Deseret Book, 1976.
—"Enduring Well," *Ensign*, April 1997.
—*Even As I Am.* Salt Lake City, UT: Deseret Book, 1991.
—*If Thou Endure It Well.* Salt Lake City, UT: Bookcraft, 2002.
—*Lord, Increase Our Faith.* Salt Lake City, UT: Bookcraft, 1994.
—*Men and Women of Christ. Salt Lake City, UT: Deseret Book, 1991.*
—*Notwithstanding My Weakness.* Salt Lake City, UT: Deseret Book, 1981.
—*One More Strain of Praise.* Salt Lake City, UT: Deseret Book, 2003.
—"Patience," *Ensign*, October 1980.
—*That Ye May Believe.* Salt Lake City, UT: Bookcraft, 1994.
—*The Promise of Discipleship.* Salt Lake City, UT: Deseret Book, 2001.
—"These Are Your Days," *New Era*, January 1985.
McConkie, Bruce R. *A New Witness for the Articles of Faith.* Salt Lake City, UT: Deseret Book, 1985.
—*Doctrinal New Testament Commentary.* Salt Lake City, UT: Deseret Book, 1972.
—*Doctrines of Salvation: Sermons and Writings of Joseph Fielding Smith,* Salt Lake City, UT: Bookcraft, 1954–1956.
—*Mormon Doctrine.* Salt Lake City, UT: Bookcraft: 1966.
—"Obedience, Consecration, and Sacrifice," *Ensign*, May 1975.
—"The Doctrine of the Priesthood," *Ensign*, May 1982.
—*The Mortal Messiah: From Bethlehem to Calvary.* Salt Lake City, UT: Deseret Book, 1981.

—"*The Probationary Test of Mortality.*" Address delivered at the University of Utah Institute, January 10, 1982.
—*The Promised Messiah: The First Coming of Christ.* Salt Lake City, UT: Deseret Book, 1981.
—"The Ten Blessings of the Priesthood," *Ensign,* November 1977.
McConkie, Joseph Fielding and Robert L. Millet. *Doctrinal Commentary on the Book of Mormon.* Salt Lake City, UT: Deseret Book, 1987–1993.
—*Joseph Smith: The Choice Seer.* Salt Lake City, UT: Bookcraft, 1996.
—*Revelations of the Restoration.* Salt Lake City, UT: Deseret Book, 2000.
McKay, David O. *Gospel Ideals: Selections from the Discourses of David O. McKay.* Salt Lake City, UT: Deseret Book, 1993.
---*Pathways to Happiness.* Salt Lake City, UT: Bookcraft, 1957.
McMullin, Keith B. "Come to Zion! Come to Zion!" Salt Lake City, UT: *Ensign,* November 2002.
Merriam Webster's New World Dictionary, Third Edition. New York, NY: Simon and Schuster, 1998
Middlemiss, Clare. *Man May Know for Himself: Teachings of President David O. McKay.* Salt Lake City, UT: Deseret Book, 1967.
Millet, Robert L. "Quest for the City of God: The Doctrine Of Zion In Modern Revelation," *1989 Sperry Symposium on the Doctrine and Covenants.* Salt Lake City, UT: Desert Book, 1989.
—*The Capstone of Our Religion: Insights into the Doctrine and Covenants.* Salt Lake City, UT: Deseret Book, 1989.
—*The Life Beyond.* Salt Lake City, UT: Deseret Book, 1986.
—*The Power of the Word: Saving Doctrines from the Book of Mormon. Salt Lake City, UT: Deseret Book*, 2000.
Monson, Thomas S. "In Quest of the Abundant Life." *Ensign,* March 1988.
Nelson, Russell M. "Personal Priesthood Responsibility," *Ensign,* October 2005.
—*The Power within Us. Salt Lake City, UT: Deseret Book, 1989.*
Nelson, William O. "Enoch and His Message for Latter Days," *Deseret News,* Feb. 5, 1994.
Neuenschwander, Dennis. "Ordinances and Covenants," *Ensign,* August 2001.
Nibley, Hugh. *Abraham in Egypt.* Salt Lake City, UT and Provo, UT: Deseret Book and FARMS, 2000.
—*An Approach to the Book of Mormon.* Salt Lake City, UT: Deseret Book, 1988.
—*Approaching Zion.* Salt Lake City, UT: Deseret Book, 1989.
—"Educating the Saints—A Brigham Young Mosaic." Provo, UT: *BYU Studies,* Vol. 11, Autumn 1970.
—*Nibley on the Timely and the Timeless. Provo, UT: Religious Studies Center, Brigham Young University, 2004.*
—*Teachings of the Book of Mormon.* Provo, UT: Covenant Communications, 2004.
—*Temple and Cosmos: Beyond This Ignorant Present.* Salt Lake City, UT: Deseret Book, 1992.
Nibley, Preston. *Brigham Young: The Man and His Work,* 4th ed. Salt Lake City, UT: Deseret Book, 1960.

Nielsen, Donna B. *Beloved Bridegroom.* Salt Lake City, UT: Onyx Press, 1999.
Nyman, Monte S. and Charles D. Tate, Jr., eds. *Fourth Nephi through Moroni: From Zion to Destruction. Salt Lake City, UT: Bookcraft, 1992.*
—*The Capstone of Our Religion: Insights into the Doctrine and Covenants.* Salt Lake City, UT: Bookcraft, 1989.
Oaks, Dallin H. "Good, Better, Best," *Ensign,* November 2007.
—"He Heals the Heavy Laden," *Ensign,* November 2006
—"Preparation for the Second Coming," *Ensign,* November 2004.
—"Taking Upon Us the Name of Jesus Christ," *Ensign,* May 1985.
—"The Challenge to Become," *Ensign,* November 2000.
—"Timing," *Ensign,* October 2003.
Oaks, Robert C. "The Power of Patience," *Ensign,* November 2006.
Otten, L. G. and C. M. Caldwell. *Sacred Truths of the Doctrine and Covenants. Salt Lake City, UT: Deseret Book, 1982–1983.*
Pack, Frederick J. "Was the Earth Created in Six Days of Twenty-Four Hours Each?" *Improvement Era,* October 1930.
Packer, Boyd K. "Personal Revelation: The Gift, the Test, and the Promise," *Ensign,* November 1994.
—"Restoration," *First Worldwide Leadership Training Meeting.* Salt Lake City, UT: The Church of Jesus Christ of Latter-day Saints, January 2003.
—*That All May Be Edified.* Salt Lake City, UT: Bookcraft, 1982.
—"The Candle of the Lord," *Ensign,* January 1983.
—"The One Pure Defense (An Evening with President Boyd K. Packer)," Intellectual Reserve, 2004. Address to CES Religious Educators, 6 February 2004, Salt Lake Tabernacle.
Parry, Donald W., ed. *Temples of the Ancient World: Ritual and Symbolism. Salt Lake City, UT and Provo, UT: Deseret and FARMS, 1994.*
—*Understanding the Book of Revelation.* Salt Lake City, UT: Deseret Book, 1998.
Peterson, H. Burke. "Your Special Purpose," *New Era,* October 2001.
Pratt, Orson. *Times and Seasons,* vol. 6. no. 10, 1 June 1845.
Riddle, Chauncey C. "The New and Everlasting Covenant," 1989 *Sperry Symposium on the Doctrine and Covenants.* Salt Lake City: Desert Book, 1989.
Roberts, B.H. *Comprehensive History of the Church of Jesus Christ of Latter-day Saints.* Salt Lake City, UT: Church of Jesus Christ of Latter-day Saints, 1930.
—*Seventy's Course of Theology.* Salt Lake City, UT: Deseret Book, 1931.
Romney, Marion G. "Church Welfare Services' Basic Principles," *Ensign,* May 1976.
—"Church Welfare—Temporal Service in a Spiritual Setting," *Ensign,* May 1980
—"Priesthood," *Ensign,* May 1982.
—"'In Mine Own Way,'" *Ensign,* November 1976.
—"The Celestial Nature of Self-reliance," *Ensign,* November 1982.
—"The Oath and Covenant Which Belongeth to the Priesthood," *Ensign,* November 1980.
—"The Purpose of Church Welfare Services," *Ensign,* May 1977.

—"The Royal Law of Love," *Ensign*, May 1978.
—"Unity," *Ensign*, May 1983.
—"Welfare Services: The Savior's Program," *Ensign*, October 1980.
Salt Lake School of the Prophets Minutes. Salt Lake City, UT: The Church of Jesus Christ of Latter-day Saints, 1899.
"Sermon Given to Different People," *LDS Church News,* Feb. 18, 1995.
Skidmore, Rex A. "What Part Should a Teenager Play in a Family?" *Improvement Era,* 1952.
Skinner, Andrew C. *Temple Worship: 20 Truths That Will Bless Your Life.* Salt Lake City, UT: Deseret Book, 2008.
—*The Old Testament and the Latter-Day Saints.* Salt Lake City, UT: Deseret Book, 2005.
Smith, Hyrum M. and Janne M. Sjodahl. *Doctrine and Covenants Commentary.* Salt Lake City, UT: Deseret Book, 1960.
Smith, Joseph. *Evening and Morning Star,* July, 1833.
—*History of The Church of Jesus Christ of Latter-day Saints.* Salt Lake City, UT: Deseret Book, 1980.
—*Lectures on Faith.* Salt Lake City, UT: Deseret Book, 1993.
Smith, Joseph F. *Gospel Doctrine: Selections from the Sermons and Writings of Joseph F. Smith. Deseret News Press, 1919.*
—*Teachings of Presidents of the Church.* Salt Lake City, UT: The Church of Jesus Christ of Latter-day Saints, 1998.
Smith, Joseph Fielding. *Church History and Modern Revelation.* Salt Lake City, UT: The Church of Jesus Christ of Latter-day Saints, 1946.
—"Our responsibility as Priesthood Holders," *Ensign,* June 1971.
—*Teachings of the Prophet Joseph Smith.* Salt Lake City, UT: Deseret Book, 1938.
—"The Duties of the Priesthood in Temple Work," *The Utah Genealogical and Historical Magazine,* vol. 30, no. 1, January 1939.
—*The Restoration of All Things.* Salt Lake City, UT: Deseret News Press, 1945.
Snow, Lorenzo. *The Teachings of Lorenzo Snow,* Salt Lake City, UT: Bookcraft, 1984.
Sorensen, A. D. "No Respector of Persons: Equality in the Kingdom," ed. Mary E. Stoval, .*As Women of Faith: Talks Selected from the BYU Women's Conferences.* Salt Lake City, UT: Deseret Book, 1989, 55.
Stevenson, Edward. "Life and History of Elder Edward Stevenson." Provo, UT: Special Collections, Harold B. Lee Library, Brigham Young University, n.d.
Stuy, Brian H., comp., *Collected Discourses.* Burbank, CA: B.H.S. Publishing, 1988.
Summerhays, James T. "The Stripling Elect." *MeridianMagazine.com,* February 20, 2009.
Talmage, James E. *Articles of Faith.* Salt Lake City, UT: Deseret Book, 1984.
—*Jesus the Christ.* Salt Lake City: Deseret News Press, 1915.
—"The Eternity of Sex," *Young Woman's Journal*, October 1914.
—*The House of the Lord.* Salt Lake City, UT: Bookcraft, 1962.
Tanakh: A New Translation of the Holy Scriptures According to the Traditional Hebrew Text. Philadelphia, PA: Jewish Publication Society of America, November 1985.
Tanner, N. Eldon. "Constancy Amid Change," Ensign, November 1979.
Tanner, Susan W. "All Things Shall Work Together for Your Good," *Ensign,* May 2004.

—"My Soul Delighteth in the Things of the Lord," *Ensign*, 2008.
Taylor, John. *Teachings of the Latter-day Prophets*. Salt Lake City, UT: Bookcraft, 1998.
Times and Seasons, vol. 6. no. 10, 1 June 1845.
Thomas, M. Catherine. "Alma the Younger, Part 1," Provo, UT: Neal A. Maxwell Institute for Religious Scholarship, 1996.
—"Alma the Younger, Part 2," Provo, UT: Neal A. Maxwell Institute for Religious Scholarship, 1996.
—"Benjamin and the Mysteries of God," *King Benjamin's Speech*. Provo, UT: Foundation for Ancient Research and Mormon Studies, 1998.
Turner, Rodney. *Woman and the Priesthood*. Salt Lake City, UT: Deseret Book, 1972.
Tvedtnes, John A. *The Church of the Old Testament*. Salt Lake City, UT: Deseret Book, 1967.
—"They Have Their Reward," *MeridianMagazine.com*, February 21, 2007.
Van Orden, Bruce A. and Brent L. Top. *Doctrines of the Book of Mormon: The 1991 Sperry Symposium*, Provo, UT: Maxwell Institute, 1993.
Watt, George D., ed. *Journal of Discourses. Liverpool, England: F.D. Richards, et al., 1854–1886.*
Whitney, Newell K. in *Messenger and Advocate*, 3 September 1837.
Whitney, Orson F. *Gospel Themes*. Salt Lake City, UT: n.p., 1914.
—*Life of Heber C. Kimball*. Salt Lake City, UT: Bookcraft, 1975.
—*Saturday Night Thoughts*. Salt Lake City, UT: Deseret News, 1927.
Wickman, Lance B. "Today," *Ensign*, May 2008.
Widtsoe, John A. *An Understandable Religion. Salt Lake City, UT: The Church of Jesus Christ of Latter-day Saints, 1944.*
—*Priesthood and Church Government*. Salt Lake City, UT: Deseret Book, 1939.
—*Utah Genealogical and Historical Magazine*. Salt Lake City, UT: October 1934.
Williams, Clyde J. *The Teachings of Lorenzo Snow, Fifth President of the Church of Jesus Christ of Latter-day Saints*. Salt Lake City, UT: Bookcraft, 1984.
Wilson, Marvin. *Our Father Abraham*, Grand Rapids, MI: Eerdmans Publishing Co., 1989.
Winder, Barbara W. "Finding Joy in Life," *Ensign*, November 1987.
Wirthlin, Joseph B. "The Great Commandment," *Ensign*, November 2007.
—"The Law of the Fast," *Ensign*, May 2001.
Woodruff, Wilford. *The Discourses of Wilford Woodruff*. Salt Lake City, UT: Bookcraft, 1946.
Yarn, David H. *The Gospel: God, Man, and Truth. Salt Lake City, UT: Deseret Book, 1965.*
Yorgason, Blaine M. *I Need Thee Every Hour*. Salt Lake City, UT: Deseret Book, 2003.
—*Spiritual Progression in the Last Days*. Salt Lake City, UT: Deseret Book, 1994.
Young, Brigham in *Deseret News*, 10 October 1866.
—*Discourses of Brigham Young*. Salt Lake City, UT: Deseret Book, 1926.
—*Journal History*. 28 September 1846.
—*Millennial Star, Vol. 16*. Salt Lake City, UT: The Church of Jesus Christ of Latter-day Saints, 1840–1970.

Index and Concordance

This is a master index of the book series. The page number is specific to the book in which it is located. For example: 101:3 means page 101 in book 3. Marker "P" refers to Portrait of a Zion Person.

About the Author

Larry Barkdull is a longtime publisher and writer of books, music, art, and magazines. For nine years, he owned Sonos Music Resources and published the Tabernacle Choir Performance Library. He was also the owner and publisher of Keepsake Books. Over the past thirty years, he's published some six hundred products for numerous authors, composers, and artists. He's founded two nonprofit organizations: The Latter-day Foundation for the Arts, Education and Humanity (to promote LDS arts), and Gospel Ideals International (to promote the gospel of Jesus Christ on the Internet).

His books have sold in excess of 300,000 copies, and they have been translated into Japanese, Korean, Italian, and Hebrew. He is the recipient of the American Family Literary Award; the Benjamin Franklin Book Award; and *Foreword Magazine's* GOLD Book of the Year Award for best fiction. His most recent books are *Priesthood Power—Blessing the Sick and the Afflicted*; *Rescuing Wayward Children*; and *The Shepherd Song.*

He and his wife, Elizabeth, have ten children and a growing number of grandchildren. They live in Orem, Utah. Read more of his writings at Meridian Magazine.com.

13290838R00105

Made in the USA
San Bernardino, CA
17 July 2014